Girls' Violence

SUNY series in Women, Crime, and Criminology
Meda Chesney-Lind and Russ Immarigeon, editors

Girls' Violence

Myths and Realities

Edited by
Christine Alder and Anne Worrall

STATE UNIVERSITY OF NEW YORK PRESS

Published by
State University of New York Press, Albany

For information, address State University of New York Press,
90 State Street, Suite 700, Albany, NY 12207

Production by Kelli M. Williams
Marketing by Fran Keneston

Library of Congress Cataloging-in-Publication Data

Girls' violence : myths and realities / edited by Christine Alder and Anne Worrall.
    p. cm.—(SUNY series in women, crime, and criminology)
  Includes bibliographical references and index.
  ISBN 0-7914-6109-2 (hardcover)—ISBN 0-7914-6110-6 (pbk.)
    1. Female juvenile delinquents—Cross-cultural studies.   2. Female offenders—
  Cross-cultural studies.   3. Teenage girls—Psychology.   I. Alder, Christine, 1950–
  II. Worrall, Anne.   III. Series.

HV6046.G565   2004
364.36'082—dc22

                                                            2004007184

10 9 8 7 6 5 4 3 2 1

We dedicate this book to

Marissa and Kirra
And
Jennifer, Natalie, and Sharon

Contents

Acknowledgments

We are both grateful to the following people who helped with the preparation of the manuscript: Joel Spencer, Melissa Klein, Jack Fagan and Di Brown.

Anne Worrall would also like to thank the Crime Research Centre at the University of Western Australia for its support in the editing of this collection.

The chapter entitled "Capturing Girls' Experiences of 'Community Violence' in the United States" by Laurie Schaffner was originally published as "Violence and Female Delinquency: Gender Transgressions and Gender Invisibility" © 1999 by the *Berkeley Women's Law Journal*. Reprinted from the *Berkeley Women's Law Journal*, Vol. 14, pp. 40–65. Used by permission of the University of California, Berkeley.

Chapter One

A Contemporary Crisis?

Christine Alder and Anne Worrall

Two runaway schoolgirls took over a pensioner's home in Manchester, covered her walls in graffiti, bandaged her face so tightly that she choked, then pushed her body through the streets in a wheelie [rubbish] bin and dropped it into a canal.

—Rebecca Fowler, *The Guardian*, 12 July 1999

Four young women beat a 17-year-old girl with gardening tools to warn her off a boy she was seeing. She suffered minor injuries. Police said, "These girls are known for hanging around the area."

—"Crimestoppers," *The West Australian*, 17 July 1998

Just what is going on? Does the new freedom that women have rightly gained include the freedom to act as foully as men?

—Paul Barker, *Evening Standard*, 1 May 1996

Some girls now carry guns. Others hide razor blades in their mouth. . . . The plague of teen violence is an equal-opportunity scourge.

—C. Leslie et al., *Newsweek*, 2 August 1993

Teenage girls are becoming more violent, with rising crime figures shattering the image of females as the gentler sex. Experts say it is the ugly side of the greater freedom and equality enjoyed by girls and young women today. Boys and girls are becoming similar.

—*Sunday Mail*, 27 July 1997

1

The idea for this book began in September 1998 when the editors met for the first time in Melbourne and realized that both had been researching attitudes toward, and work with, troubled and troublesome girls and young women for several years. Despite working on opposite sides of the world, we found that we shared identical concerns about the increasingly punitive attitudes that were being displayed toward these multiply disadvantaged but nevertheless resourceful young women by the criminal justice system and the media, based on what appeared to us to be spurious evidence of an increase in violent and disorderly behavior by this group. We both felt thwarted in our attempts to investigate this phenomenon by an absence of reliable information and a paucity of sound qualitative research. Although there are many texts on "youth and crime," girls are rarely mentioned in these. Similarly, there are many texts concerned with "women and crime" which pay little attention to girls. This book represents our efforts to rectify this situation. It aims to bring together some of the best existing research from four English-speaking areas of the world (Australia, Britain, Canada, and the United States) on the perceived increase in girls' violence. It is a critical collection that seeks to challenge official definitions and media representations by asking such questions as:

- Has violence by girls really increased at the end of the twentieth century?
- Exactly what kind of behavior by girls is now classified as "violent" and has this classification changed?
- What is the process whereby girls' behavior is criminalized and is this different for boys?
- How have attitudes toward girls' behavior changed?
- How do different perspectives seek to explain the apparent increase in girls' violence?
- In what contexts do girls behave violently?
- What are the links between violence by girls and the broader issues of the social construction and social control of adolescent femininities?

Definitions of the terms *girls*[1] and *violence* are each sufficiently contested to warrant chapters, if not complete books, in their own rights. Juxtaposing them in the title of this collection may seem to invite the immediate questions, "What do you mean by 'girls'?" and "What do you mean by 'violence'?" Much of this collection is focused on answering precisely those questions, but, as editors, it is incumbent to offer an explanation of what was in *our* minds when we chose the title. The remainder of this introductory chapter will attempt to unravel some of the threads that have resulted in the construction of the "new" social category of "violent girls" in the four geographical regions we have identified. We aim to achieve this, first, by challenging official definitions of the "violence" committed by girls and, second, by examining the construction of "girlhood" and the ways in which girls "do femininities."

The Unchallenged Statistics

The sort of newspaper reports with which we started this chapter are most often followed by stories drawing on evidence from official statistics of one form or another, and/ or stories of selected incidents. Police, court, and prison statistics are presented as "facts" about the incidence of crime and changing crime patterns. The writers of such reports are apparently unaware of the elementary cautions about the interpretation of crime statistics that would be familiar to any novice in criminology.

The reasons for the need for caution in interpreting official statistics are well documented. Gibbons (1982: 85) has noted that crime statistics "are among the most unreliable and questionable social facts." Other analysts have shown that crime statistics may not so much disclose "facts" about "criminal acts" as they do changes in police policies and the political maneuvering of criminal justice agencies as a response to such issues as changes in management objectives, budget structures, and other organizational issues (Taylor 1999). However, "the traces of the storyteller cling to the story the way the handprints of the potter cling to the clay vessel" (Benjamin 1955: 92 cited in Tait 1994: 60). Thus, official statistics are not necessarily "worthless" but rather they can provide valuable insights into the "organizational constraints and priorities of the criminal justice system" (Muncie 1999: 14). One of the purposes of this chapter is to challenge the interpretation of official statistics that underpins accounts of increasing girls' violence. We begin with an overview of the observations about girls' violence suggested by official statistics in Britain, Canada, the United States, and Australia before turning to consideration of alternative explanations and forms of analysis.

Media reports of girls' violence most often draw upon selected statistics and particular interpretations of them to support their story. Before beginning a discussion of these statistics it needs to be noted that youth crime in general, and the crimes committed by young women in particular, are predominantly less serious property crimes. An Australian study found that between 1990 and 1996 most girls' offending was minor, with half consisting of Good Order offenses (known as Public Order offenses in Britain—offenses such as being "drunk and disorderly") most (70 percent) of which were transit offenses (such as traveling without a ticket or having their feet on a seat) (Alder & Hunter 1999). The same study found that while there had been an increase (81 percent) in the number of criminal cases involving girls across this time period (compared to a 26 percent increase in boys' offenses), most of this increase was accounted for by an increase in Good Order offenses (114 percent increase for girls).

In general, violent crimes account for a small proportion of all youth crimes and an even smaller proportion of crimes committed by young women (Muncie 1999: 15; Alder & Hunter 1999; Chesney-Lind 1997). In the United States in 1994, 3.4 percent of girls' arrests were for serious crimes of violence (Chesney-Lind 1997: 39). In Victoria, Australia, Children's Court statistics, which you would anticipate would reflect a higher proportion of serious offenses than police arrest statistics, indicate that violent offenses have consistently accounted for less than 10 percent of girls' offending. Although this is a slightly higher percentage than for boys (7–8 percent), the absolute numbers for boys (around 450 offenses per year) is more than four times that for girls (around 100 offenses per year) (Alder & Hunter 1999), demonstrating the potential posed by the use of percentages to distort the presentation of the "facts."

Further, girls account for a small proportion of all youthful violent crimes and this proportion has changed little across time. In the United States in 1985 girls accounted for 11 percent of all arrests of youth for serious violent offenses; by 1994 the figure was 14 percent (Federal Bureau of Investigation 1995, 222) (Chesney-Lind 1997: 39). Similarly, in Australia the proportion of youth violent offenses for which girls are responsible has remained relatively stable at around 20 percent (Alder & Hunter 1999).

At the same time, the broader statistical picture of youth violent offending across several Western nations indicates a rise in youthful violent crimes across the late 1990s. This observation applies to levels of robbery and assault offenses, but not to homicides, which have remained at relatively stable levels since the 1980s (Pfeiffer 1997; Cook, Leverett, & Mukherjee 1999). For example, Pfeiffer (1997: 20) presents data on trends for violent crimes in Germany that suggest a sharp increase in violent crimes among the fourteen to twenty-one age group beginning in 1991 through to 1995. In the Netherlands, for the twelve to eighteen year-old population the violent crime rate doubled from the beginning of the 1990s (Pfeiffer 1997: 22–23). In Finland, a similar trend is observed with an increase in violent crimes for the fifteen to twenty year-old population, particularly since 1993. In Britain, James (1995: 122–23) found an increase between 1987 and 1993 in the rates of violent offending by the ten to thirteen and fourteen to sixteen year-olds. Such statistics, suggesting an increase in youth violence generally, form a backdrop for speculation about increases in violent offending by young women.

Some statistics also suggest an increase in violent offending by young women in particular. In Victoria (Australia), an analysis of Children's Court statistics indicated a 52.9 percent (40.1 percent for boys) increase between 1990 and 1996 in crimes of violence for girls. An almost identical pattern can be found in data from the Children's Court in New South Wales. In the five year period between 1992–1993 and 1996–1997, assault among boys almost doubled, while for girls there was a three-fold increase in the level of assaults over the same period. Similarly, a study of robbery and assaults in Germany for the period 1993–1997 concluded that the increases in violence tended to be greater for girls than for boys. In Canada and the United States, where there is no overall increase in youthful violent offending, there is nevertheless a statistical indication of increasing levels of violent offending by young women (Leschied, Cummings, Van Brunschot, Cunningham, & Saunders 2000).

Media analyses tend to take such statistics at face value and use them to fuel speculation about "new" violent young women. However, such statistics are as much an indication of definitions of particular behaviors, and criminal or juvenile justice system responses to them and to particular individuals, as they are about the actions of young women. We turn now to an overview of some of the issues that need to be taken into account in interpreting official statistics and a consideration of alternative explanations.

What Constitutes, Officially, Violent Offending by Girls?

Most aggregate analyses of trends in official statistics tend to use very broad categories of offenses. In relation to increases in violent crimes by girls for example, the two categories often used as the basis of analysis are robbery and assault. These broad terms tend to invoke in the popular imagination some of the most feared of crimes: from the balaclava-headed, knife-wielding stranger who enters our home in the dark of night, to the random assault of our person as we go about our everyday business. However, a broad range of offenses is subsumed under these general categories, from the most serious armed robberies to minor assault with intent to rob, and an even greater breadth of action is deemed to *constitute* these offenses.

In an effort to clarify further the interpretation of statistical trends some researchers have attempted to investigate the more precise nature of the crimes committed by girls that have resulted in charges for violent offenses. From their analysis of violent offenses in the youth court cases in Canada between 1991 and 1996, Doob and Sprott (1998: 185) concluded that for girls, as for boys, there had been "large increases in minor assaults and no increase in the most serious assaults."

Two Australian studies had similar findings. In Queensland, following media attention regarding increases in predatory girl violence, a more detailed analysis revealed that girls' violent offenses were of the "less serious" nature, frequently involving fights between girls in public spaces such as shopping centers (Beikoff 1996). In Victoria, a study of Children's Court statistics found that, of the 9 percent of girls' offenses that were offenses against the person, assaults comprised 39 percent. Of these, 33 percent involved assault of a police officer or a person assisting the police. In comparison, 13 percent of boys' assaults were committed against the police (Alder & Hunter 1999). On the face of it, it seems unlikely that girls are actually more likely to assault police than boys. Rather, these figures suggest the need to look more closely at the ways and circumstances in which the offense of assault against police is defined in practice.

Also in Victoria, Australia, Rechtman (2001) analyzed police descriptions of the events that formed the basis of charges against girls for assaults and for robberies for the period between 1993 and 1999. Almost no change was found in the sorts of violent crimes with which girls were charged, with the most common offense being the less serious charge of "unlawful assault." Further, there was very little discernible difference in the nature of the events leading to these charges as described in the police descriptions of the event. One shift, which we will return to discuss later in the chapter, was in the number of victims who were "professional care workers." Rechtman provides the following example of the events that most frequently led to a charge of unlawful assault:

> The victim had been hassled by the offender for approximately five to six weeks prior to the assault. The harassment included telephone calls, and torment at school by offenders and unknown friends of the offender. The reason for the harassment was that the offender believed that the victim has been spreading rumours about her which were slanderous. The harassment climaxed with a minor assaulting which took place when the offender believed the victim had been insolent to the offender's mother. The assault consisted of approximately four punches with a closed fist, and the victim having her hair pulled. The victim's injuries included a

minor asthma attack, and one minor scratch on the face approximately 2 centimetres long on the left cheek. (Rechtman 2001: 43)

This account is very similar to accounts of girls' violence described in the chapters in this book. That is, most often they are of the less serious form of assault. Most often the victims are girls about the same age or younger who are known to the offenders, and the offense most often does not involve a weapon. In the United States, girls' assaults are more likely than boys' to involve other family members (Chesney-Lind 2001: 39,42).

Similar conclusions regarding the less serious nature of girls' violent offending were drawn from a study of robberies in Hawaii between 1994 and 1996. While the statistical data indicated an increase in robbery arrests involving girls, a more detailed analysis of the events leading to the charges found that this was the result of "less serious offences being swept into the system" (Chesney-Lind 2001: 42). The increase in robberies was predominantly accounted for by crimes that were characterized as, "slightly older youths bullying and 'hijacking' younger youths for small amounts of cash and occasionally jewelry" (Chesney-Lind 2001: 44).

Together these pieces of research from Canada, the United States, and Australia suggest that while statistical analyses of the broad categories of offending indicate an increase in girls' violent offending, more detailed analyses of the forms and nature of that offending indicate that this increase is accounted for by more of the same, that is, the less serious forms of violent offending in which some girls have always been involved. As Horowitz and Pottieger (1991, 81) conclude from their Miami research, analyses of overall arrest rates can be deceptive and the complexity of the ways in which gender and race are involved in arrest decision making requires much more detailed analyses before we can draw meaningful conclusions from arrest statistics.

What Constitutes, in Self-Report Studies, Violent Offending by Girls?

Self-report studies are another form of research that can shed some light on the nature of girls' violent offending. Such studies were founded on the observation that official statistics as a measure of juvenile offending behavior were confounded by the juvenile justice responses to the behavior. They are intended to provide a measure of offending as reported by young people themselves.

In comparing the results of such studies with official statistics it has long been noted that official statistics tended to oversexualize and underreport girls' offending. That is, self-report studies suggested that offenses related to concerns regarding sexual behavior tended to be overrepresented in official statistics, and girls engaged in more criminal offending, including less serious assaults, than was recorded in official statistics. Chesney-Lind (2001: 39) observes that "self-report data, particularly from the 1970s and 1980s, always have shown higher involvement of girls in assaultive behaviour than official statistics would indicate." For example, Campbell (1981) found that 89 percent of sixteen-year-old girls in her study had been involved in at least one physical fight. Further, contrary to the conclusions drawn from official statistics that violent offending by girls is *increasing,* Chesney-Lind (2001: 39) reports that a self-report study in the United States "revealed significant *decreases* in girls' involvement in felony assaults, minor assaults, and hard drugs, and no change in a wide range of other delinquent behaviours—including felony theft, minor theft, and index delinquency."

Self-report studies are not without their problems (Muncie 1999: 20) but they do indicate that a good deal of the "crime" committed by young people does not result in arrest. Consequently, changes in arrest statistics may not so much represent changes in young women's behavior as changes in responses to that behavior.

Shifting Definitions and Responses

Central to any interpretation of official statistics is consideration of the ways in which the categories are defined and understood. From their extensive review of the literature on "female adolescent aggression," Leschied, Cummings, Van Brunschot, Cunningham, and Saunders (2000: 8) observe that "what all studies suggest, however, is that estimating the rates for youth violence and gender is complicated by the definition of what is considered violent."

Juvenile justice legislation in the United States, Canada, England, and Australia has undergone extensive change in recent years. Potentially, these changes have had an impact on the definitions and processing of youth crime and thus on the patterns of youth crime as reflected in official statistics, including the increase in violent crimes committed by girls. A thrust of many of these changes has been to separate the handling of welfare matters or "status" offenses (that is, "offenses" that pertain only to young people under a certain age and relate to their own well-being, such as "runaway," "incorrigible," and "in need of care and protection") from criminal offenses. It has been suggested that as a consequence of such reforms, girls' actions that might previously have been dealt with as a "welfare" matter or a "status offense" are now processed as criminal offenses (see, for example, Worrall 2000).

In Australia such a practice has been postulated as having some impact on the official statistics regarding girls' offending in Queensland (Beikoff 1996). An analysis of violent offenses indicated that, as previously mentioned, they were predominantly of a "less serious" nature and, in a third of the cases, the police were named as victim. The author ponders whether this indicates that common public order offenses for juveniles—obscene language, resisting arrest, and assaulting police— are replacing the "care and protection" applications of the past. It has also been suggested in Australia that the more limited availability of "care applications" as a response to girls' unruly behavior has meant that girls involved in incidents, or "acting out" in welfare placements or foster care, are now being charged with criminal offences such as property damage, with subsequent bail refusal, guilty plea, and control orders, resulting in the girl being characterized as a "serious offender" (Alder 1998a). Such a scenario may be an explanation for Rechtman's (2001) finding of an increase in the number of "unlawful assaults" in which the victim was a "professional carer."

In the United States, Chesney-Lind (2001) also argues that the relabeling of behaviors that were once categorized as status offenses into violent offenses cannot be ruled out as an explanation for the observed statistical increase in girls' violence and may also reflect changes in the criminal justice system's handling of domestic violence. Noting that girls' aggression is often in the home or "intra-family" and therefore traditionally less likely to be reported to authorities, she suggests that increasing awareness of, and changing practices in relation to, domestic violence in recent years may have contributed to the increasing levels of girls' arrests for violence. Chesney-Lind (2001: 42) cites the findings of two studies that provide some evidence in support of this suggestion. In one of these studies of "person-to-person" offenses by girls referred to Maryland's juvenile justice system in 1994, virtually all were "assaults," about half of which were "family centered." Similarly a more recent California study of girls' assault charges found that most were the result of "non-serious, mutual combat with parents" (Chesney-Lind 2001: 42).

As this research makes evident, it is not only changing legal definitions that impact on the defining of girls' actions. Parents, teachers, welfare workers, and neighbors have always played a significant part in the defining of girls' behavior as unacceptable and bringing it to the attention of the welfare and juvenile justice systems. For example, Chesney-Lind (2001: 42) suggests that an increase in girls' arrests for robbery in Honolulu may have resulted from changes in school policy and parental attitudes, since many of the offenses occurred as the youths were traveling to and from school, and the victims were peers who were robbed of small amounts of cash and occasionally jewelery.

In Australia, Hancock (1980) found that parents are responsible for bringing their child to the attention of police in a far higher proportion of female than male cases (21 percent compared with 1 percent of boys). Similarly, in England, Gelsthorpe (1986: 139) observed that police were "inundated with requests from parents for officers to go and speak to their 'difficult' children. The majority of these requests . . . came from parents who were concerned about the difficult behaviour of their daughters." In developing their case, police will also draw upon the reports of other people who have had contact with the young women such as teachers, welfare workers, and doctors. Thus, Carrington (1993) has argued, the policing of young women is not only a function of police officers, but is also the responsibility of a range of other people in their environment.

Thus, shifts in definitions of young women's actions as unacceptable or even violent can be brought about not only by legislative or policy changes, but by cultural shifts in understandings of either what is acceptable behavior on the part of girls or what constitutes a violent offense worthy of reporting to police. It is, therefore, important to recognize that the apparent statistical increase in girls' violence may be accounted for, at least in part, by (a) increased visibility of girls' violence, (b) increased categorization of girls' unacceptable behavior as "violence" and/or (c) inappropriate use of percentages to distort increases from a very low initial base (after all, an increase from 1 to 2 is an increase of 100 percent, whereas an increase from 100 to 120 is an increase of only 20 percent!). All these factors will potentially have an impact on recorded crimes and, as the following section seeks to argue, on the answers to two more theoretical questions:

- Under what material and ideological conditions are girls required to "do femininities" in Australia, Britain, Canada, and the United States?
- What resources are available to girls to perform nonpassive femininities and in what ways do they utilize these in their daily routines?

Constructing Girlhood

Kathleen Daly (1997,37) has asked the seemingly rhetorical question:

> Would the claim that crime is a "resource for doing femininity"—
> for women and girls "to create differences from men and boys or
> to separate from all that is masculine"—have any cultural reso-
> nance? Probably not.

Our view, five years on, is that the answer may now be a very tentative "Yes" (see Jody Miller and Norman White in chapter 9). Daly's
concern is that, in theorizing crime within a framework of "doing gender" or "situated accomplishment" (West & Zimmerman 1987) there is
the danger of employing a spurious sex/gender symmetry (or engaging in what Worrall [2002] refers to as the "search for equivalence").
Nevertheless, the evidence provided in this collection suggests that
girls growing up in particular material conditions of existence—far
from trying to be *more like boys*—are routinely looking for ways of
claiming (or reclaiming—see Godfrey's descriptions of "rough girls" a
century ago, in chapter 2) the "resources" of youth in order to demonstrate their *difference* from boys. That the practices that result from this
can only be conceptualized and responded to as crime (a concept that is
always-already gender-laden as a resource for "doing masculinities") is
indicative of the restrictive discourses within which girls are required to
accomplish adolescent femininities.

More specifically, our reading of the essays in this collection leads
us to argue that, wherever girls fail to accomplish the approbated adolescent femininities of scholastic achievement and/or domestic docility,
their alternative behaviors are constructed no longer in terms of emotional "neediness" but in terms of "crime"—and, in particular, in terms
of "disorder" and "violence." There is little tolerance of youthful female
resistance, no indulgent acceptance that "girls will be girls." Girls who
occupy public spaces (see Jenny Pearce in chapter 7), celebrate racial
and cultural differences (see Sheila Batacharya in chapter 4), prioritize
loyalty to female friends (see Michele Burman in chapter 5), express
their sexualities (see Laurie Schaffner in chapter 6) and are generally
boisterous and rebellious, are defined as *threat*, as being *violent*. They are
being *like boys* (see Anne Worrall in chapter 3). The only socially approved alternative resources available to girls are those from within the
discourses of *victimization*. Girls who are the *survivors* of nonsexual and
sexual physical and emotional abuse have permission to be "damaged"
and even to "retaliate" within circumscribed limits. Girls who adopt a

victim identity may be afforded greater leniency when their behavior is considered disorderly or violent, but girls who "take risks" or embark on dubious "adventures," especially in groups, put themselves beyond the reach of positive description. Being "nondescript" (literally, "not easily classified"—see Worrall 1990) these girls are *muted*. And, as Ardener (1978: 21) famously said:

> The theory of mutedness . . . does not require that the muted be actually silent. They may speak a great deal. The important issue is whether they are able to say all that they would wish to say, where and when they wish to say it. Must they, for instance, re-encode their thoughts to make them understood in the public domain? Are they able to think in ways which they would have thought had they been responsible for generating the linguistic tools with which to shape their thoughts? If they devise their own code will they be understood?

The ways in which girls talk about their experiences of violence are often not "re-encoded" in ways that are readily understood and accepted by dominant groups in society (see Burman in chapter 5).

But, as Batacharya argues in chapter 4, the concept of "violent girls" is a construct of white, middle-class culture. Girls of color (whether indigenous or nonindigenous) are constructed as always-already "violent," regardless of their presenting behavior. They are always-already a threat, regardless of their scholastic achievement or domestic docility. For them, we would argue, the only alternative discourse resides within exotica. "Oriental" girls may be viewed as "cute but deadly" (see Worrall in chapter 3). Girls of color who fail to be alluring in this way are routinely assumed to be verbally and physically aggressive.

Aboriginal girls in Australia and African American girls in the United States fare particularly badly in the juvenile justice systems in both countries. In Australia, although indigenous youth comprised approximately 2.6 percent of the youth population, in June 1996 they made up 36 percent of all juveniles held in juvenile detention centers (Atkinson 1996: 3). One study reports that "in one state 77% of inmates in maximum security institutions for juvenile girls were Aboriginal" (Paxman 1993: 156). In the United States the weight of evidence suggests that African American girls are treated more harshly than their European American counterparts at all stages of the juvenile justice system. In terms of policing, Visher found the influence of race and age on arrest decisions was greater for female than male suspects (Visher 1983: 15). Further, African American females represent the fastest growing category of young people adjudicated for delinquent offenses (Girls Incorporated 1996: 20).

Both historical and contemporary research indicates that understanding of African American women as "strong and threatening" (Rafter 1985: 143) and "dominant and nagging" (Daly & Stephens 1995: 204) has informed correctional and court officials punitive responses. A more punitive response to African American girls was evident in Miller's Los Angeles study of probation decision making. Miller (1996: 233) concluded that middle-class African American girls were more likely to receive a detention-oriented placement, while poor white girls were more likely to be recommended to an explicitly treatment-oriented facility. It was in the discursive frameworks of the justifications for these recommendations that Miller found "the most striking differences in the framing of delinquent girls by race" (1996: 235). As a general pattern she observed that "paternalistic discursive frameworks were frequently called upon to explain the behaviour of white and Latina girls, while punitive constructs were more likely to be used to describe African-American girls" (Miller 1996: 239).

In Australia, Pettman notes different versions of femininity and sexuality are portrayed in racialized stereotypes so that "Aboriginal women may be portrayed as loose and easy, and Asian women as sexually exotic, passive and used to male domination" (Pettman 1992: 74). Kerry Carrington has argued that for Aboriginal girls, their gender and their Aboriginality as constructed in a discourse of sexuality, constitute their public visibility as somehow "harmful to the local community" (an oft-quoted phrase in court records) (Carrington 1990: 8). Consequently, their public behavior is more closely policed than that of white girls. The blending of discourses of sexuality, race, and gender was also apparent in the frequent reports by Aboriginal girls of the use by police of such terms as "black sluts," "black bitches," and "black moles" in their interactions with Aboriginal girls (Cunneen 1990).

What It Means to Be a Girl

Christine Alder (1998b: 96) urges:

> We have yet to explore the multiple constructions of femininities and sexualities, their relationship to understandings of girlhood, and their implications for the experiences of girls of differing class and race backgrounds in the juvenile justice system.

Given that "girlhood is produced in the practices in which girls are regulated" (Walkerdine 1993: 15), are we in a position to participate in a reworking of what it means to be a girl in Australia, Britain, Canada, and the United States at the beginning of the twenty-first century? This collection attempts to address a number of the dimensions of that experience by exploring: media representations of girls' behavior and criminal justice responses to it; girls' presence in public space; girls' definitions of violence and their relationships to it; girls' relationships with each other and their behavior in groups.

Barry Godfrey (chapter 2) demonstrates that many contemporary concerns about the behavior of girls are by no means "new" concerns. Using oral evidence, newspaper trial reports, and statistical data, he shows how, in England and in Australia and New Zealand, the deceptively low number of prosecutions for violence by girls in the 1880–1930 period mask the active participation of working girls in street gangs and public brawls. But arresting a girl was not "a good collar" for a constable and might invite ridicule from colleagues, so few appeared in official statistics. Even a century ago it was clear that it was attitudes toward a girl's behavior, rather than the behavior itself, that dictated the extent to which it was made visible. It was not that girls did not engage in risk-taking behavior but it was their risky *sexual* behavior that created more anxieties among respectable citizens than their propensity for drunken brawling. (In contrast, one might argue that, with sexual behavior being less risky a century later—at least in terms of pregnancy and *some* sexually transmitted diseases—it is the propensity for drunken brawling that causes more alarm).

Anne Worrall (chapter 3) examines the evidence that media representations of girls' violence have both reflected and reinforced changing official responses to troublesome girls. Noting the discrepancy between declining overall rates of juvenile female offending and increasing rates of incarceration of girls, she attributes the latter to changing perceptions of the *threat* posed by girls' presence in public spaces and the reconstruction of girls' friendship groups as "girl gangs." While the application of actuarial justice continues to assess girls as a "low risk" category, ideological pressure to render them "auditable" has resulted in the creation of "violent girls" as a penal category to which increasing numbers of disorderly "ladettes" can be assigned.

If Anne Worrall argues that traditional assessments of girls as "low risk" in terms of criminality have been replaced by assessments of them as "high risk underclass youth" (who just happen to be female), then Sheila Batacharya (chapter 4) argues powerfully that "girl violence is an empty concept." Analyses of girls' violence routinely neglect issues of racism, ableism, and heterosexism. When Reena Virk was murdered, the media attributed the violence to a freak failure of gender socialization, to girls being uncharacteristically aggressive. But these were *white* girls attacking a South Asian girl; these were attractive girls attacking a "plain" and "overweight" girl; these were "sexy" girls attacking a lonely, unhappy girl who made false claims about having boyfriends. The femininities that were being played out in this scenario were too complex to be reduced to a mono-causal explanation. What was being reenacted here was a brutal colonialism that constructed "immigrants" as inferior and "immigrant girls" as a "servant" class to be punished for having the audacity to think themselves deserving of relationships with superior white males. This was no "girl-on-girl" violence, but white girls protecting white boys from the insult of being the subjects of black girls' fantasies and competing with black girls for the affections of white boys.

In chapter 5, Michele Burman reports on research into girls' own definitions of, and attitudes toward, violence in Glasgow, Scotland. In their "turbulent talk," girls' definitions of violence are fluid. "Violence" is denounced when it is physically *and* verbally aggressive behavior which cannot be justified; it is acceptable when the social context justifies it—when it is a reaction to insult or humiliation or when it involves "standing up" for self or close friends and family. Girls are all too familiar with violence and have to make sense of it routinely in their lives. But they do not often resort to its use themselves and, when they do, it is rarely "senseless." It is contextualized, analyzed, and explained within girls' complex, and sometimes contradictory, moral discourses.

In chapter 6, Laurie Schaffner also calls for violence by girls to be contextualized. She is more ready than some other contributors to accept that violent behavior by girls has increased (in North America) but argues that this can only be understood through the concept of "community violence" and the gendered impact of this on the daily lives of girls. This is not to argue that violent girls are always direct victims of violence themselves, though this is often the case. Rather, Schaffner argues that we need to explore the extent to which girls absorb or internalize the devaluing messages of domestic violence, routine misogyny, homophobia, and sexual harassment. Schaffner draws our attention to the blurred boundary between girls as perpetrators of violence and girls as victims, survivors, or witnesses of violence.

If Burman and Schaffner urge us to listen to girls' voices and contextualize their violence, then Jenny Pearce explores, in chapter 7, the resourcefulness of girls (in London) in dealing with routine violence and their strategic use of public space to reduce the restrictions on their movement imposed at home. Breaking free from overcrowded and sometimes abusive home environments, Pearce found that girls use streets, estate stairways, and landings to gain knowledge of, and participate in, routine violence and disorder. At times they are actively involved but, more often, they learn to avoid it or negotiate noninvolvement. This is all part of a complex, and historical, engagement of girls in "street life" (as Barry Godfrey demonstrates in chapter 2). Often it is no more than "roughness" or "nuisance"—risky play, testing the boundaries; sometimes it turns into something nastier; sometimes more vulnerable young women become the victims of violence and exploitation themselves. If we read Pearce's contribution aright, she urges us not to perceive "violent" girls as somehow "different" from "nonviolent" girls. Violence inheres in the everyday life of many girls—to be "played with," tested, avoided, negotiated with, and, occasionally, indulged in. Until we understand more about the complexities of gendered street life, we will be unable to explain or situate apparently violent and disorderly behavior by girls.

Sibylle Artz confirms, in chapter 8, that much of the behavior by girls that is classified as "violent" takes place at school. Reporting on a school-based violence prevention program, she notes the greater receptivity of girls to such programs and, though using a different terminology, reinforces the arguments of other contributors that girls' violence emerges from experiences that are different from those of boys and that girls set their own violent behavior in a context of moral judgments. Girls who utilize physical and verbal violence, Artz argues, have a disproportionate experience of violence in their own lives and view themselves through the "hegemonic male gaze," internalizing male expectations of women and judging their own worth by male standards.

Many of the themes that run throughout this collection are summarized and theorized in the final chapter (chapter 9) by Jody Miller and Norman White. Exploring the complexities of girls' use of gender resources in the male-dominated urban street scene, they demonstrate that, while violence may, in some situations, be a resource for girls to accomplish gender, there are many situations in which girls use gender as a resource to negotiate with or avoid participation in violence (as either a victim or a perpetrator). The context of girls' violence on the street, in groups and gangs, is always one of gender power inequalities. Whether engaging in the instrumental violence required for robbery or the symbolism of gang violence, it is power imbalance and sexual double standards that dictate the agenda.

The contributions in this collection are written from differing disciplinary and geographical perspectives. They contain contradictory evidence and, at times, conflicting views. But the common concerns are clear, as is the common commitment to the adventure of excavating the continuities and discontinuities in the struggles of girls and young women to take control of their own lives and futures in material and ideological conditions that continue to restrict their options and opportunities.

Notes

1. We use the term *girls* partly to distinguish teenagers from "older" young women and because the term *young women* tends to mask this younger age group. We also use the term out of respect for the move by some girls to reclaim their power as girls and give the word a new and nontraditional connotation (see Alder 1998).

References

Alder, C. 1998a, "Young women and juvenile justice: Objectives, frameworks, and strategies," in C. Alder (ed), *Juvenile crime and juvenile justice*, Australian Institute of Criminology (Research and Public Policy Series No. 14), Canberra.

———. 1998b. "'Passionate and willful' girls: confronting practices", *Women and Criminal Justice, vol.* 9 no. 4, pp. 81–101.

Alder, C., & Hunter, N. 1999, *Young women in the juvenile justice system,* Criminology Department, University of Melbourne, Melbourne.

Ardener, S. 1978, *Defining women,* Croom Helm, London.

Atkinson, L. 1996, *Detaining Aboriginal juveniles as a last resort: Variations from the theme,* Trends and Issues no. 64, ACT, Australian Institute of Criminology, Canberra.

Beikoff, L. 1996, "Queensland's juvenile justice system: equity, access and justice for young women?" in C. Alder & M. Baines (eds), *And when she was bad? Working with young women in juvenile justice and related areas,* National Clearinghouse for Youth Studies, Tasmania.

Benjamin, W. 1955, "The storyteller," in *Illuminations,* Fontana, London.

Carrington, K. 1990, "Aboriginal girls and juvenile justice: What justice? White justice," *Journal of Social Justice Studies,* no. 3, pp. 1–18.

———. 1993. *Offending girls: Sex, youth, and justice,* Allen and Unwin, St. Leonards, NSW.

Chesney-Lind, M. 1997, *The female offender,* Sage, Thousand Oaks.

———. 2001. "What about the girls? Delinquency programming as if gender mattered." *Corrections Today,* February, pp. 38–44.

Cook, B., Leverett, S., & Mukherjee, S. 1998, *Australian crime: facts and figures 1998,* Australian Institute of Criminology, Canberra.

Cunneen, C. 1990, *A study of Aboriginal juveniles and police violence,* Report Commissioned by the National Inquiry into Racist Violence, Human Rights and Equal Opportunity Commission, Sydney.

Daly, K. 1997, "Different ways of conceptualising sex/gender in feminist theory and their implications for criminology," *Theoretical Criminology,* vol. 1, no. 1, pp. 25–51.

Daly, K., & Stephens, D. J. 1995, "The 'dark figure' of criminology: Towards a black and multi-ethnic feminist agenda for theory and research," in N. Hahn Rafter & F. Heidensohn (eds), *International feminist perspectives in Criminology: engendering a discipline,* Open University Press, Buckingham.

Doob, A. N., & Sprott, J. B. 1998, "Is the 'quality' of youth violence becoming more serious?" *Canadian Journal of Criminology,* April, pp. 185–94.

Gelsthorpe, L. 1986, "Towards a sceptical look at sexism," *International Journal of the Sociology of Law,* no. 14, pp. 125–53.

Gibbons, D. 1982, *Society, crime, and criminal behavior,* Prentice-Hall, Englewood Cliffs, N.J.

Girls Incorporated 1996, *Prevention and parity: Girls in juvenile justice,* Girls Incorporated National Resource Center, Indianapolis.

Hancock, L. 1980, "The myth that females are treated more leniently than males in the juvenile justice system," *Australian and New Zealand Journal of Sociology,* no. 16, pp. 4–14.

Horowitz, R., & Potteiger, A. E. 1991, "Gender bias in juvenile justice handling of seriously crime-involved youths," *Journal of Research in Crime and Delinquency,* no. 28, pp. 75–100.

James, O. 1995, *Juvenile violence in a winner-loser culture,* Free Association Press, London.

Leschied, A., Cummings, A., Van Brunschot, M., Cunningham, A., & Saunders, A. 2000, *"Female adolescent aggression: a review of the literature and the correlates of aggression (User Report No. 2000-04),"* Solicitor General Canada, Ottawa.

Miller, J. 1996, "An examination of disposition decision-making for delinquent girls," in M. Schwartz & D. Milovanovic (eds), *Race, gender, and class in criminology: the intersection,* Garland Publishing, New York.

Muncie, J. 1999, *Youth and crime,* Sage, London.

Paxman, M. 1993, "Aborigines and the criminal justice system: women and children first," *Alternative Law Journal,* vol. 18, no. 4, pp. 153–57.

Pettman, J. 1992, *Living on the margins: racism, sexism, and feminism in Australia,* Allen & Unwin, St. Leonards, NSW.

Pfeiffer, C. 1997, "Jugendkriminalitaet und Jugendgewalt in europaeischen Laendern" an unpublished paper, Hannover: Kriminologisches Forschungsinstitute Niedersachsen e. V. (KFN), Leutzeroderst. 9, 30161 Hannover, Germany.

Rafter, N. 1985, *Partial justice: Women in state prisons, 1800–1935,* Northeastern University Press, Boston.

Rechtman, K. 2001, "Is the Nature of Violent Offending by Girls Changing?" Masters Thesis, Criminology Department, The University of Melbourne, Australia.

Tait, D. 1994, "Cautions and appearances," in R. White & C. Alder (eds), *The police and young people in Australia*, Cambridge University Press, Cambridge.

Taylor, H. 1999, "Forging the job: A crisis of 'Modernization' or redundancy for the police of England and Wales, 1900–1939," *British Journal of Criminology*, no. 39, pp. 113–35.

Visher, C. A. 1983, "Gender, police arrest decisions, and notions of chivalry," *Criminology*, no. 21, pp. 5–28.

Walkerdine, V. 1993, "Girlhood through the looking glass," in M. de Ras & M. Lunenberg (eds), *Girls and girls' studies in transition*, Het Spinhuis, Amsterdam.

West, C., & Zimmerman, D. H. 1987, "Doing Gender," *Gender and Society*, vol. 1, no. 2, pp. 125–51.

Worrall, A. 1990, *Offending women*, Routledge, London.

———, 2000, "Governing bad girls: changing constructions of adolescent female delinquency" in J. Bridgeman & D. Monk (eds), *Feminist perspectives on child law*, Cavendish Publishing, London.

———. 2002, "Rendering women punishable: the making of a penal crisis," in P. Carlen (ed), *Women and punishment: The struggle for justice*, Willan Publishing, Collumpton.

Chapter Two

Rough Girls, 1880–1930: The "Recent" History of Violent Young Women

Barry Godfrey

Recent debates on young women's criminality and capacity for violence have a familiar ring to historians. Public statements concerning the viciousness of youth gangs, both male and female, some of which are discussed in this volume, are reminiscent in tone and content to those made in the late Victorian and Edwardian era (Humphries 1981; Pearson 1983; Pearson 1989). The easy complacency of journalists and moral commentators who have posited the emergence of the violent street or "gang" girl at the start of the third millennium can be corroded away by historical research. This chapter weaves together oral evidence, newspaper trial reports, and statistical data in order to present an integrated view of "normal" and "deviant" girls in the 1880–1930 period. It will attempt to answer one central question: Why did girls constitute a small number of those prosecuted for violent offenses in the fin de siècle period? The study will be underpinned by analysis of the Chief Constables' reports for northwestern cities (1880–1920), which, unlike the national governmental statistics, contain a breakdown of offenses by age and gender of perpetrators. Additionally, the essay will draw on evidence from outside of the English experience but within the English-speaking world.[1] In this period, Australia, New Zealand, and England all shared similar common law systems, laws, and legal procedures, and the populations of those countries also appear to have shared common assumptions about the nature and sociopolitical position of girls within their societies.

Gender, Youth, and Gang Activity

Nineteenth- and twentieth-century historians have often examined criminal justice through the prisms of class, gender, or both. However, although gender has come to the forefront in criminological and historical
research in the last twenty years or so (See Heidensohn 1997; King 1999),
age as a critical factor has seldom been integrated into historical studies
of power relations and the operation of the criminal code. Moreover,
the historiography of youth violence has mainly, and for girls almost
exclusively, focused on their involvement in gang-related activities.

Internationally in the 1880 to 1900 period there was unease about
the state of youth. Far from carrying the world forward to a bright
new twentieth-century dawn, many moral commentators were convinced that the seemingly dissolute and irresponsible nature of their
young people would bring an end to the progress made over the
last century. Concerns centered on visible youth problems, such as
teenage prostitution, and, particularly, the groups of youths that hung
around the streets. Labeled as "hooligans," they took names of their
own choosing—Birmingham's "Peeky Blinders" and Liverpool's
"corner-men" for example. Pearson (1983) has written on the nature of
these gangs and the moral panics that accompanied them by reference
to Victorian newspapers for whom these gangs held particular fascination, and Davies has deepened our knowledge by detailed study of
the Manchester Scuttlers (Davies 1999; 2000). This notorious fighting
gang was responsible for a number of violent affrays in the late nineteenth century, and they deserved their tough reputation (they committed numerous woundings and five homicides between 1870 and
1900). However, below this "hooligan aristocracy," most urban centers
had their own gangs; indeed, neighborhoods could hold ten or twenty
competing gangs of boys who fought over territory, prestige, and reputation as the toughest of the local "mobs." John Drummond, for example, listed tens of gangs all based in a small area of Sydney in the
1920s (Tape 68, *Bicentennial Oral History Project, Australian National Library,* hereafter *ANL tape*). These groups were responsible less for
murder and mayhem, than small-scale street-fights, playing street
football, pushing over dustbins, and numerous public nuisances as
they roamed the parks, coffee-stalls, and railway arches of the English
and Australian cities (Burt 1925; Fishman 1988).

The Australian media were equally active in describing their "Larrikins"[2] as the latest scourge of society. The *Sydney Quarterly Magazine*
went as far as to query whether the only answer to "the uniformly dangerous and pestilent" larrikin element was the arming of the population

(*Sydney Quarterly Magazine,* January 1884). But the Australian and English newspapers of both countries were prone to hyperbole and exaggeration, which makes their assessment of gang activity problematic. The few literary descriptions of gangs, such as the extract from an anonymous poem below, are interesting, but similarly problematic.

The Bastard of the Bush (c. 1880–1914)[3]

As night was falling slowly on city town and bush,
From a slum in Jones's Alley came the Captain of the Push,[4]
And his whistle, loud and piercing, woke the echoes of the
   Rocks,[5]
And a dozen ghouls came slouching round the corners of the
   blocks.

So down in Jones's Alley all the members of the Push
Laid a dark and dirty ambush for that Bastard from the Bush.
But up against the wall of Riley's pub the Bastard made a stand,
A nasty grin upon his dial;[6] a bike chain in each hand.

However, oral history can offer another route into this inquiry. The majority of people interviewed in the 1980s for oral history projects in England and Australia were all young men and women at the turn of the century, and, despite the problems associated with the analysis of people's reminiscences, memories of episodes of childhood play and teenage criminality can reveal much about adolescent youth in the 1880–1930 period.

In those days there were mobs around Sydney. There was the Railway gang and the Renny St mob, the Waterloo mob, the Surry Hill's mob and these mobs used to combat in parks with fist-fights for the sake of fighting. (Walter Tulloch, b.1900, *ANL tape* 112)

Will Sarnoch also highlighted the fighting nature of the gangs, stating that whenever rival gang members met they aimed to pelt their enemies with "blue metal" road covering—"to hit some poor kid with a piece of blue metal." "It was wonderful stuff," added another, "get a handful and you could aim to kill somebody at fifty yards away. And many times they did nearly kill someone, hit them on the head. I don't think there ever was a fatality but some pretty bad injuries." (William Sarnoch, b.1904, *ANL tape* 72 and Mr. Hickey, b.1905, *ANL tape* 114)

A Yorkshireman remembered similar maneuvers to protect "progging" wood before Guy Fawkes night from other groups of bonfire builders: "It was always a great thing to, em, guard your, em, bonfire because rival gangs from maybe three or four streets away they used to try and light your bonfire if they could, see. And we used to have semi-pitched battles, I mean there was never anybody really got hurt at all, well maybe they did" (Tape E0003K/01/07, *Bradford Central Library*).

Few of the men interviewed mentioned the involvement of girls in gang-life. "There'd be fifteen to twenty boys . . . no girls were allowed then," said one man, and when pressed on the point by his interviewer, he reiterated, "No, no, the girls . . . oh they were different to what they are today. They kept to themselves the girls, not like they are today. You know, how they mix together today. But them days it was just the opposite. They never interfered with it, whatever, you know, like all the boys were doing . . . they kept to themselves the girls" (George Cairns, *Pyrmont and Ultimo Oral History Project, State Library of New South Wales,* hereafter *PUOHP*). Indeed, asked about girls' participation in gangs, male respondents often grew a little flustered, as if they had never considered that possibility, and some had trouble talking coherently about the issue. The female respondents never spoke unprompted about gangs, and when they did, not one of the two hundred English and Australian women surveyed claimed to know much about gangs—it was something that boys and "bored young men" did (Millie Weston, b.1893, *ANL Tape* 131). So was there a female presence in gangs at the turn of the century, and, if so, what part did girls play in gang activities?

Girls in the (Victorian) Gang?

Davies has greatly informed our understanding of both youth leisure activities and gang-related violence in the late Victorian period, and he is one of the very few to have written on the involvement of young women in late Victorian street disorders (Davies 1999; 2000). Neither he, nor any other commentator, has found much evidence for there being all-girl gangs. From trial reports and prosecution records, Davies calculates that female members constituted a minor grouping of about 6 percent of total membership.

In Rickard's brief exploration of Australian masculinity, he mentions the "donah" or "clinah," the female counterpart to the larrikin, who never disputed territorial control of the streets alongside the boys, but remained "a gaudily dressed auxiliary" (Rickard 2000). The women members wore similar dress, though it was not entirely dissimilar from the attire of young female factory workers, from whose ranks they were mainly drawn (Violet Douglas b.1903, Sydney discussed cliques of female factory workers). They may have stood out from the norm to contemporaries who could pick up visual cues missed by the modern historian, but they were not as instantly recognizable as some of their male counterparts. The most flamboyant male gang member was resplendent in his pointed brass-tipped clogs, flared trousers, bright silk scarf, and rakishly tilted peaked cap (Russell 1905). Australian gang members too had a penchant for loud fashion styles. But it is likely that most gang members would have blended in with the mass of working-class youth. One Australian remembered that his gang

> wore clothes as cheaply as they could buy them to fit the occasion. Now we were all tough we didn't have too many clothes. It was mostly a thin singlet and a thin shirt at the most and in winter you were lucky if you had one of those heavy braided coats. You had them but you didn't need them. You were tough. (Mr. Hickey, b.1905, *ANL tape* 114)

A reputation for toughness, of course, needed more to back it up than a paucity of clothing. Developing a tough reputation, competition for a girl's affection, or more likely the male intention to claim "property rights" over particular local girls, may all have provoked inter-neighborhood fights. Some girls may have celebrated a young man's attempts to impress them in this way. Girls may similarly have fought over boys' affections, or protected their interest in a boy from the girls of other neighborhoods (Campbell 1984). In other words, the female presence in youth gangs may not have been marginal, but their participation in violence appears to have been limited, at least as far as prosecuted violence goes.

Girls and Routine, "Everyday" Violence

In reviewing the historiography previously outlined, one could be forgiven for concluding that the small number of girls involved in gang activities constituted all violent young women. Were girls ever involved in violence outside of the sphere of gang activities? Before answering that question it is important not to overstate the distinctions between gang and non-gang violence, particularly when thinking of public fights. Affrays between warring neighborhood families, disputes arising from romantic jealousy, and routinely boisterous play all shared many similarities.

Many disturbances involving young women could involve large numbers of people, see the use of weapons (though often of a domestic character—fire pokers, rather than knives), and could be equally as brutal in character. Witness three examples from the 1886 *Staffordshire Advertizer:*

> *The Holy Sabbath in Tenterbanks.* The court was occupied for a considerable time arising out of a number of charges arising out of a disgraceful neighborhood quarrel in Tenterbanks on Sunday. Mary Nolan, a young woman of bad character was charged with breaking a pane of glass in a window of a house during the progress of the disturbance. The defendant's hand was cut, and the evidence was to the effect that the injury was caused by her thrusting her hand through the window. Against this the defendant alleged that her hand was cut by a knife. (*Staffordshire Advertizer,* October 9, 1886).

> Jane Lloyd was charged with assaulting her mother who she frequently abused. "On the day in question she struck her in the head with a poker. The complainant did not wish to press the charge, all she wanted was protection." (She was subsequently bound over to keep the peace. *Staffordshire Advertizer,* August 14, 1886).

> Charlotte Hall was summoned for assaulting a woman leaving Messrs. Bostock's factory with her sister at one o'clock, and the defendant, who was employed at Mr. Wycherley's factory, crossed the road and addressed her in very insulting language. They took no notice of the defendant, who became very excited, and caused a large crowd of operatives to follow them along the street. Opposite St Patrick's place the defendant struck her twice upon the breast with her fist. (Charlotte was fined 10 shillings, but, since she was unable to come up with the money, she was sentenced to spend a month in jail, *Staffordshire Advertizer,* February 26, 1881).

Gender, Life-Cycle, and Offending Behavior

Newspapers would have considered crimes involving violent young women to have been well worth reporting, and the lack of such

Fig. 2.1
Assaults, number of offenders, within age brackets,
North-West English cities, 1900–1920

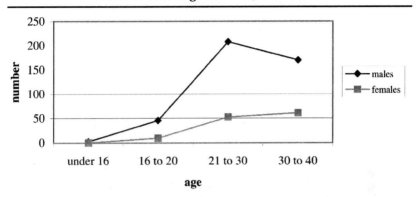

reports superficially indicates a low number of trials involving women. The statistics collected by the police courts, forwarded to the Home Office, and published in the Chief Constables' reports, provide a more reliable index.

As can be seen in the above graph, young men vastly outnumbered the young women caught at the wrong end of the criminal justice system. For every girl aged between sixteen and twenty-one, there were five boys prosecuted for violence in northwest England. For the twenty-one to thirty age bracket the ratio was still one to four.

Both in Victoria (where the statistics are dominated by the state capital, Melbourne), and in New Zealand, the different rates of offending are even more marked (1:7.5 in both jurisdictions). However, although the numbers of male and female offenders were vastly different, the age profiles of male and female offenders were similar.

Peter King has noted that the peak age of property offenders was mobile in the last decades of the eighteenth century. The sharp male peak in the 18 to 19-year-old bracket moved in 1791 to an equally pronounced peak at age 21–22 in 1821, whilst the less dramatic age profile of women moved from a peak at age 19–21 to one at 22–23 (King 1996: 65). Philips puts the peak age of offending at age 21–25 by 1853–1855 (Philips 1977: 161), and in the early twentieth century the peak age for violent offenses (assaults; assaults on a police officer; and aggravated drunkenness) was 21 to 30 for men, and, for women, between 30 and 40. The latest Home Office figures (2000) show that the peak age of offending for men is 18, and the female peak between 14 and 18. So, although

Fig. 2.2
Assaults, percentage of offenders within age brackets,
North-West English cities, 1900–1920

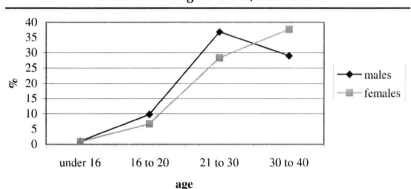

the peak age of offending shifted back and forth over the last two hundred years, it is unsurprising that the peak remains in the lower age brackets. As King states:

> For both sexes, the often highly mobile period between the usual age of leaving home (mid-teens) and the most frequent age at marriage (early to mid-twenties) was the key period of vulnerability to prosecution. . . . For various social and psychological reasons adolescents and young unmarried adults in many societies and periods have been perceived as both more likely to commit property offenses and more likely to antagonize victims and control agencies and therefore more vulnerable to prosecution. (King 1996: 61–90)

Most noticeable, however, is that from the eighteenth century onward, the divergence in offending between the sexes is most marked in the number of offenses being committed in the age range twelve to twenty-one. During that adolescent life-stage, boys and young men outpaced young women in the judicial statistics to a considerable degree (Davies 1999).

Only a small proportion of law breakers ever reach the courts. Various official and informal practices in the criminal justice system often intruded to either accelerate or inhibit a person's progress through the prosecution process. Were "violent" girls prevented from reaching the courts by the action/inaction of formal authorities, or was the socialization and control of young women sufficient to prevent them from committing offenses?

Fig. 2.3
Assaults, percentage of offenders within age brackets, Victoria 1901 and New Zealand 1915 to 1920

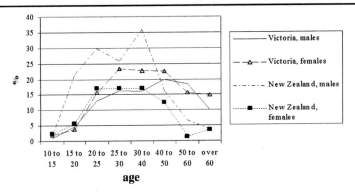

The Socialization of Young Women

"Have you been a good girl?"
"Have you been a good girl?"
I go to a party, I go out to tea,
I go to an aunt for a week at the sea,
I come back from school or from playing a game;
Wherever I come from, it's always the same:
"Well? Have you been a good girl, Jane?"

—A. A.Milne, *Now That We Are Six*

Though Milne poked fun, and Hilaire Belloc stretched a point (Belloc 1907), Matilda told lies and was burned to death, Sarah didn't learn to study and was gored by a bull, and Rebecca, who slammed doors, "perished miserably." Popular literature of the mid-nineteenth century overwhelmingly praised modesty and politeness in girls (Percival 1939) and posited severe sanctions for those who transgressed these expectations. In comic books and children's novels girls were convenient chums who could have the plot explained to them, be endangered and subsequently saved by our hero. Even the most independent and aggressive women required rescuing by male companions (Elmira the Female Pirate, for example [Springhall 1998: 49]). By the twentieth century most heroines were not pirates but priggish public schoolgirls out on amateurish detective ventures. Such heroines and chums could never truly compete with the boy-hero, they were not even fully rounded sexual characters: "All these girl chums as featured in the illustrations had a tendency towards flat chests and low heels. Their faces were pretty in a chocolate box style, but their figures were strictly non-voluptuous . . ." (Turner 1948: 124).

Boys might go soppy over their chums, they might take them to their dens, but they never took them to bed. They were preoccupied with more pressing matters in any case. Sons of the Empire relived past wars and practiced for the next: "Oh we used to go every Saturday. We'd have great fun at the pictures, we'd come home and Sunday would be the pictures all over, in the backyard. We'd always play Cowboys and Indians, and Robinson Crusoe—make a bit of wood up . . . and the sword, we'd be fighting in the yard" (George Burns, *PUOHP*). It must be remembered that few British and Australian boys born between 1880 and 1914 would have reached their twenty-first birthday without being entreated to fight in the Somme, Gallipoli, or some other corner of a foreign field. It is small wonder that, in literature as in real life, boys who acted aggressively often had their behavior praised by friends, parents, and schoolteachers, since it demonstrated their preparations for adult life, where masculine toughness in wartime and peacetime (within limits) was a quality to be admired. As for the young female readership, tales of schoolgirl exploits and adventuresome naughtiness were written for the well-brought-up girl, not her working-class counterpart who, in reality, would likely have been far closer to danger, risk, and sexual activity.

The gendered ideological position evident in contemporary literature was buttressed by familial and societal controls over the leisure and home activities of younger women designed to protect them and their reputation. Enid Ross's mother, for example, thought her daughter should learn to dance at a well-governed respectable dance hall.

> So I went on two occasions. . . . But my father learned of my going and stopped it immediately. I was not to dance. I think he was over-protective really and it was a fear that I might get into the wrong company and I think that he perhaps, he loved us well and therefore wished to save us from any harm that may have come but I, being young, didn't think of such things. (Enid Ross, *ANL tape* 20)

One winter's night in 1910, whilst sitting in front of the fire with a group of her mother's friends, Martha Hallinan let slip that she had heard that one of the neighbors was pregnant. Her mother immediately took her to the back room for a "dressing down" for her rudeness

(Martha Hallinan, *ANL tape* 28). Indeed, many women looked back to "very unhappy" (Jeanette Clear, *ANL tape* 27) home lives, remembering strict, occasionally cruel, punishments handed out (mainly) by their fathers. One woman summed up the whole situation thus:

> My father had the greatest authority. . . . I think his actions, his looks and perhaps one word or two we would know we had to behave. Not that it was necessary to do a great deal because we had been trained from an early age, the beginning you might say, to do what was correct as well as we might and he would see to it that we didn't stray from that path. (Enid Ross, *ANL tape* 20)

Much of the above evidence refers to the disciplining of younger girls, however, and both the ideology of girlhood and the ability to enforce its principles may have been increasingly tested as girls grew into young women. The young women employed in mills, factories, and shops, for example, may not have needed to heed the dictates of home quite so closely. Their financial contributions to the family budget allowed some measure of freedom from the routines of domestic dicta. Like the boys, they spent some of their wages on new clothes and frequenting the cinema (which was entering its "Golden Age" in the 1920s and 1930s). However, for most boys and girls, entry to "the pictures" was merely a pleasant change from their nightly colonization of the public streets (for modern similarities see Chesney-Lind and Sheldon 1998: 72), though others viewed these social activities less benignly:

> I have the misfortune to traverse the High Street frequently in the evenings, and am sometimes foolish enough to imagine the footpath is intended for respectable persons, and not only for youths and girls to promenade; but I speedily observe my error by being jostled onto the roadway. Then in addition to this, I since heard language uttered by young women so foul and filthy that I felt ashamed to belong to the same sex, and this is an everyday occurrence. (Letter to *The Nantwich Chronicle*, 9 April 1881)

Home discipline, familial control, and the impact of gendered socializing influences, may all have kept a lot of girls out of "mischief," off the streets, and out of the public eye. However, as the above examples, and a number of other studies make clear (Dyehouse 1981; Davies 1992; Bourke 1994; Tebbutt 1995; Davin 1996; and Roberts 1995), girls seem to have joined the boys on the streets in significant enough numbers to make them vulnerable to police attention. When they did fall foul of the police, were girls treated differently from boys?

The Policing of Young Women

A witness to "An Amazonian Quarrel" between two young women declared he "knew nothing about the disturbance, because, like a wise man, when he saw there was likely to be a row between women in the street he had kept close within doors" (*Staffordshire Advertizer,* July 10, 1884). Policemen may not have been so shy, but that is not to say that constables arrested every woman who disturbed the peace. Police officers considered dangerous or violently drunken men to be higher on their list of priorities than women, and certainly higher than girls. After all, constables were as anxious to preserve their status as "hard men" as the rest of the male working population, and the arrest of a dangerous man could be admired by colleagues—"a good collar"—which enhanced their reputation within the station house, and the neighborhood generally. There were few kudos in "bringing in" drunken women or girls committing minor infringements of the law. To arrest a girl invited ridicule. Police officers in England and Australia often assaulted young men who they thought undermined their authority (Male, b.1909, K0011/01/15, *Bradford Central Library).* For example, the police in 1920s Sydney waited for nearly two years to catch the Mad Digger, leader of the locally notorious Dirty Dozen gang, on his own. When they did, they beat him so badly that he was in hospital for six months (G. Cairns, *PUOHP,* NSW Library, Sydney). Though this police operation was covert, and the level of violence exceptional, the public generally accepted and approved of the physical disciplining of teenage boys by the police. The "clip round the ear" which has now become a symbol of a past Golden Age of policing, when deferential youths were reminded of their place without recourse to the courts or formal police action, was often employed by local policemen.

No wonder that, when asked about how her community viewed the police in the 1920s, Evelyn Goodwin (*ANL tape* 90) replied, "oh, very good . . . children were all frightened of the police, if they ever saw a policeman they'd run for miles because they were all frightened." Yet the physical disciplining of girls on the public streets seems not to have been a viable option. Boys faced casual violence or a trip to the magistrates' court for their misdemeanors, but many girls who had jostled, pushed, threatened, and abused fellow youths may have escaped both informal police action and judicial attention.

It is true that women who had stabbed or severely beaten adversaries were likely to be arrested, and appear before the courts, and also women who came from populations the police considered problematic, such as the Irish communities in English cities, or the lowest socioeconomic strata of society. Frances Heywood, for example, was a young working-class woman charged with assaulting Arabella Mason. The newspaper that reported her trial could not bring itself to print the "opprobrious" language the defendant had used, but stated that Frances was fined five shillings and costs for the assault, which had amounted to a few whacks with a wet umbrella, but was also fined twenty shillings and costs for the bad language. After another case of abusive language, Frances yet again appeared in the courts, charged with assaulting her female neighbors. She was acquitted both times though her reputation had already been made (*Staffordshire Advertizer*, April 9, 1887 and June 21, 1890). However, many hundreds, possibly thousands, of lesser conflicts between young women were ignored or downplayed by police officers, so that they never reached the courts.

It appears that police policy followed the public conception that males and not females posed an aggressive threat to public order. The anxieties that swept through England and much of the "Western world" in the 1880–1914 period (Godfrey 2001a), especially the youth moral panics of the 1890s, touched but lightly and sporadically on the subject of girls. In contrast to contemporary anxieties about unrestrained or unchanneled male aggression, anxieties about women focused on unlicensed female sexuality. During the first decades of the century there was a cluster of concerns that revolved around the new, liberated woman, the massive increase in venereal disease, and the rise of underage sex, all of which seemed to threaten the stability of family life (Humphries and Gordon 1994: 14). The attempted curbing of male aggression had been an objective of the state since the early nineteenth century (Weiner 1995), and it is unsurprising that boys were targeted in that process. Moreover, boys posed specific problems due to their marginality in the labor market at the height of the adolescent phase of their life. Pearson believes that "boy labor" was a transient period of employment and the move to man's labor was difficult for many, since they were plunged into competition with younger boys who would labor for less money. It was greatly feared, in fact, that the structure of employment was such that it supplied the rising generation with little discipline and even less skill, and that it threatened to produce an endless tide of loafers, unemployables and ne'er-do-wells who had been thrown on to the scrap heap in their late teens or early twenties.

The employment opportunities for working-class girls—whether in factory work or in domestic service—would not appear to have excited either the same sympathy or alarm (Pearson 1983, 60). Of course, the workless girl in her early twenties was always assumed to be able to rely on matrimony for her economic support. Only when some young women turned to prostitution as an alternative source of income, or when young mothers were accused of rearing delinquent (male) children, did the public gaze turn their way again.

Conclusion: Young Women, Offending, and Risk Taking

So were girls violent; were they fighters; were they aggressive risk takers? The socialization of girls, and the restrictions placed on their liberty whilst living at home with parents, meant that women in their late teens were less likely to be seen in the public streets (especially at night). During the day when girls played skittles, skipping, and other street games they were not considered as problematic as boys playing football or cricket. Nor was their behavior scrutinized for signs of future disorder. Boys were expected to be rough, and it was no surprise when roughness strayed over into intolerable aggression, and the police stepped in. Girls, however, were denied this conceptual space. The ideological polarization permitted girls only to be either essentially good or intrinsically bad. No doubt this detrimentally affected girls accused of more serious crimes who were cast as folk devils, but the girls who were occasionally rough were kept out of the clutches of the police (and consequently they were also kept out of the cycle of repeat offending that seems to have affected young lads).

Moreover, from the evidence considered in this chapter, it appears that young women were only occasionally involved in gang-related affrays, and not to the same extent as were young men. Girls were consigned in gang hierarchies to subsidiary roles (molls, hangers-on, trophies), and only occasionally did some girls overcome the strictures of those roles to participate in episodic disorders. But although subordinated under this system, many believed that their best interests were served by collaboration. Boys could advantage themselves in the local hierarchies by claiming to be "hard men," and by backing up their claims by assaulting rival gang members, passers-by who caught their attention, and the police. The successful commission of more serious assaults could rapidly elevate a youth to an admired position within a neighborhood, and a jail sentence may not have harmed that reputation either. It is difficult to see how young women could have gained prestige under that system, since the more violent they were, the less attractive they were both to potential "normal" decent young suitors and to male gang leaders (who, for the most part, would have shared the general view that women should conform to feminine conventions).

None of the above, however, means that young women did not have a capacity for violence when they felt it warranted. Defending or protecting the rights of the family, the neighborhood, or some other imagined community was traditionally a male activity. Nevertheless, whenever and wherever young women found themselves "pitched" into neighborhood or family feuds, the newspaper and oral evidence confirms that they were as intent on causing injury as the boys. In those circumstances girls showed no natural psychological or biological disinclination to hitting someone when kith and kin were threatened. Nor does it mean that young women were not natural risk takers.

Violence is very often associated with risk taking—fighting, for example, offered not only the promise of victorious triumph but the possibility of ignominious defeat. Risky behavior for boys often involved interaction between them and the natural environment (climbing, hanging onto trams, and so on), or between them and their peers (fights, football matches, wrestling contests, and so on). The supporting role of female gang members, and the marginality of young women in the statistics of prosecuted violence superficially suggests that they held conservative attitudes and were wary of taking risks. However, girls, when they had the opportunity and the inclination, often risked two valuable commodities—their health and/or their reputation (hence they risked their chances of securing employment and a "good" marriage). In both respects it was in the sexual realm that risks were taken. For example, of the women who had no desire to become pregnant, nearly one-fifth (19 percent) used no form of contraceptive method at all, or abstained completely from penetrative sex; and nearly one-third (30 percent) used the unreliable *coitus interruptus* or "safe period" method (Bone 1973, quoted in Bourke 1994: 58).

As the oral accounts make clear, in England and Australia, unmarried women often turned to abortions when those "natural" methods of birth control had failed them, and, in this period, abortions were not only illegal, but frequently fatal. For example, three Nottinghamshire women spoke to interviewers about self-performed abortions using Lysol (bleach), crochet needles, and by throwing themselves down stairwells. They all survived, though two were hospitalized, and one subsequently needed a hysterectomy (Nottingham Oral Archive, tapes 84, 84a, 84b). Others told of even more horrifying consequences:

There was this girl at school. . . . She looked sick and we were asking what was the matter, she said her sister—she was pregnant—

and this girl had put a hat pin up her and it caused her terrible pain. She died. She had septiceamia and the doctor said he could put her in gaol but he thought she had suffered enough. He was nice, but he couldn't do much about it. The girl was dead. (Ella Gibson, *ANL tape* 56)

Dramatic and desperate home-grown medical procedures may have represented the pinnacle of risk for some women (it is impossible to even make a guess at the total figure), but even having the faintest local reputation for being a woman of easy virtue could have disastrous effects on a woman's chances of getting married. Premarital sex was illicit, may have been exciting, and fraught with the danger of attracting a bad name. If it was to be approached at all, girls were wise to choose a young man who would go on to make "an honest woman" of them through marriage. However, the young women partners draped on the arm of "Hooligan Harry" or "Larrikin Larry," by choosing to associate themselves with men for whom society had not a good word to say, virtually removed themselves from respectable society (Mahood and Littlewood 1994: 567). Therefore, in risking their health, reputation, and future economic security, the many thousands of young women who may have chosen "unsuitable" partners, or to experiment sexually before marriage, proved the equal of men as risk takers—even if that route did not carry them into the courts. The police, magistrates, journalists, policy makers, and moral entrepreneurs all had their heads turned toward boys' activities. Unfortunately, until recent days, so too have the criminologists and the historians.

Notes

This essay arises from research projects funded by the Economic and Social Research Council research (award no. R000223300) and The British Academy (award no. APN 30187). Part of this research was carried out in the Oral History Collection of the Australian National Library during a fellowship at the Humanities Research Centre, Australian National University.

1. The study is underpinned by analysis of Staffordshire and Cheshire newspapers, 1880–1920; the Chief Constables' Reports for Chester, Liverpool, Manchester, Stafford, Victoria (Australia), and Christchurch (New Zealand). Of particular use have been the oral history collections held in England County Records Offices and Libraries, and the Bicentennial Oral History Project transcripts held in the National Library of Australia.

2. This term was coined in the 1890s after a violent gang rape in Melbourne. The term gradually lost its impact when it began to be used indiscriminately to label young working-class youths who gathered on the streets at night.

3. Sometimes attributed to Henry Lawson, the Australian poet.

4. Australian term for the hooligan "gang."

5. The Rocks area of the Sydney waterfront had developed a reputation as a dangerous area since the early days of settlement. See Karskens, G. (1997), *The Rocks, Life in Early Sydney*, Melbourne; Godfrey, B. (2001b), "Rethinking attitudes towards violence: England, New Zealand and Australia, 1880–1920," International Conference on the History of Violence, Liverpool, July 2001.

6. Cockney slang for a person's face.

References

Oral History Primary Sources

John Drummond, b.1903, Bicentennial Project, *Australian National Library*, tape 68.
Walter Tulloch, b.1900, Bicentennial Project, *Australian National Library*, tape 112.
William Sarnach, b.1904, Bicentennial Project, *Australian National Library*, tape 72.
Mr. Hickey, b.1905, Bicentennial Project, *Australian National Library*, tape 114.
Millie Weston, b.1893, Bicentennial Project, *Australian National Library*, tape 131.
Violet Douglas, b.1903, Bicentennial Project, *Australian National Library*, tape 121.
William Dunlop, b.1899, Bicentennial Project, *Australian National Library*, tape 113.
Enid Ross, b.1896, Bicentennial Project, *Australian National Library*, tape 20.
Martha Hallinan, b.1896, Bicentennial Project, *Australian National Library*, tape 28.
Jeanette Clear, b.1897, Bicentennial Project, *Australian National Library*, tape 27.
Evelyn Goodwin, b.1899, Bicentennial Project, *Australian National Library*, tape 90.
Ella Gibson, b.1896, Bicentennial Project, *Australian National Library*, tape 56.
George Cairns, Pyrmont and Ultimo Oral History Project, *State Library of New South Wales, Sydney.*
George Burns, Pyrmont and Ultimo Oral History Project, *State Library of New South Wales, Sydney.*
Anonymous interviewee, *Bradford Central Library, Local Studies Section*, E0003K/01/07.
Anonymous interviewee, *Bradford Central Library, Local Studies Section*, A0026/01/01.
Anonymous interviewee, *Bradford Central Library, Local Studies Section*, K0011/01/15.
Anonymous interviewees, *Nottingham Central Library, Local Studies Section*, 84, 84a, 84b.

Contemporary Printed Sources

Staffordshire Advertiser, February 26, 1881.
Staffordshire Advertiser, July 10, 1884.
Staffordshire Advertiser, August 14, 1886.

Staffordshire Advertiser, October 9, 1886.

Staffordshire Advertiser, April 9, 1887.

Staffordshire Advertiser, June 21, 1890.

Crewe and Nantwich Chronicle, April 9, 1881.

Sydney Quarterly Magazine, January 1884, quoted in J. Birmingham (2000) Sydney, Leviathan, Vintage, Sydney.

PP. 1882 Select Committee on the Law Relating to the Protection of Young Girls.

42nd Annual Report of the Inspector of Reformatory and Industrial Schools in Great Britain, *PP* (1899) vol. XLIV.

45th Annual Report of the Inspector of Industrial Schools in Great Britain, *PP* (1902) vol. XLVIII.

Published Sources

Belloc, H. 1907, *Cautionary tales,* Duckworth, London.

Bone, M. 1973, "Family planning services in England and Wales, London," reproduced in Bourke 1994, *Working class cultures in Britain, 1890–1960,* Routledge, London.

Bourke, J. 1994, *Working class cultures in Britain, 1890–1960,* Routledge, London.

Burt, C. Sir. 1925, *The young delinquent,* London University Press, London.

Cale, M. 1993, "Girls and the perception of sexual danger in the Victorian reformatory system," *History,* vol. 78, pp. 73–96.

Campbell, B. 1984, *The girls in the gang,* Blackwells, Oxford.

Chesney-Lind, M. & Shelden, R. 1998, *Girls, delinquency, and juvenile justice,* 2nd edition, West/ Wadsworth, New York.

Davies, A. 1992, *Leisure, gender, and poverty. Working-class culture in Salford and Manchester, 1900–1939,* Open University, Buckingham.

———. 1999, "'These viragoes are no less cruel than the lads': Young women, gangs, and violence in Late Victorian Manchester and Salford," *British Journal of Criminology,* vol. 39, no. 1, pp. 72–89.

———. 2000, "Youth gangs, gender, and violence, 1870–1900," in S. D'Cruze, *Everyday Violence in Britain, 1850–1950,* Longman Pearson, London.

Davin, A. 1996, *Growing up poor: Home, school, and street in London 1870–1914,* Rivers Oram, London.

Dyhouse, C. 1981, *Girls growing up in late Victorian and Edwardian England,* Routledge, London.

Fishman, W. 1988, *East End, 1888,* Duckworth, London.

Godfrey, B. 1999, "Sentencing factors: do they explain gender differential patterns of punishment for assault in the late nineteenth-century?" Paper presented at North-West Crime Historians Conference, Liverpool University, April.

———. 2001a, "Jack the Ripper and fin de siecle anxieties: relocating historical specificity," *Newsletter Moderne,* March.

———. 2001b, "Rethinking attitudes towards violence: England, New Zealand, and Australia, 1880–1920." Paper presented at International Conference on the History of Violence, Liverpool, July.

Heidensohn, F. 1997, "Gender and crime," in *Oxford Handbook of Criminology*, Oxford University Press, Oxford, pp. 761–84.

Home Office Digest 2000, Her Majesty's Stationary Office, London.

Humphries, S. 1981, *Hooligans or rebels? An oral history of working-class children and youth 1889–1939*, Blackwell, Oxford.

Humphries, S. and Gordon, P. 1994, *Forbidden Britain: our secret past*, BBC books, London.

Jackson, L. 2000, *Child sexual abuse in Victorian England*, Routledge, London.

Karskens, G. 1997, *The Rocks, life in early Sydney*, Melbourne University Press, Melbourne.

King, P. 1996, "Female offenders, work, and life-cycle change in late-eighteenth-century, London," *Continuity and Change*, vol. 11, no. 1, pp. 61–90.

Mahood, L. and Littlewood, B. 1994, "The 'vicious' girl and the 'street-corner' boy: sexuality and the gendered delinquent in the Scottish child-saving movement, 1850–1940," *Journal of the History of Sexuality*, vol. 4, no. 4, pp. 549–78.

Milne, A. A. 1927, *Now that we are six*, Methuen, London.

Newburn, T. 1997, "Youth, crime, and justice," in *The Oxford Handbook of Criminology*, Oxford University Press, Oxford, pp. 613–61.

Pearson, G. 1983, *Hooligan: a history of respectable fears*, Macmillan, London.

———. 1989, "A Jekyll in the classroom, a Hyde in the street: Queen Victoria's hooligans," in D. Downes (ed), *Crime and the City*, Macmillan, London.

Percival, A. 1939, *The English miss to-day and yesterday. Ideals, methods, and personalities in the education and upbringing of girls during the last hundred years*, George Harrap, London.

Philips, D. 1977, *Crime and authority in Victorian England, 1835–60*, Croom Helm, London.

Rickard, J. 2000, "Lovable larrikins and awful ockers," in R. Nile (ed), *The Australian legend and its discontents*, Queensland University Press, St. Lucia, Queensland, pp. 297–310.

Roberts, E. 1995, *A woman's place: an oral history of working-class women, 1890–1940*, Blackwells, Oxford.

Russell, C. 1905, *Manchester boys: sketches of Manchester lads at work and play*, Manchester University Press, Manchester.

Springhall, J. 1998, *Youth, popular culture, and moral panics*, Macmillan, London.

Tebbutt, M. 1995, *Women's talk? a social history of "gossip" in working-class neighbourhoods, 1880–1960*, Scholar, London.

Turner, E. 1948, *Boys will be boys: the story of Sweeney Todd, Deadwood Dick, Sexton Blake, Billy Bunter, Dick Barton et al*, Micheal Joseph, London.

Weiner, M 1995, "Changing attitudes to violence in nineteenth-century Britain." Paper for International Association of Historians of Crime and Criminal Justice, Paris, June.

Zedner, L. 1991, *Women, crime, and custody in Victorian England*, Clarendon, Oxford.

Chapter Three

Twisted Sisters, Ladettes, and the New Penology: The Social Construction of "Violent Girls"

Anne Worrall

Slowly but surely a new problem population is being constructed from which the public requires protection. In the actuarial language of the new penology (Feeley & Simon 1992), a group that hitherto has been assessed as too small and too low-risk to warrant attention is now being reassessed and recategorized as high-risk and dangerous. No longer "at risk" and "in moral danger" from the damaging behavior of men, "violent girls" now exist as a category within penal discourse—a category to which increasing numbers of young women can be assigned and, within which, can be subjected to the same objectives and techniques of management as young men. This process of reconstructing "troublesome young women" as "nasty little madams" has been barely perceptible. This is partly because the theorizing of adolescent femininity and its relationship to state intervention has a complex history with many twists and turns. But it is also because, in actuarial terms, gender is one of the most certain predictors of offending. It is therefore not easy to adjust to the realization that youth (another sound predictor), class, and race (less reliable predictors) may be displacing gender in the categorization and management of violent offending. Violence is increasingly predicted to be something engaged in by poor, young, black people of both sexes.

Some examples may serve to demonstrate this subtle shift toward gender neutrality. Rutter et al. (1998: 254) claim that the sex ratio of males to females in relation to offending in England and Wales has declined from 11:1 in the 1950s to less than 4:1 in the late 1990s (though most of that decline took place between 1950 and 1980). The ratio has also been affected by ethnicity, being even less than 4:1 for black young people and more for Asian young people. Although acknowledging that the violence committed by young women represents only a small fraction of that committed by young men, Rutter et al. argue that violence by young women has increased, especially in America and especially where girls have been exposed to gang membership (1998: 74).

It may be that girls are becoming more violent, Rutter et al. (1998: 278) argue, because they are increasingly exposed to social contextual influences where violence is a risk rather than because girls, in some general sense, are becoming more violent. Steffensmeier and Haynie (2000) similarly dispute the claim that the structural disadvantage normally associated specifically with *being a woman* (poverty, income inequality, joblessness, single parenthood [see also Pantazis 1999]) has significant effects on *juvenile* female homicide. Rather, they argue that homicides by young women (though rare) are more likely to be caused by either individual desperation (for example, killing an unwanted newborn baby) or exposure to social contexts more usually associated with homicide by young men (firearms, gangs, and drugs). Again, the argument is that being a young woman per se is not the issue.

Finally, a study of the extent of weapon carrying among school-age children in England (Balding et al. 1996) showed that, although girls were less likely (16 percent) than boys (27 percent) to carry weapons for protection (including sound alarms and sprays), the ratio was less than 2:1 and the carrying of weapons was closely related to lifestyles (drugs, drink, smoking), concerns (bullying, assault), and attitudes (especially toward protecting disposable income). So the potential for violence was predictable more by these latter factors than by gender alone. At the same time, however, the study showed that girls were most likely to carry defensive sound alarms, while boys were most likely to carry weapons with blades—a rather important difference that was overlooked by a subsequent television program (Channel Four Television 1996) arising from the study.

These examples indicate, I would suggest, that postfeminist explanations of violence by girls are taking one of two forms: a return to individually based psychological explanations (albeit informed by feminist psychotherapy, as will be discussed later) or a "liberation hypothesis" which refutes the role of gender in women's and girls' offending. These explanations share a belief in the moral agency of women and the importance of "empowering" them to take responsibility for their own actions (Hannah-Moffat 1999). The corollary of this "responsibilization" is that the "welfarization" and "soft policing" of young women's behavior by both formal and informal social control mechanisms has now given way to the straightforward "criminalization" of that same behavior, with increasing numbers of young women being incarcerated, not on spuriously benevolent welfare grounds, but on spuriously equitable "justice" grounds.

Barbara Hudson foresaw this danger more than fifteen years ago:

If we rescue girls from the rigidities of notions of orthodox femininity embodied in our judgements of girls as "beyond control," or "in moral danger," we do not eliminate girls from being judged by the double standard we apply to girls' and boys' behaviour; rather we transfer judgement from a set of stereotypes connected with girls' behaviour within the family to another set connected with female delinquency. (B. Hudson 1984: 108 cited in Howe 1994: 185)

But this warning was overlooked because, at the same time, Annie Hudson (1983) had written a groundbreaking article entitled *The Welfare State and Adolescent Femininity*, which provided the theoretical underpinnings of the "sexualization" analysis of state intervention in the lives of young women in the United Kingdom for the rest of that decade. This resulted in practitioners looking for alternatives to traditional welfare approaches without necessarily heeding Barbara Hudson's warning.

The "sexualization" theory of welfare regulation posited that

the majority of girls do not get drawn into the complex web of the personal social services because they have committed offenses. It is more likely to be because of concerns about their perceived sexual behaviour and/or because they are seen to be "at risk" of "offending" against social codes of adolescent femininity. (A. Hudson 1989: 197)

According to the "sexualization" theory, "troublesome" girls have always provoked anxiety in those who work with them, and fear and suspicion in those who look on (Baines & Alder 1996; Brown & Pearce 1992). Chesney-Lind and Okamoto suggest that girls are "much more emotional than boys in the treatment setting . . . have distinctly different needs . . . and elicit unique counter-transference reactions from practitioners" (2000: 20). They have been socially constructed within a range of legal, welfare, and political discourses as, on the one hand, deeply maladjusted misfits and, on the other (and more recently), dangerous folk devils, symbolic of postmodern adolescent femininity.

Although welfare concerns have always dominated professional responses to girls "in trouble," concerns to provide protection to girls have always been mingled with anxieties about the wildness and dangerousness of girls who are "out of control." "Passionate and willful girls"(Alder 1998) have always aroused as many respectable fears as have hooligan boys (Pearson 1983; Davies 1999). In particular, bad girls who become pregnant, engage in prostitution, get drunk, are generally "unruly" (Belknap & Holsinger 1998), "rough" (see chapter 2), or commit acts of violence run the risk of no longer being socially constructed as children or even as troubled young women, but rather as witting threats to the moral fabric of society.

I have argued elsewhere (Worrall 2000) that, in recognition of the problems highlighted by feminist critiques of traditional approaches to adolescent female delinquency (the "sexualization" paradigm of juvenile justice), three alternative discourses have (re)emerged in the late twentieth century: informality (in the specific form of restorative justice), just deserts, and a renewed appeal to the "lost" innocence of childhood, as a result of the victimization of girls (predominantly by men). These alternative approaches to dealing with bad girls, which attempt to divert them from incarceration, have proved no more successful than traditional welfare interventions. Instead, I have argued that we have seen a number of indicators of a paradigm shift in the treatment of bad girls: more girls who offend are being dealt with by the criminal justice rather than by welfare systems; more bad behavior by girls is being redefined as criminal, particularly fighting; more immoral behavior by girls is being constructed as "near criminal" (for example, so-called "early" pregnancy and lone parenthood). As a consequence of these changing attitudes, there has been a shift away from the "welfarization" of troublesome girls toward their criminalization.

In this chapter, I want to extend that analysis, specifically in relation to the perception that "girls are getting more violent." In particular, I argue here that the key concepts of the new penology—risk assessment and dangerousness—have taken on new meaning for girls. The discursive attempts, described above, to foreclose the debate about female juvenile delinquency have between them created a lacuna from which has emerged the "violent girl"—the ungovernable, "nasty little madam"— who can *only* be dealt with by risk assessment and management within the formal criminal justice system.

From Tank Girl to Twisted Sisters—or, Cute but Deadly?

In its policy proposal paper, "Crime, Justice and Protecting the Public," which preceded the Criminal Justice Act 1991 in England and Wales, the Conservative Government suggested that the number of girls under the age of eighteen years sentenced to custody by the courts was so small that the abolition of detention in a young offender institution for this group might be feasible in a civilized society. The 150 or so girls in custody (compared to more than seven thousand boys) could be dealt with quite adequately by the "good, demanding and constructive community programmes for juvenile offenders who need intensive supervision." Those few who committed very serious crimes could still be dealt with by means of section 53 (of the Children and Young Person Act 1933)[1] detention in local authority secure accommodation.

The ascendancy of the "just deserts" model of criminal justice, coupled with the inclusion of a supposedly antidiscriminatory clause in the 1991 Criminal Justice Act,[2] might have resulted in fewer girls being incarcerated. The principle of proportionality in sentencing should have led to the fairer sentencing of women (since their offending behavior is generally less serious than that of men) and this trend should have been buttressed by greater access for women to community sentences. But any such optimism was short-lived. A decade later custody in young offender institutions for girls remains and has expanded and the reason, we are led to believe, is that girls are committing more crime, especially violent crime.

The 1990s saw the emergence of several moral panics in relation to juvenile delinquency (Worrall 1997). The first was "rat boy," the elusive persistent offender who laughed at the system. The "discovery" that a small number of children were committing a disproportionate amount of not-so-trivial crime, especially burglary and criminal damage, led to public outrage that, because of their age, these children could not be given custodial sentences. The government's response to this was to announce the introduction of secure training units for twelve to fourteen year olds, the first of which opened in April 1998. But this concern was to prove merely a precursor to the second moral panic, which followed the murder of Jamie Bulger in 1993. After this appalling event, serious questions were asked about the retention of a system of justice for children which was based on a belief in the still developing understanding of right and wrong between the ages of ten and fourteen years (the principle of "doli incapax") and the consequent need to protect such children from the full weight of the criminal law. Increasingly, the media demanded that so-called "adult" offenses should be dealt with by "adult" sentences, regardless of the age and maturity of the offender. The vexing issues of the age of criminal responsibility and doli incapax became matters of public and parliamentary debate until the latter was finally abolished in the Crime and Disorder Act 1998.

This level of media-fueled public anxiety was based on the scantiest of empirical evidence. Hagell and Newburn (1994), for example, found far fewer persistent young offenders (and virtually none of them girls) than the then Home Secretary had claimed existed. Nevertheless, it was against this backdrop that the third moral panic emerged.

In 1994 Lisa Brinkworth wrote an article in the *Sunday Times* entitled "Sugar and spice but not at all nice." The article claimed to have discovered "all-girl gangs menacing the streets" and "cocky, feminist, aggressive" superheroines targeting vulnerable women and other girls. Moreover, this "new breed" of criminal girl apparently "knows" that the criminal justice system is lenient on her. She knows how to work the system, dressing smartly for court and playing up to the magistrates. The illustration for the article was "Tank Girl"—an American cartoon fantasy heroine who turned the tables violently (and frequently to their surprise) on repressive and sadistic men. The reasons for this supposed upsurge in young female crime are, however, confused. On the one hand, Brinkworth argues that women's liberation has raised women's expectations but has not delivered in terms of careers and wealth. Consequently, frustration and anger lead to street violence. On the other hand, women are supposedly sick of feeling unsafe in the home and are now fighting back (but why then are the targets so often not men but other young women?). Either way, according to Brinkworth, the responsibility for all this lies with feminism. This is what happens when you loosen the controls on women. This is what happens when adolescent girls are allowed to think themselves equal or superior to boys. It is every mother and father's nightmare—their daughter's sexuality rampant and violent.

Brinkworth, in both this and a subsequent article (1996), was in the business of creating a third moral panic alongside those of "rat boy" and "child killer" (Worrall 1997). At the time there was no evidence at all to support her argument other than one or two celebrated "nasty" incidents which were only newsworthy *because* of their rarity. Feminist analyses of violence by women had revealed that the overwhelming majority of "violent" women were themselves victims of violence. "Battered woman syndrome"—though a highly contentious concept—was slowly being accepted by courts as, at the least, a mitigating factor in domestic violence committed by women. Campaigning groups such as "Women in Prison" demonstrated that violent young women (such as Josie O'Dwyer—see

Carlen et al. 1985) had been abused by individual men and by the prison system from an early age. Yet this was not the kind of "girl violence" that Brinkworth was talking about. She was clearly on a different mission—the "search for equivalence." Her concern was to demonstrate that "girls do it too." And in so doing, she set in train a particular media "hunt" characterized by the oft-repeated themes—younger and younger girls becoming increasingly aggressive, mushrooming girl gangs, increased use of drugs and, especially, alcohol, and the wilful abandonment of gender role expectations.

In 1996, Jo Knowsley in *The Sunday Telegraph* used the manslaughter of thirteen-year-old Louise Allen by two girls of a similar age to claim the mushrooming of "girl gangs, apeing American gangs . . . fuelled by cheap, strong wine . . . [who] travel in pairs or packs, carry baseball bats, mug for money and jewellery, and stage shoplifting raids on designer shops" (see also Archer 1998). No, that was *not* what happened with poor Louise Allen (where an argument between a group of schoolgirls got disastrously out of hand), but who cares? It makes for a good, coherent news story that offers some, albeit distorted, explanation for a horrible but rare incident.

Such distorted reporting was not confined to the UK. The following year, in Canada, a fourteen-year-old south Asian woman called Reena Virk, was attacked and killed by a group of young women and one young man. According to Sheila Batacharya's account (2000) the media coverage appears to have been very similar to that surrounding the death of Louise Allen in England. The difference was that Virk was a young woman of color and "the narrative of girl violence obscures race" in the analysis of her death. By constructing a category of "girl violence" the media was able to proffer explanations devoid of dimensions of racism, classism, ableism, and heterosexism (Batacharya 2000). The sole relevant risk factor to be considered was that of gender.

Journalists are now warning us that "psychologists have projected that by the year 2008, the number of girls reverting [*sic*] to violence will outnumber boys if they carry on lashing out at this rate" (Fowler 1999). This prediction is, it seems, based on a claim that the number of women sentenced for violence against the person "has quadrupled from just a handful of cases in the 70s." The fact that the numbers (according to Fowler's own, inaccurate, statistics)[3] are now 460, compared with more than 11,000 crimes of violence committed by men, does not cause her to reflect on her hypothesis. In fact, although there has been an increase in violent crime committed by young people (Home Office 2000), the gender ratio of such offenses has remained that of around one female to five males throughout the 1990s (Rutter et al. 1998). Arrest rates of girls for serious crimes of violence in the United States have also remained largely unchanged (Chesney-Lind & Brown 1998, cited in Belknap & Holsinger 1998: 43).

In August 2000, *The Guardian* reported on an eighteen-year-old girl charged with rape (Chaudhuri 2000) and asked, "A shocking lone incident or a sign of rising woman-on-woman violence?" Again, we hear the garbled statistics about the apparent increase in violence by women; again, the attribution of bad behavior to girl gangs and alcohol misuse; again, the role of feminism in making women more aggressive yet, because of their continued powerlessness in relation to men, causing that aggression to be displaced onto other women. These are no longer fantasy Tank Girl figures; these are the girls "next door." In their more benign form, these are "ladettes;"[4] in their more sinister form, the sisters have become "twisted."

This shift of attitude which moves "violent girls" from fantasy to "next door" has been conceptualized by Shiokawa's (1999) analysis of the popularity of "cuteness" in Japanese cartooning. "Cute but deadly" cartoon action heroines represent, Shiokawa argues, an attempt to manage the constructed threat of powerful young women (who are not, in reality, powerful at all but can be flattered into thinking that they are):

> The repetitive formula of "cute" action heroines indicates that "cute" women are desirable and that being "cute" is advantageous to women who, in reality do not possess equal ground in the male-dominant culture. "Cute" means imperfection . . . is an achievable quality, equally available to everyone . . . if she develops fuzzy, likable flaws in her character, so as to remove the threat that her very presence poses to the general public. (Shiokawa 1999: 120)

The New Psychology of Female Violence

Media constructions of "twisted sisters" have claimed to be based on pseudo-scientific psychology, such as that reported in *Psychology Today* by journalist Barry Yeoman (1999), who quotes randomly from seemingly respectable studies to move from factual statements about the few women who commit violent acts to the generalization that:

> Violence by women has skyrocketed in the latter part of this century. Have they taken "women's liberation" one step too far, or are they just showing their natural killer instinct? (Yeoman 1999: 54)

Similarly, James (1995) reproduces the cliché that men are socialized to be violent and women to be depressed (and that depressed mothers produce violent sons) but predicts that:

> If women are not genetically prone to depression, then, as the restraints on their expression of aggression are lifted, so their rates of depression should drop to those currently found in men. Likewise, if men are not genetically prone to violent externalizations of frustration, as their role changes and if the much-heralded "New Man" ceases to be a myth, their rates of violence should drop, and of depression rise proportionately. (James 1995: 90)

While it may be relatively easy to dismiss populist psychologizing, it is perhaps more important to confront *a* new discourse of causation that has emerged from the tradition of feminist psychotherapy and, in particular, the work of Estela Welldon (1988). Welldon's concept of "female perversion"[5] and the "intergenerational transmission of perverse and abusive mothering" (Motz 2001: 4) has been further developed by Anna Motz to challenge the denial of women's capacity to commit acts of violence. "It is essential," Motz argues, "to recognise the violence which is done to [women] through the denial of their capacity for aggression, and the refusal to acknowledge their moral agency" (2001: 3–4). The idealization of motherhood and subsequent denigration of women who do not fulfill gender role expectations contribute to this denial, as does the private nature of much female violence. Female violence is more likely to be against children (physical and sexual abuse, infanticide, and Munchausen's syndrome by proxy), against abusive partners, or against themselves (self-harm and eating disorders). In all these situations, Motz argues, women use their bodies to communicate distress and anger (2001: 7).

The women about whom Motz and others with similar views (Bailey 2000) talk are undoubtedly extreme cases and the development of a feminist psychotherapeutic approach to understand and help such women is arguably extremely valuable. The emphasis on exploring the meaning of the violent act for the woman who engages in it, rather than imposing preconceived categories and explanations on it, is an important contribution to the discourse of prevention. It is also true that theorizing about women's uses of their bodies to convey negative rather than positive emotions offers an insight into the "physicality" of girls' public behavior, which so alarms the socially constructed "decent citizen."

What is more concerning, however, is Motz's view that psychological explanations of this kind can be given for *all* manifestations of violence by women, including, for example, gang violence. By including this term, Motz invites the reader to view all violence by women as being "linked to a developmental failure to conceptualise one's own and other people's states of mind" (2001: 2). Despite Motz's concern not to classify and manage all acts of female violence, the effect of her work is to hold out the positivistic possibility of precisely this—a new taxonomy of female violence. By constructing an implied continuum of female violence ranging from public incivility to homicide, Motz reinforces, however unwittingly, journalistic stereotypes of ladettes and twisted sisters.

Invisible Girls?

One of the problems in analyzing trends in the behavior of girls is the absence of reliable and comparable statistics. The problem is an international one:

> Assembling statistics and demographics in the field of juvenile justice can produce a confusing muddle that renders the comparison of "rates" meaningless. . . . Data specifically for girls are even more difficult to obtain. (Shaffner et al.1997: 191)

Because the numbers involved are so small, very little attempt seems to be made to present the data in a systematic form. For example, in England and Wales (Home Office 2000), it is possible to identify trends in violence and robbery for *all* women over ten years from one set of annual statistics, but to identify trends for girls, one has to refer to ten different sets of statistics.[6] However, even with these difficulties, it is possible to state that:

- The number of women (all ages) found guilty or cautioned for offenses of violence against the person was 7,900 in 1989 and 8,200 in 1999, compared with 62,300 men in 1989 and 48,700 men in 1999;
- The number of women (all ages) found guilty or cautioned for offenses of robbery was 300 in 1989 and 500 in 1999, compared with 4,700 men in 1989 and 5,700 men in 1999;
- The number of girls (under eighteen years) found guilty or cautioned for offenses of violence against the person in 1999 was 2,900, compared with 11,500 boys;
- The number of girls (under eighteen years) found guilty or cautioned for offenses of robbery in 1999 was 300, compared with 2,300 boys.

For a more detailed analysis of trends, I have selected two offense classifications that include the offenses of which the public seem to be most fearful in relation to girls—"other wounding" and "robbery."[7] Here some very interesting figures emerge for girls under eighteen years of age:

- Although the number of "other wounding" proceedings started increased from 1,360 in 1996 to 1,530 in 1999, the numbers actually sentenced increased from 810 to only 880 (the remaining charges being discontinued, withdrawn, or dismissed).
- In relation to "robbery," proceedings actually *declined* from around 500 in 1996 to around 400 in 1999 and numbers sentenced declined from 240 to 190.

What has changed, though, are rates of cautioning for girls: from 100 to 96 percent for 10–11 year olds; from 94 to 87 percent for 12–14 year olds; and from 77 to 64 percent for 15–17 year olds. (Cautioning rates for boys have always been rather lower). The fall in cautioning rates has led to an increase in the numbers of girls appearing in court and being sentenced.

In addition to changes in cautioning, patterns of sentencing have also changed. Most significantly, use of immediate custody rose from 3 to 6 percent. In 1999 approximately four hundred girls under the age of

Table 3.1
Changes in Treatment of Young Women Offenders
Aged 15–17 Years 1994–1999

	1994	1999
Total found guilty or cautioned	16,200	14,500
Rates of cautioning	77%	64%
Total sentenced	3,800	5,200
Rates of discharges	50%	39%
Rates of supervision/probation	24%	28%
Rates of community service	3%	4%
Rates of combination orders	1%	2%
Rates of custody	3%	6%
Total in custody	200	400

Ref: Home Office (2000) *Criminal Statistics England and Wales 1999, Cm50* eighteen years were sentenced to immediate custody—double the number in 1994, as can be seen from Table 3.1 above. Unfortunately, it is not possible to identify how many of these are in custody for all offenses of violence but the figure in relation to "other wounding" and "robbery" is 91—compared with 59 in 1994 and 74 in 1996.

It has been suggested to me that the apparent underrepresentation of girls in Young Offender Institutions may be accounted for by their overrepresentation in local authority secure accommodation.[8] In 2000 there were 459 places in 32 secure units for boys and girls (an increase of 32 percent since 1997) (Department of Health 2000). On 31 March 2000 there were 377 children in secure units, of whom 275 were boys and 102 were girls. Although the numbers of boys increased slightly from 1997, the numbers of girls more than doubled in that period, suggesting that a very high proportion of the increased capacity has indeed been taken up by girls. There are two main routes into secure accommodation—the "welfare route" and the "justice route" (Goldson 1995: 66). Children being looked after by a local authority may be placed in secure accommodation if they have a history of absconding from other accommodation *and* if they are likely to suffer "significant harm" if they abscond, or are likely to injure themselves or others if not placed in secure accommodation. The "justice route" has two distinct pathways—remands pending criminal trial or sentence and detention for "grave offenses" under section 53 of the Children and Young Person Act 1933. On 31 March 2000 there were 69 boys and 11 girls on section 53 orders. Of the remaining children, a large majority of the boys were on remand; the girls were slightly weighted toward the "welfare route" though, as one manager pointed out to me, that does not mean that the girl does not have a criminal history—it simply refers to her legislative status. It does appear that the pattern of admission to secure units has changed (see Worrall 1999) and that we are locking more of our daughters up (Carlen & Wardaugh 1991) for criminal rather than welfare matters.

"Nasty Little Madams"

Whatever promise the "just deserts" approach might have held for young women in the early 1990s, it has, in practice, resulted in a greater criminalization of girls' bad behavior and has proved no more successful in diverting them from incarceration than traditional welfare intervention. Instead, the construction of "violent girls" has resulted in at least two indicators of a paradigm shift in the treatment of bad girls:[9]

More girls who offend are being dealt with by criminal justice rather than welfare systems.

There has been a disproportionate increase in the number of girls being brought to court, placed on community service and combination orders, and sentenced to Young Offender Institutions in England and Wales since 1993. Similar patterns are identifiable in Australia (Alder & Hunter 1999), Canada (Reitsma-Street 1999), and the United States (Schaffner 1999; Chesney-Lind & Okamoto 2000). In Canada and the United States there is evidence that the much criticized use of "status offenses" to justify the incarceration of girls on welfare grounds has now been replaced by "failure to comply" charges. The latter, which may concern breaches of noncriminal court orders (curfews, residence and association conditions) allow the courts to reclassify status offenders as delinquent and incarcerate them in penal, rather than welfare, facilities. Both Chesney-Lind and Okamoto (2000) and Schaffner (1999) suggest that increasing numbers of girls may find themselves in court following family disputes. In the UK there is anecdotal evidence[10] that girls are being transferred from "ordinary" children's homes to Secure Units (on "welfare" grounds) for assaults on house-parents, which would perhaps have been tolerated in the past.

More bad behavior by girls is being redefined as criminal, particularly fighting.

Frances Heidensohn (2001) has pointed out "that we do not have notions of 'normal' uses of force and violence by women and girls," which contrasts with our acceptance of "rough play and fighting" among men and boys. Sibylle Artz (1998) has demonstrated that a certain level of "hitting" among mainstream (as opposed to marginalized) schoolgirls is commonplace to settle disputes about boys and enhance reputations as "tough girls." Yet this violence is very different from the violence of "hitting" among school boys (who formed a much more distinct group in her research) and invariably arose out of friendship situations. The significance of friendship for girls has been noted in many studies and, most recently in Burman et al.'s study of the experiences of violence among Glasgow girls (2000). It is this, however, which has also provoked the media constructions of "girl gangs"—where two or three girls are gathered together, a gang is formed in the eyes of the media. The Howard League Report "Lost Inside" found that half the girls imprisoned for "violence" were there for fighting with other girls. Beikoff (1996) has identified another pattern among Australian girls charged with assault. The assault charge is frequently one of "assaulting a police officer," accompanied by a charge of "resisting arrest," arising out of a public order incident involving drunk and disorderly behavior. She refers to this as the "public space trifecta" and asks whether this has replaced the "care and control" applications of the past. What all these studies, and others, also make clear is that girls' violence is almost always borne out of experiences of violence. Burman et al. (2000) for instance, conclude that 98.5 percent of their sample of girls had witnessed at first hand some form of interpersonal violence and 41 percent had experienced someone deliberately hitting, punching, or kicking them. Only 10 percent of their samples described themselves as "violent." Most girls, Burman et al. argue, handle the routine experience of low-level violence and intimidation without resorting to violence themselves.

As a consequence of these changing official attitudes, however, there has been a shift away from the "welfarization" of troublesome girls toward their criminalization. Talking to prison officers in women's prisons about the inappropriateness of imprisoning girls, the response one invariably receives these days is that they are *not* lost and bewildered souls, but "nasty little madams."

At Risk, in Danger and in Prison

The plight of girls in prison in England was highlighted in 1997 by three events: a thematic review of women in prison by HM Chief Inspector of Prisons, a report by the Howard League on the imprisonment of teenage girls, and a High Court ruling that a teenage girl should not be held in an adult female prison.[11] There are no institutions in the female prison estate designated solely as Young Offender Institutions. There are two standard Prison Service justifications for mixing young and adult offenders in the female prison estate: first, there are too few young offenders to warrant separate institutions, which would, in any case, exacerbate the problem of women being imprisoned at unreasonable distances from their homes; second (and conveniently!), adult women are regarded as having a stabilizing influence on young women (though, strangely, adult men are seen as having a corrupting influence on young men!). Setting aside the complaints of adult women that young women have a disruptive influence on their lives, reports from the Chief Inspector and Howard League present a rather different picture of girls and young women being bullied, sexually assaulted, and recruited as prostitutes and drugs couriers:

> There are serious child protection issues in mixing young prisoners with others who may include Schedule 1 offenders (women convicted of offenses of violence against children under the 1933 Children and Young Person Act) which covers a multitude of behaviours. . . . We noted, for example, women convicted of procuring being held alongside 15 and 16 year olds. (HM Inspector of Prisons 1997: 26)

The exposure of girls to an environment that is seriously damaging is explored in detail by the Howard League. In particular, the "culture" of self-harm, or "cutting up," which is endemic in most women's prisons, can socialize vulnerable girls into dangerous and violent ways of expressing their distress:

> For the vast majority of the young girls we interviewed it was the first time they had come across self-mutilation and we were told by staff that it was rare a 15, 16 or 17 year old would come in self-harming. The danger is that they will copy this behavior partly as a way of creating some control in their distressed and chaotic lives and partly because it is part of the culture of prison life to which they now belong. (Howard League 1997: 33)

The special needs of adolescent women are not being addressed. Prison officers reported to the Howard League that girls in prison had disproportionate experience of sexual abuse, poor or broken relationships with parents, local authority care (between one-third and one-half of women in prison having been in care), drug or alcohol abuse, prostitution, school exclusion, and truancy. If one has any lingering doubts about the "special needs" of girls and young women in prison, one has only to consider the statistics of offenses against prison discipline. The rate of disciplinary offending is considerably higher in all Young Offender Institutions than in adult prisons, but the rate for female young offenders is the highest (Home Office 2000b). By far the most common offense is that of "disobedience or disrespect." However one chooses to explain this phenomenon (as being an indicator of either very badly behaved young women or of overly controlling female prison officers), it is clear that there is a very real risk that young women who are no more than ladettes outside prison can quickly become twisted sisters inside it.

Risk, Dangerousness, and Justice

The history of juvenile justice has been a history of the conflict between justice and welfare concerns (Worrall 1997) and girls have tended to experience both the advantages and disadvantages of welfarism to a greater extent than boys, on the grounds that they are "at risk," "in moral danger," and "in need of protection." In particular, under the "old penology" criminal girls were regarded as girls "in need"—*individuals* requiring *individual* attention and treatment (Gelsthorpe 1989; Holsinger 2000). They were too few in number to warrant categorization and were more often seen as "misfits"—as "non-descript women" who could not readily be categorized (Worrall 1990). Feminist critiques of welfarism in the 1980s resulted in moves toward "just deserts" for girls, which promised much (Elliott 1988) but delivered greater criminalization and incarceration in the 1990s. Within this general trend, there has been a barely perceptible move toward the classification of delinquent girls and, in particular, a specific category of "violent girls" has been constructed. This has been necessary because, as Muncie points out (2000, 29), the political agenda for the New Youth Justice is no longer based on matters of guilt, innocence, deterrence, and rehabilitation, but on the actuarial principle of risk assessment and techniques of "identifying, classifying and managing groups sorted by levels of dangerousness." So while common sense (and official statistics) may tell us that girls—even violent ones—are neither high-risk (in terms of the predictability of their violence) or dangerous (in terms of the harm they cause), they must nevertheless be made "auditable." They have to be given a risk classification and be subjected to objectives and techniques of management. Kemshall (1998: 39) has suggested that "there is the possibility that the pursuit of risk reduction may eventually outweigh the pursuit of justice." She warns that concerns for public protection and victims' rights may eventually lead to an unacceptable (though to whom?) erosion of the rights of the offender. In the case of violent girls it could be argued that, rather than the pursuit of risk *reduction*, it is the pursuit of risk *amplification* that is outweighing justice. No one would deny that young women are capable of acts of violence but the category "violent girls" is a social construction that serves as a mechanism "for the colonisation of the future and for managing the uncertainty of contingency" (Kemshall 1998: 38). It is a way of managing the anxiety, fear, and suspicion that troubled and troublesome girls and young women provoke in respectable citizens. It is a form of insurance against the perceived threat of ever-increasing numbers of Myra Hindleys, Rose Wests, and Josie O'Dwyers.[12] Yet nothing is more certain to ensure the enlargement of the next generation of such women than locking up increasing numbers of our teenage daughters.

Notes

1. Detention under section 53 of the Children and Young Person Act 1933 provides for the long-term detention of children and young persons under eighteen for certain grave crimes such as murder, manslaughter, and other serious crimes of violence—the numbers of girls incarcerated under this provision will be discussed later in this chapter.

2. Section 95 of the Criminal Justice Act 1991 required the Home Secretary to monitor the administration of criminal justice to ensure the absence of discrimination on grounds of race, sex, or other "improper" grounds.

3. I am not sure where Fowler's statistics come from. Official criminal statistics indicate that young women of 14–17 years accounted for about 1,800 offenses of violence and robbery in 1996, compared with 11,000 young men. The figure of 460 seems to refer only to robbery committed by young women (Home Office 1997).

4. Ladette: A young woman characterized by her enjoyment of social drinking, sport, or other activities typically considered to be male-oriented, and often by attitudes or behavior regarded as irresponsible or brash; (usually) one of a close-knit social group (Draft entry in OED Online, June 2001).

5. Welldon defines the "perverse" woman as one who "feels that she has not been allowed to enjoy a sense of her own development as a separate individual, with her own identity; in other words she has not experienced the freedom to be herself. This creates in her the deep belief that she is not a whole being, but her mother's part-object, just as she experienced her mother when she was a very young infant" (1988, 8–9).

6. In addition to the main Criminal Statistics for England and Wales, I have used the Supplementary Tables Volumes 1 & 2 which detail offenses in specified age categories dealt with in both the Magistrates' and Crown Courts.

7. "Other wounding" includes *inter alia* grievous bodily harm, actual bodily harm, possession of offensive weapons, breach of antisocial behavior order, and racially aggravated assault; "robbery" covers robbery and assault with intent to rob.

8. Secure accommodation for juveniles in England and Wales is staffed by social workers and is not run by the prison service.

9. I have argued elsewhere (Worrall 2000) that these two indicators have been buttressed by a third indicator reflecting "underclass" theory: more immoral behavior by girls is being constructed as "near criminal;" for example, so-called "early" pregnancy and lone parenthood.

10. Personal communication with a manager of a Secure Unit.

11. *R v. Secretary of State for the Home Department and others,* ex parte Flood. Independent Law Reports: 2 October 1997, cited in Howard League (1997) *Lost Inside.*

12. Myra Hindley, along with Ian Brady, committed the notorious Moors Murders of children in the 1960s. She died in prison in 2002 as the longest serving female prisoner in England. Rose West was accomplice to Fred West in killing numerous young women, some relatives, from the 1970s to 1990s. Fred West committed suicide, while Rose is still in prison. Josie O'Dwyer was a young woman who spent her life in and out of prison for serious acts of violence and received media attention for an attack on Myra Hindley. She died violently.

References

Alder, C. 1998, "Passionate and wilful girls: confronting practices," *Women and Criminal Justice*, vol. 9, no. 4, pp. 81–101.

Alder, C. & Hunter, N. 1999, *Young women in the juvenile justice system,* University of Melbourne (unpublished), Melbourne.

Archer, D. 1998, "Riot grrrl and raisin girl: femininity within the female gang," in J. Vagg & T. Newburn (eds), *Emerging Themes in Criminology,* The British Criminology Conferences Selected Proceedings vol.1, Loughborough.

Artz, S. 1998, *Sex, power, and the violent school girl,* Teachers College Press, New York.

Bailey, S. 2000, "Violent adolescent female offenders" in G. Boswell (ed), *Violent children and adolescents: asking the question why,* Whurr Publishers, London.

Baines, M. & Alder, C. 1996, "When she was bad she was horrid," in C. Alder & M. Baines (eds), *And when she was bad?* National Clearing House for Youth Studies, Hobart, Tasmania.

Balding, J., Regis, D., Wise, A., Bish, D. & Muirden, J. 1996, *Cash and carry? young people, their friends, and offensive weapons,* University of Exeter Schools Health Education Unit, Exeter.

Batacharya, S. 2000, *Racism, "girl violence," and the murder of Reena Virk,* unpublished MA thesis, University of Toronto.

Beikoff, L. 1996, "Queensland's juvenile justice system: equity, access, and justice for young women?" in C. Alder & M. Baines (eds), *And when she was bad? Working with young women in juvenile justice and related areas,* National Clearinghouse for Youth Studies, Hobart, Tasmania.

Belknap, J. & Holsinger, K. 1998, "An overview of delinquent girls: how theory and practice have failed and the need for innovative change," in R. T. Zaplin (ed), *Female offenders: critical perspectives and effective interventions,* Aspen Publishers, Gaithersburg, Md.

Brinkworth, L. 1994, "Sugar and spice but not at all nice," *Sunday Times,* 27 November 1994.

———. 1996, "Angry young women," *Cosmopolitan,* February 1996.

Brown, H. C. & Pearce, J. 1992, "Good practice in the face of anxiety: social work with girls and young women," *Journal of Social Work Practice,* vol. 6, no. 2, pp. 159–65.

Burman, M., Brown, J., Tisdall, K. & Batchelor, S. 2000, *A view from the girls: exploring violence and violent behaviour,* Final Report for ESRC (unpublished).

Carlen, P., Hicks, J., O'Dwyer, J., Christina, D. & Tchaikovsky, C. 1985, *Criminal women*, Polity Press, Oxford.

Carlen, P. & Wardaugh, J. 1991, "Locking up our daughters," in P. Carter, T. Jeffs & M. K. Smith (eds) *Social work and social welfare Year Book 3*, Milton Keynes, Open University Press.

Channel Four Television 1996, *Dispatches: class wars: schoolchildren, violence, and weapons*, Channel Four Television, London.

Chaudhuri, A. 2000, "Twisted sisters," *The Guardian*, 15 August 2000.

Chesney-Lind, M. & Okamoto, S. K. 2000, *Gender matters: patterns in girls' delinquency and gender responsive programming* (unpublished).

Davies, A. 1999, "'These viragoes are no less cruel than the lads': young women, gangs and violence in Victorian Manchester and Salford," *British Journal of Criminology*, vol. 39, no. 1, pp. 72–89.

Department of Health 2000, *Children accommodated in secure units, year ending 31 March 2000: England and Wales*, Statistical Bulletin 2000/15, National Statistics, London.

Elliott, D. 1988, *Gender, delinquency, and society*, Aldershot, Avebury.

Feeley, M. M. & Simon, J. 1992, "The new penology: notes on the emerging strategy of corrections and its implications," *Criminology*, vol. 30, no. 4, pp. 452–74.

Fowler, R. 1999, "When girl power packs a punch," *The Guardian*, 12 July 1999.

Gelsthorpe, L. 1989, *Sexism and the female offender*, Gower, Cambridge.

Goldson, B. 1995, *A sense of security*, National Children's Bureau, London.

Hagell, A. & Newburn, T. 1994, *Persistent young offenders*, Policy Studies Institute, London.

Hannah-Moffat, K. 1999, "Moral agent or actuarial subject: risk and Canadian women's imprisonment," *Theoretical Criminology*, vol. 3,1, no. 7, pp.1–94.

Heidensohn, F. 2001, "Women and violence: myths and reality in the 21st century," *Criminal Justice Matters*, no. 42, p. 20.

HM Chief Inspector of Prisons 1997, *Women in prison: a thematic review*, HM Inspectorate of Prisons, London.

Holsinger, K. 2000, "Feminist perspectives on female offending: examining real girls' lives," *Women and Criminal Justice*, no. 12, pp. 23–51.

Home Office 1997, *Criminal statistics for England and Wales 1996*, Cm 3764 Home Office, London.

———. 2000a, *Criminal Statistics for England and Wales 1999*, Cm 50, The Stationery Office, London.

———. 2000b, *Prison Statistics for England and Wales 1999*, Home Office, London.

Howard League 1997, *Lost inside: the imprisonment of teenage girls*, The Howard League for Penal Reform, London.

Howe, A. 1994, *Punish and critique: towards a feminist analysis of penality*, Routledge, London.

Hudson, A. 1983, "The welfare state and adolescent femininity," *Youth and Policy*, vol. 2, no. 1, pp. 5–13.

———. 1989, "Troublesome girls: towards alternative definitions and policies," in M. Cain (ed) *Growing up good: policing the behaviour of girls in Europe*, Sage, London.

James, O. 1995, *Juvenile violence in a winner-loser culture*, Free Association Books, London.

Kemshall, H. 1998, *Risk in probation practice*, Aldershot, Ashgate.

Knowsley, J. 1996, "Girl gangs rival boys to rule the streets," *The Sunday Telegraph*, 6 May 1996.

Motz, A. 2001, *The psychology of female violence: crimes against the body*, Brunner-Routledge, Hove.

Muncie, J. 2000, "Pragmatic realism? Searching for criminology in the new youth justice," in B. Goldson (ed), *The new youth justice*, Russell House Publishing, Lyme Regis.

OED Online 2001, "Ladette": http://athens.oed.com/cgi/entry_main/

Pantazis, C. 1999, "The criminalization of female poverty," in S. Watson & L. Doyal (eds), *Engendering social policy*, Open University Press, Buckingham.

Pearson, G. 1983, *Hooligan: a history of respectable fears*, Macmillan, London.

Prentice, E. 2000, "Dark side of girl power," *The Times*, 22 November 2000.

Reitsma-Street, M. 1999, "Justice for Canadian girls: a 1990s update," *Canadian Journal of Criminology*, July, pp. 335–63.

Rutter, M., Giller, H. & Hagell, A. 1998, *Antisocial behavior by young people*, Cambridge University Press, Cambridge.

Schaffner, L., Shick, S. & Stein, N. 1997, "Changing policy in San Francisco: girls in the juvenile justice system," *Social Justice*, no. 24, pp. 187–211.

Schaffner, L. 1999, "Violence and female delinquency: gender transgressions and gender invisibility," *Berkeley Women's Law Journal*, vol. 14, pp. 40–65.

Shiokawa, K. 1999, "Cute but deadly: women and violence in Japanese comics" in Lent, J. A. (ed) *Themes and issues in Asian cartooning*, Bowling Green State University Popular Press, Bowling Green, Ohio.

Steffensmeier, D. & Haynie, D. L. 2000, "The structural sources of urban female violence in the United States," *Homicide Studies*, no. 4, pp. 107–34.

Welldon, E. 1988, *Mother, madonna, whore: the idealization and denigration of motherhood*, Free Association Books, London.

Worrall, A. 1990, *Offending women: female lawbreakers and the criminal justice system*, Routledge, London.

———. 1997, *Punishment in the community: the future of criminal justice*, Longman, Harlow.

———. 1999, "Troubled or troublesome? Justice for girls and young women," in B. Goldson (ed), *Youth justice: contemporary policy and practice*, Aldershot, Ashgate.

———. 2000, "Governing bad girls: changing constructions of adolescent female delinquency," in J. Bridgeman & D. Monk (eds), *Feminist perspectives on child law*, Cavendish Publishing, London.

Yeoman, B. 1999, "Bad Girls," *Psychology Today*, vol. 32, no. 6, pp. 54–57 & 71.

Chapter Four

Racism, "Girl Violence," and the Murder of Reena Virk

Sheila Batacharya

On November 14, 1997, Reena Virk, a young South Asian woman aged fourteen, was attacked by seven young women and one young man in a planned assault under a bridge in Saanich, a suburb of Victoria, British Columbia. After the initial attack that involved eight youths and a mob of between twenty and fifty onlookers, a second fatal assault was committed by two white youths involved in the first attack: sixteen-year-old Warren Glowatski and Kelly Ellard, aged fifteen. Reena Virk's naked body was found nine days later in a river, the Gorge Waterway. Her corpse was bruised and cut, and the autopsy report found extensive "internal injuries to her back and abdomen that were consistent with being kicked and stomped" (Meissner 1999: A6). Drowning was stated as the official cause of death.

The earliest media reports did not mention that the young woman found in the Gorge Waterway was South Asian. Reena was later identified as "East Indian"; however, racism as a site of analysis or contributing factor to her murder was absent from most mainstream media reports. One article stated that "[p]olice have ruled out racism as a motive, noting that some of the accused are also non-white" (Purvis 1997: 68). This statement preempts any consideration of racism as systemic and, thus, how people of color can be implicated in racist violence. It is one of the many examples found in the mainstream media reports that served to "erase race" from the murder of Reena Virk (Jiwani 1998: 3).

Even though racism was "ruled out," Reena Virk's racial difference and class disadvantage were repeatedly commented on. Both served to mark her, however, only as "a troubled teen who tried desperately to fit in" (Jimnez 1997: A1).

Reena Virk, like many fourteen-year-old girls, had a hard time fitting in where she grew up, in her case the middle-class suburb of Saanich on the outskirts of Victoria, B.C. It didn't help that she was slightly overweight and the dark-skinned child of immigrants who were not well-to-do. Her home life was troubled. She had shuttled between three foster homes and her own family residence; at one point she attempted suicide. She had accused her father of sexual abuse, though he denied it and the charges were later withdrawn (1997: A4).

This description of Reena as just another "troubled teen" obscures the connection between the constructed difference of "overweight," "dark skinned," and "not well-to-do" with the systemic relations of power such as racism and classism. Furthermore, although Reena is described as "like many fourteen-year-old girls," the information that follows conveys that she was not like other fourteen-year-old girls. She was not thin, white, and middle class, which is the dominant definition of a "girl" in Western culture. However, for the narrative of girl violence to remain secure, Reena must be portrayed as just a girl precisely because the narrative of girl violence depends on a generic construction of girlhood. In this respect the narrative of girl violence obscures race as it simultaneously depends on it for the construction of the "girl" in "girl violence." Thus, in the media reports Reena remains just a "girl" who, along with her attackers, are the victims and perpetrators of "girl violence."

In order to understand how and why racism was obscured in the media coverage, it is necessary to interrogate the construction of white femininity in both hegemonic and feminist discourses. The media frenzy surrounding girl violence revealed a public concern with the erosion of normative heterosexual, middle-class gender roles. For example, the supposed rising trend of girl violence is explained as resulting from the work of feminists who in the struggle for equality have now made girls more like boys and led them astray from their preordained roles as mother, wife, daughter.

The mainstream feminist rebuttal to this argument charges patriarchy with driving young women to violence. They argue that violent girls are the victims of patriarchy who, lacking other options, use violence in response to gender oppression. Both of these perspectives hinge on the notion that girls are, by nature, nonaggressive and nonviolent. Absent from both of these explanations is a theorization of how girls and young women perform themselves as dominant. In other words, these explanations do not address how racism, sexism, classism, ableism, and heterosexism place girls in dominant and subordinate relationships to one another as well as contextualizing the violence they commit. In the media coverage of the murder of Reena Virk the construction of white femininity as intrinsically nonaggressive informs the discourse of girl violence and obscured issues of race, class, gender, ability, and sexuality.

Interlocking Systems of Oppression and Hegemonic Femininity

The violence of white women is unnameable in both hegemonic and feminist discourses because constructions of white femininity position women as having no agency or as only demonstrating agency as resistance. My aim is to interrogate the dichotomy whereby white women are seen as property/objects (no agency) in patriarchal discourse or as victims/resisters (having agency) in gender-centric feminist discourse—both of which exclude the role of white women as agents of domination.

An analysis of interlocking oppressions is central to my project. An interlocking analysis of oppression keeps in view the multiple forms of violence and oppression that work interdependently to support elite hegemony: "Interlocking systems need one another, and in tracing the complex ways in which they help to secure one another, we learn how women are produced into positions that exist symbiotically but hierarchically" (Razack 1998b: 13). I argue that the only way to understand the murder of Reena Virk, and the media coverage surrounding it, is to question the symbiotic functioning of racism, sexism, classism, ableism, and heterosexism that created the context for, and the dominant explanations of, this crime. By examining hegemonic femininity using an interlocking framework, we also see the collaborative functioning of hegemonic and gender-centric feminist discourses.

Complicating feminist theory and activism to include an analysis of the systematic operation of all systems of oppression is risky. If white women acknowledge their role as oppressors, it weakens their claims for justice. Fellows and Razak (1998b: 4) point out that women must race to a position of innocence or risk being dismissed and their claims for justice invalidated. Another risk associated with addressing white women's violence is that it will fuel a backlash against feminism. Holmes and Ristock (1998) identify the ways in which women's violence is taken up in dominant discourses and argue that hegemonic narratives regarding violent women, or women who are categorized as deviant, are central to backlash strategies that maintain systems of oppression:

Backlash writers are not interested in widening the analysis from
gender to include race, class or sexuality in any way. Yet their crit-
icisms of feminist discourse allow for a reflexive moment for us to
ask, do our current discourses let us speak about women who
abuse their children or their elderly? or lesbians who have experienced abuse within their relationships? . . . or the ways in which
women use racist, classist, ableist violence against other women?
(1998: 26)

These authors argue that by not addressing women's violence, the
violence against women that cannot be "explained by sexism" (Kadi
1996: 74) is rendered invisible.

Historically, white women have been positioned as the weaker/
fairer/gentler sex in need of protection. This hegemonic construction of
femininity is central to patriarchy and justifies gender oppression by
positioning white women as objects, dependents, and property. Within
this construction white women are denied agency as social actors and
subjects (Razack 1998a: 346). Feminists have countered hegemonic constructions of femininity by citing women's agency in resistance to patriarchal oppression but have been reluctant to acknowledge white
women's agency in oppression. This uncomplicated picture of women's
oppression has sometimes enabled white women to rely on white supremacy in order to advance their claims for equality. For example,
American suffragists in the nineteenth century argued that granting
white women the vote was not only fair and just but would also help to
maintain a white nation and thus secure notions of white citizenship.
Suffragists profiled claims for justice for women using a single axis
analysis that required that the violence of racism be minimized if not
rendered invisible altogether (Davis 1983: 118–21; Hammond 1997: 173).

In Amina Mama's discussion of African women, she cites specific
legal, administrative, military history and policies that structured the development of white femininity. She argues that African women were, and
still are, "counterpoised" to constructions of white femininity: "the
pedestalization of upper-class white womanhood was counterpoised to
an inferiorized construction of blackness" (1997: 49). Mama shows how
colonialism and imperialism organized and produced violence against
African women as simultaneously racist, sexist, heterosexist, and capital-
ist and argues that constructions of white femininity and black sexuality
are inseparable from this history.

In order to understand "what kind of racialized gendered selves get
produced" (Razack 1998b: 13) through colonialism we must address issues of subject formation and agency in terms of the violence required

to secure categories of subordination and domination. For Meyda Yegenoglu this means acknowledging how:

> It is in the east that the Western woman was able to become a full individual, which was the goal desired and promoted by the emerging modernist ideology. Hence, for Western women it was possible to achieve the desired subject status against a devalued cultural difference. Rosemary M. George, in examining the impact of imperialism on women's attainment of an authoritative self-hood, notes that the "modern individual woman was first and foremost an imperialist." (1998: 107)

Yegenoglu's work can be read as a challenge to feminist scholarship that places emphasis on the subordination aspect of subjectivity formation for white women in the colonial settings by overlooking the violence that they participated in amidst the multiple identities they negotiated.

Other examples of scholarship addressing white women's role in imperialism include Vincent Rafael's work on colonial rule in the Philippines. In his discussion of the deployment of domesticity as a gendered form of imperial violence he argues that "by making a home away from home"(1995: 643) white women were in direct contact with servants whose labor is necessary to create an ordered home and leisure time for imperial women and men (1995: 659). As managers of domesticity in the Philippines, white women engaged in acts of violence as a means of controlling "their" servants and producing the imperial home (1995: 656).

Rafael identifies that simultaneously exploiting and obscuring the servant's labor requires a range of actions that include racist objectification, condescension and mimicry, and physical violence (1995: 675–79). The violence performed by white women in colonial Philippines included economic exploitation and physical violence against their male servants. This violence was mediated by imperialism and capitalism and should not be reduced to their response to gender oppression. "As both captive and empowered by the structures of empire, American women in the Philippines invariably participated in the simultaneous enactment and disavowal of the everyday violence of colonial rule"(1995: 641).

Toni Morrison (1992) also addresses colonial violence committed by white women in *Playing in the Dark: Whiteness in the Literary Imagination*. Morrison examines the racialization of black women by addressing the racist heterosexist violence committed by a white woman in the novel *Sapphira and the Slave Girl*, by Willa Cather. In this story Sapphira is a disabled woman who, convinced of her husband's "aching to have a liaison with Nancy, the pubescent daughter of her most devoted slave," plans to orchestrate Nancy's rape as a means of reclaiming the "full attentions of her husband"(1992: 19). Morrison's work illustrates a key point relevant to the construction of white femininity. Heterosexism and racism interlock to produce constructions of black women as a threat to white female control over "their" men and their stake as partners in imperialism and white supremacy.

Morrison's critique of *Sapphira and the Slave Girl* illustrates how Sapphira's violence against Nancy is contextualized by racism, patriarchy, and slavery. The construction of the character of Sapphira as a disabled woman is not addressed by Morrison; however, I argue that Cather attributes Sapphira's violence to her disability rather than to her whiteness. Addressing the association of deviance with disability would have made Morrison's critique fuller by further illustrating the ways in which white women's violence is perpetually attributed to their subordination or deviance when they are constructed as not white by discourses of class, disability, and sexuality.

In the Canadian context, Adel Perry addresses the role of white women in early-twentieth-century British Columbia. In her article titled "Fair Ones of a Purer Caste: White Women and Colonialism in Nineteenth Century B.C.," Perry writes: "Indeed, white women's role as agents of white supremacy was a matter for celebration, not a problematic issue for reflection" (1997: 508). Seen as moral guardians necessary for warding off the vices of men such as drinking, gambling, and marrying Native women, white women were seen as the catalyst for establishing a white, hetero-normative, settler culture in nineteenth-century British Columbia (1997: 504). Along with Morrison, Perry illustrates how relations of power between white women and Native women are structured by racial conflict and sexual competition that frequently contextualizes white women's violence against women of color (1997: 508). Perry's work also illustrates how violence was mobilized by white women. She writes:

> In constructing a definition of white women in contrast to primitivist understandings of First Nations women, these representations reinforced, rather than disrupted, the colonial discourse that positioned white women at the center of the effort to enforce normative standards of whiteness and masculinity. Rather than rejecting the inherent racism and bounded definitions of womanhood explicit in this discourse, they celebrated it in a bid to enlarge white female power. (1997: 519)

As Perry mentions elsewhere, this bid to enlarge white female power was not a unified cohesive strategy employed by all white women in the colony, nor did it benefit white women who failed to meet the requirements of white femininity based on bourgeois heteronormativity (1997: 517). However, for the purposes of my project I am concerned with how discourses of race afforded white women colonial agency in their role as perpetrators of imperial violence whether the violence was systemic, physical, or economic.

"[I]n the context of feminist politics, the white female gaze often sustains rather than disrupts white supremacy, capitalism and patriarchy" (Razack 1998b: 15). I have focused on violence committed by white women in order to make the point that imperialism has left a legacy that has made addressing women's violence theoretically and politically challenging. The fact remains that white women have and do commit acts of violence against people of color. Dominant discourses have insisted that violent men are pathological individuals not in any way produced by patriarchy. Feminist antiviolence work has targeted this explanation and theorized links between individual acts of violence and the social context that supports and generates male violence against women and children. However, the absence of work that identifies and addresses violence committed by women is in large part because we do not want to look at how we are implicated in, or agents of, violence (Razack 1998b: 20).

The narrative of girl violence is constructed around the idea that violent white girls are a new phenomenon. This new trend is explained as either a result of eroding gender roles or due to violence against women that causes otherwise nonviolent white girls to be violent. When Reena Virk was murdered, journalists, academics, and policy makers marveled at the fact that young (white) women were involved in her assault and murder. The papers and television accounts of this crime focused on what they asserted is a rising trend of girl violence. For example, the cover of *Maclean's* magazine carried the headline "Bad Girls, A Parents' Nightmare: missing the danger signs. The brutal murder of Reena Virk, 14, sounds an alarm about rising violence among teenage girls" (Chisholm, P. 1997). Headlines such as this are reminiscent of other moral panics in the twentieth century. In her research on young South Asian women Amita Handa discusses how moral panics of the early twentieth century were linked to anxieties over immigration and an increase in the youth population. She argues that moral panics articulate notions of white citizenship and regulated bourgeois sexuality that are central to Canadian nationalism (Handa 1997: 40). In a similar fashion the narrative of girl violence, as it is used to explain the murder of Reena Virk, is based on the belief that a tear in the moral fabric of society has occurred because of the erosion of normative gender roles.

In hegemonic discourses the narrative of girl violence is defined as evidence that girls are just as bad as boys and used to deny the pervasiveness of systemic male violence against women. In response to these claims, feminists such as Sibylle Artz have argued that the violence committed by girls is a result of the violence they have been subjected to (1998: 200–203). While I acknowledge that the experience of violence should be addressed as a factor in perpetrating violence, I am critical of stopping at explanations that attribute violence committed by girls to the cycle of violence. The term *"the cycle of violence"* (Rafiq 1991) is often used to describe a pattern of abuse as well as a way of describing how violence is learned through the experience of violence. In the girl violence narrative the cycle of violence is taken up as an explanation of why young women commit acts of violence—that is, because they have been targeted for violence they turn to violence as a means of resistance or out of a lack of options. This explanation does not address how young women who commit acts of violence could be demonstrating or vying for dominance and power over their subordinates.

Other explanations of violence among girls assume all girls are horizontally positioned to each other despite differences in power between them. Violence occurs among girls along lines of systemic relations of power—race, class, nationality, language, body size and appearance, skin color, and disability. Feminists have struggled to address the systemic features of male violence and challenge individualistic explanations that focus only on individual pathological behavior and histories of abuse rather than the context of patriarchy and misogyny. For example, feminist writing and activism regarding the Montreal Massacre focused on the fact that the murder of fourteen women in Montreal by Marc Lepine was not an isolated act of violence committed by a madman, but rather consistent with systemic misogyny and patriarchy (Malette & Chalouh 1991). It would make sense then, that when addressing the violence of girls and women, a systemic approach also be adopted to interrogate the power relations that contextualize their acts of violence.

Counter-Hegemonic Frameworks—
The Murder of Reena Virk Re-Framed

Rather than trying to answer the question "Who Was Reena Virk?" (Tafler 1998), I ask, how can we understand her murder in ways that counter hegemony? In this section I do not attempt to tell the story of what "really" happened. The counter-hegemonic reading I offer here is one that takes up the media reports through an interlocking analysis informed by the work of researchers and scholars producing work on violence against South Asian women and girls. I do not know what "really" happened any more than I know who Reena Virk "really" was. The aim of my research is to address the media representation of her life and murder and the narrative of girl violence that, I argue, has been used to construct who Reena was, or was not, without attending to the systems of oppression that contextualized this crime. The counter-hegemonic reading I argue for in this section is one that resists the "erasure of race" (Jiwani 1998) and the narrative of girl violence. The murder of Reena Virk was an act of racist, heterosexist, classist, ableist violence—not an example of what has been erroneously termed girl violence.

Since the initial media coverage of this crime six young women have been tried and convicted for assault (April-May 1998) and Warren Glowatski and Kelly Ellard were convicted of second degree murder (June 1999 and March 2000 respectively). An article by Guy Lawson published in the U.S. version of *Gentlemen's Quarterly* (1999) indicated that Reena was lured to Shoreline Park by two young women. Lawson writes that these young women intended to teach Reena a lesson for calling boys using phone numbers acquired from one of the young women's phone book:

> Reena didn't know, couldn't know that Amber and Cherelle [pseudonyms] were going to fuck her up. But they were. It was part wild fury at Reena for trying to claim the attention of boys Amber and Cherelle liked, and it was partly because Reena had dark skin and a loud mouth and she was plain and she was always telling stories about herself. Like how she was going out with some cute guy. (1999: 162)

In this passage and in other writing about this murder, the young women who participated in the attack on Reena are described as doing so out of a sense of outrage that Reena dare to consider having sexual or other kinds of relationships with boys in their social group. The attack on Reena echoes the historical research presented earlier in this chapter whereby competitive heterosexuality frames white women's violence against women of color.

In "Reckless Eyeballing: Being Reena in Canada," Tess Chakkalaka (2000) names this murder as a Canadian lynching. She writes: "Given the intersection of race, or more accurately, ethnicity, gender and sexuality in the Reena Virk case, the term lynching—in its contemporary *decontextualized* manifestations, make sense" (2000: 166). The accusation that Reena called the boys in another girl's phone book would be considered a violation of the code of conduct outlined in Sibylle Artz's research on violent white girls (1998: 183). Artz states that young women police each other's sexual conduct and that to be called a slut is often enough justification for physical assault (1998: 175). In this case, the violation was not just about trying to steal someone else's boyfriend, which is seen as the highest crime according to the rules of conduct in Artz's book, (1998: 175), but also about a young South Asian woman daring to express the desire to have a boyfriend at all.

In "Who Fancies Pakis? Pamella Bordes and the Problems of Exoticism in Multiracial Britain," Gargi Bhattacharyya writes:

> At various points, from the late 1980's onwards, I have suspected that some changes have been occurring in popular conceptions of Asian women. . . . When I was growing up, although ethnic identity was clearly sexualized in some manner, you were not supposed to fancy pakis. Asian was not a sexy identity. (1994: 87)

Bhattacharyya writes this to contextualize the media treatment of Pamella Bordes, who was the focus of a tabloid scandal in the summer of 1989. Bordes was profiled as "a young and good-looking House of Commons researcher, and the allegation [was] that she had been sexually involved with a number of eminent men—perhaps for money, and perhaps endangering state security" (1994: 89). Similar to the murder of Reena Virk, Bordes's ethnicity was erased in the media because of the incompatibility of sexual agency and hegemonic definitions of "Asianness":

> At the time of Bordes' fame, most people I spoke to were surprised to find out that she was Asian. Although this quickly became apparent through the references to the "Indian-born beauty" and "former Miss India," this seemed incongruous material for a British sex scandal. . . . As far as I can tell, Asian women have not been associated with the category "whore" recently in Britain. If they are fetishised, it is in their status as "virgin"—this signaling not only sexual inexperience but also a wider awkwardness, and inability to enjoy the pleasures of Western civilization without help. (1994: 92)

Bhattacharyya raises some important points in her reading of the Pamella Bordes scandal that are relevant to a counter-hegemonic reading of the murder of Reena Virk. The British and Canadian contexts are similar with respect to constructions of South Asian female sexuality. In her interviews with Canadian young South Asian women Handa also identifies the desexualization of young South Asian who are seen as "undesirable," "asexual," and "passive" (1997: 285). Virk was simultaneously portrayed as a "bad girl" who demonstrated sexual agency as well as an unwanted, rejected, unattractive, not-sexy young South Asian woman. Both of these narratives coexisted and were activated in contradictory ways that nonetheless supported the narrative of "girl violence." It is not enough to say that the youth that attacked and murdered Reena did so because of her transgression—to pursue boys who were forbidden to her—she was punished because, as a young South Asian woman, she had no right to be sexual at all.

As we address narratives such as "girl violence" using an interlocking analysis, it is important to recognize how seemingly contradictory claims can be made to support hegemonic narratives. The media coverage of the murder of Reena Virk is replete with such inconsistencies, yet the narrative of girl violence survives and anchors the interlocked systems of oppression on which it simultaneously depends. If telephoning boys is seen as a transgression of the code of conduct upheld by the youth who attacked and murdered Reena Virk, what also needs to be addressed is the fact that for this trespass she was punished with death. Even if one believes that the youth who committed this crime just got "carried away," at the very least, we must recognize the violence inherent to heterosexism and the resulting precarious place women of color hold in relation to white men and women within the context of white supremacy. I argue that Reena was murdered because she was a South Asian woman *and* because she did not fit the hegemonic definitions of female "Asianness." She was constructed as deviant because of who she was, and who she would not be for those around her. The fact that Reena was South Asian was a key factor in the brutality of the punishment she received for transgressing heterosexist, racist, and sexist boundaries.

Many of the articles and editorials written about this crime describe racist acts but then "dismiss" racism as a site of analysis in this crime:

> East Indian kids in Victoria usually face a few racial taunts, quickly dismissed as the grunts of the ignorant. But Reena's size and physical maturity made her different. Tall and heavy, she towered over other girls her age. . . . She was targeted by bullies, humiliated by her peers. (Tafler 1998: 16)

Racism is mentioned as an aside but not a central part of the investigation of this crime. Instead, it is Reena's "difference" of size and physical maturity that sets her apart from other girls her age. Size oppression was a key factor in the brutality of the harassment and violence against Reena; however, size oppression is interlocked with racism. Size and physical characteristics take on specific meaning when racialized bodies are targeted for violence. Women of color are subjected to racism through scientific discourses that are concerned with the shape, size, texture, and color of our bodies. Ann Laura Stoler describes the "scientific pornography" experiments conducted by Dr. C. H. Stratz in 1897 who photographed, measured, and categorized the skull, pelvis, and other body parts of Javanese women (Stoler 1995: 184). The incarceration of Sara Baartman, an African woman subjected to medical experiments in Britain in 1810, and the fascination with her body shape expressed in the empirical documentation and finally the formaldehyde preservation of her genitals upon her death in 1814 is another case that demonstrates the direct linkage between size oppression and discourses of race that dehumanize, scrutinize, inspect, and pathologize women of color (Webster 2000: 26). Although the media coverage asserts that Reena's difference revolved around her body size and maturity these constructions are in no way separate from racial discourses.

Even though Reena's social location as a young South Asian woman is not explicitly discussed in the media coverage, she is described in ways that allude to hegemonic constructions of South Asian femininity. For example, Reena is described as trying to escape her strict home environment by running away and lying about sexual abuse charges as a means of attaining freedom from parental control. The Virk family was described repeatedly in the newspapers as Jehovah Witnesses as a way of de-racing them; however, the media also evoked South Asian stereotypes and narratives of cultural inferiority regarding South Asian women and culture that have permeated representations of South Asian people particularly in British Columbia (Jiwani 1992).

Hegemonic narratives construct young South Asian women as caught between cultures or experiencing bicultural stress as they are pulled between "traditional" South Asian culture and "modern" Western culture. Amita Handa argues that the notion of "culture conflict" obscures the systemic sources of violence against young South Asian women (1997: 4). She argues that racism, sexism, heterosexism, and ageism configure various violences directed toward young South Asian women and that while it is important to acknowledge the specific cultural experiences of young South Asian women, culture is not a static essential phenomenon that "naturally" produces conflict (1997: 28). Similarly, Sherene Razack writes:

Culture talk is clearly a double-edged sword. It packages difference as inferiority and obscures gender-based domination within
communities, yet cultural considerations are important for contextualizing oppressed groups' claims for justice, for improving
their access to services, and for requiring dominant groups to examine the invisible cultural advantages they enjoy. (1994: 896)

When young South Asian women are described as caught between
cultures, multiculturalism, liberalism, and the discourse of "difference"
work to maintain Canadian nationalism and obscure systems of oppression that are present in both South Asian communities and in the
dominant society. Thus, young South Asian women are used as symbols of South Asian community integrity and respectability within the
South Asian patriarchal discourses and as symbols of South Asian
depravity and backwardness within the dominant Canadian culture.

Reena is described in the media coverage as being shuttled back
and forth between her family and social services or running away in her
attempt "to find a comfortable place for herself" (Tafler 1998: 15).
Handa documents the displacement of young South Asian women who
struggle to negotiate between hegemonic and minority oppositional
narratives (1997: 342). She mentions that young South Asian women are
perceived as needing to be rescued from their backward families and
communities. This discourse operates in the media coverage to construct Reena as both a captive of the home environment and a runaway
who seeks to partake in the "freedom" of Western culture. There has
been no acknowledgment in media of how interlocking oppressions
shaped the circumstances of Reena's life in such a way that she would
face violence and oppression in various contexts. For example, at school
and in the foster care system she faced racism, sexism, ageism, size oppression, and heterosexism and within her home she struggled to address sexual abuse. The media coverage conveys the sense that Reena
needed to be rescued from her family situation without attending to the
fact that she faced violence in other social spaces. There was no one there
to rescue Reena the night she was killed. Perhaps abandoning rescuing
as a strategy and instead adopting "anti-subordination" (Razack 1998b:
170) and anti-oppression tactics would have been a more effective way
of addressing Reena Virk's situation.

Handa discusses the experiences of young South Asian women and
the violence and oppression they live with as well as the many acts of
resistance they demonstrate. Her work is significant in that it further
documents the existence of sexual abuse, assault, racism, sexism, and
heterosexism in the lives of young South Asian women as well as their

agency in negotiating their life circumstances. Handa's work makes it clear that the negotiations demonstrated by the young South Asian women she interviews both support and disrupt hegemony. Her work also indicates that the maneuvering through interlocking systems of oppression takes a toll on them. Handa argues that young South Asian women move between identities and that this shifting subjectivity can be both a resistance to racist stereotypes and patriarchal roles as well as an ambivalent acceptance of certain status quos in both South Asian and mainstream contexts (1997: 325). She goes farther to state that while the shifting of subjectivity provides a context for self- and cultural esteem it also causes fragmentation and a constant "hiding of selves" (1997: 354). The risks for young South Asian women in this act of concealment means that they can be more vulnerable to racist and sexist violence of the dominant culture, peers, and community.

In the South Asian and mainstream community/environment, young South Asian women face a "double jeopardy" or as Amita Handa writes, they are "doubly displaced by hegemonic and minority oppositional narratives" (1997: 342). When young South Asian women experience physical, emotional, and sexual violence they may face victim blaming from both family/community as well as from mainstream social services where racist (and sexist) stereotypes about South Asian women and culture are pervasive. There are few, if any, places where young South Asian women can get support regarding both the racism and sexism they experience. This seems to also have been the case for Reena Virk who entered the foster care system at the age of thirteen. From the often vague and sensational media coverage, there is much evidence that illustrates the difficult negotiations Reena made between mainstream social services, the education system, and her family. For a young woman such as Reena, entering the foster care system may have been a way of seeking support regarding sexual abuse; however, it also exposed her to other forms of abuse particularly with regard to racism.

The media portrayed Reena as both a sad lonely victim and a messed-up "bad girl." To deny that Reena struggled to negotiate the various forms of violence again denies the agency that she demonstrated. The charges she laid against her father for sexual abuse, moving in with a foster care family, vying for the attention and affection of friends, asking for help from her family and social workers must be viewed as attempts to survive. When she screamed for her attackers to stop their assault and tried to escape the mob of youth that confined and beat her, she was trying to survive. By leaving the scene of the first assault and heading for home, she was trying to survive. To deny her will to survive is also to deny the fact that Warren Glowatski and Kelly Ellard followed her from the scene of the first attack, beat her unconscious, drowned her of their own volition. The actions of Glowatski and Ellard were acts of violence that can never be separate from the interlocking systems of oppression that allowed them to perform this violence and think that what they did made sense within the context of their social code and that in the end they would get away with murder even as they boasted to numerous strangers, acquaintances, and close friends that they killed Reena Virk. Witnesses testified that Ellard bragged about murdering Virk. Glowatski also was said to boast about his participation in Virk's murder, however, he also told a friend that he killed a "native guy" when he was asked about the blood on his pants (Lawson 1999: 192). The fact that Glowatski claimed he murdered a native man, as perhaps a cover story, indicates that on some level he thought that violence against a native person would not only be acceptable, but that it would also demonstrate his prowess. I do not believe that Glowatski's choice of lie is separate from racism and the act of racist violence he actually did commit when he beat and drowned Reena Virk.

The violence committed against Reena Virk for transgressing heterosexist and racist codes and boundaries was enacted as murder because as a young South Asian woman, Reena was racialized and, therefore, dehumanized. She could not be recuperated into the racial and gendered identity of girlhood. No amount of correction would make Reena into a white girl. This was a punishment with the aim of annihilation. The youth who attacked and killed Reena Virk carried out what they perceived as a logical expression of their outrage against a young South Asian woman who wanted to survive, make decisions, have friends, and express herself emotionally and sexually to those around her.

The Trial of Kelly Ellard

The concept of girl violence secures hegemonic femininity and systems of oppression. It will not help to end violence against girls or the violence girls perform. This was clearly demonstrated in the trial of Kelly Ellard that I attended in Vancouver, March 2000. In "A Guilty Verdict Against the Odds: Privileging White Middle-Class Femininity in the Trial of Kelly Ellard for the Murder of Reena Virk," Brenna Bhandar writes that the defense counsel relied on hegemonic femininity to cast Ellard as a good middle-class girl who "had merely fallen into a 'bad peer group' who were now framing her for the crime" (2000: paragraph 3). This framework was used to discredit crown witnesses (particularly young men and women of color) as deviant based on their failure to meet the requirements of hegemonic femininity or masculinity. The extreme manifestation of this surfaced in the defense counsel's arguments that crown witnesses were unreliable based on racial, sexual, class, and age characteristics or histories of abuse and/or criminalization. They also suggested that a young black woman charged in the initial assault on Virk actually murdered her and then conspired to frame Ellard with other youths as part of an alleged gang membership and romantically founded loyalty to Warren Glowatski (the alleged leader of the gang).

The defense banked on notions of white femininity as a means of denying that Ellard could be capable of murder—a belief that was further demonstrated in the judge's comments at the sentencing in which she described Ellard as a "person who loves animals, had positive and caring relationships with her family and friends, and posed a low risk to society in general" (Jiwani 2000: 1). Ellard's violence is unimaginable not because of the brutality of her crime, but because of her social location as a white middle-class girl. Ironically, in a videotaped interview with police on the night that she was arrested Ellard claims that she could not have been involved in the murder of Reena Virk because "This is Victoria. Nobody gets murdered in Victoria." It is as if her location both in terms of identity and environment—Victoria, a quaint town of tea drinkers and her place in it—will make invisible the violence in which she participated.

The Ellard trial exemplified how hegemonic femininity makes it unfathomable that the universal girl can be capable of violence. It also revealed the ways girls of color are "counterpoised" (Mama 1997: 49) to white femininity and the racist heterosexist violence they face as a result. In the trial of Kelly Ellard the tacit acceptance of hegemonic femininity and the narrative of girl violence served to minimize the brutality of the murder of Reena Virk *and* the violence against young women of color who testified at the trial. It also obscured the fact that this murder was a racist hate crime inseparable from sexual and class hierarchies. Tess Chakkalakal writes:

> Calling this event a lynching opens up the possibility of interpreting and locating the effects of Canadian Racism. . . . It is crucial to call the Reena Virk case by its proper name, so that it may affect our view of the way racism works in Canada. It is clear that the case has been erroneously construed by the Canadian news media as a sensational example of the rising trend in "teen" violence, an error that has systematically erased Reena Virk's death at the hand of racists from everyday life in Canada. (2000: 167)

Conclusion

Girl violence is an empty concept. It is an attempt to make simple something that is not simple. It will not help us to stop violence against young women any more than it will stop the racist, heterosexist, ableist, classist acts of violence committed by youth or adults. Because the narrative of girl violence relies on good girl/bad girl dichotomy, violence against girls is made invisible; those labeled as "bad girls" are seen as intrinsically debased rather than trying to negotiate survival within a context of violence and oppression. (Kadi 1996: 64)

Reena Virk was not a "bad girl." It is crucial to acknowledge her agency as she tried to negotiate between family, friends, teachers, and social workers in an effort to cope with the violence to which she was subjected. She was never only a victim and never only an agent (Handa 1997: 78) but a young South Asian woman "caught between omissions" (1997: 58) trying to maneuver between various systems of oppression and the violence that was, and continues to be, simultaneously virulent and invisible. Labeling Kelly Ellard as a "bad girl" is also problematic because her act of murder becomes defined through hegemonic notions of female deviance rather than analyzed with respect to her position of racial and class dominance.

By "erasing race" (Jiwani 1998: 3) from the media coverage of the murder of Reena Virk hegemonic systems remain intact. By bringing race to our interrogation of this crime I have argued that we must also insist that all other systems of oppression be afforded saliency and attention in our inquiry and discussions. Failure to do this maintains systems of domination. This has been most clearly demonstrated by gender-centric/exclusive research and theory that misses the ways in which racism is supported by notions of hegemonic femininity and the belief that women are the gentler sex. As educators and activists working to end all forms of violence and oppression we must choose carefully the tools we use in this endeavor.

The circumstances of the life and murder of Reena Virk can be traced using an interlocking analysis of oppression and in doing so, strategies must be developed to assist young South Asian women like Reena who experience multiple forms of violence. As we work to provide support for young women and adult women facing violence it is not enough to adopt a paternal approach that seeks to rescue them. Rather, we must rigorously interrogate the very notions that antiviolence theory and activism are based on. Our resistance strategies will ultimately fail until we can fully incorporate an anti-racist/colonial perspective into all facets of antiviolence work.

The murder of Reena Virk calls our attention to the inadequacies of social service agencies when it comes to providing support to young women of color. It also makes salient the danger of gender focused/ exclusive theory that fails to identify the insidious presence of white supremacy in the form of hegemonic femininity that can be found in some feminist theorizing and activism.

Feminists committed to abolishing violence against women must utilize an interlocking approach as opposed to an additive one (Razack 1998b: 20). This will require realizing that the fight to end violence and oppression cannot be won without acknowledging the interdependency of white supremacy, heterosexism, ableism, ageism, classism, and sexism. As we address specific gender forms of oppression we must also interrogate our strategies to ensure that we are not supporting other systems of oppression.

Finally, in order to explain violence that cannot be "explained by sexism" (Kadi 1996: 74) we must address racist, classist, heterosexist, ableist, and ageist violence committed by women against those in subordinate positions. As we acknowledge women's capacity to resist, we must also acknowledge our capacity for violence and domination. The legacy of imperialism and colonialism has made acknowledging white women's agency a complicated task, one that has all too often upheld a dichotomy between victim of patriarchy or a resister to oppression. Feminist antiviolence theory and activism must disrupt notions of essential womanhood based on constructions of white femininity. Our "anti-subordination" work must address interlocking systems of oppression because failure to do so cements elite hegemony (Razack 1998b: 170). The concept of girl violence will not help to end violence against girls or the violence girls perform nor will it address the racist violence prevalent in Canadian society.

References

Artz, S. 1998, *Sex, power, and the violent school girl*, Trifolium Books, Toronto.

Bhandar, B. 2000, "A guilty verdict against the odds: privileging white middle-class femininity in the trial of Kelly Ellard for the murder of Reena Virk," in Y. Jiwani (ed), *The FREDA Centre for Research on Violence Against Women and Children*, (ed), http://www.harbour.sfu.ca/Freda.articles/bhandar.htm.

Bhattacharyya, G. 1994, "Who fancies Pakis? Pamella Bordes and the problems of exoticism in multiracial Britian," in S. Ledger, J. McDonagh & J.

Spencer (eds), *Political gender texts and contexts*, Harvester Wheatsheaf, New York, pp. 85–96.

Chakkalakal, T. 2000, "Reckless eyeballing: being Reena in Canada," in R. Walcott (ed), *Rude: contemporary Black cultural criticism*, Insomniac Press, Toronto, pp. 161–67.

Chisholm, P. 1997, "Bad girls. A parent's nightmare: missing the danger signs," *Maclean's Magazine*, Dec. 8, pp. 12–16.

Davis, A. Y. 1983, *Women race and class*, Vintage Books, New York.

Fellows, M. L. & Razack, S. 1998, "The race to innocence: confronting hierarchical relations among women," *The Journal of Gender, Race and Justice: a Journal of the University of Iowa College of Law*, Spring Issue, vol. 1, no. 2. pp. 335–52.

Hammonds, E. M. 1997, "Toward a genealogy of black female sexuality: the problematic of silence," in C. T. Mohanty & M. J. Alexander (eds), *Feminist genealogies, colonial legacies, democratic futures*, Routledge, New York, pp. 170–82.

Handa, A. 1997, "Caught between omissions: exploring culture conflict among second generation South Asian women in Canada," OISE/University of Toronto, unpublished dissertation.

Holmes, C. & Ristock, J. 1998, "Exploring discursive constructions of lesbian abuse: looking inside and out," OISE/University of Toronto, unpublished draft.

Jimenez, M. 1997, "Slain teen misfit remembered," *Vancouver Sun*, Nov. 25, pp. A1&A4.

Jiwani, Y. 1992, "To be and not to be: South Asians as victims and oppressors in the Vancouver Sun, Canadian Media & Racism," *Sanvad*, Mississauga, Ontario, vol. 5, no. 45, pp. 13–15.

———. 1997, "The murder of Reena Virk, the erasure of race," *Kinesis*, December/January.

———. 1998, "Reena Virk: the erasure of race" *http://www.harbour.sfu.ca/freda/articles/virk.htm.*

———. 1999, "Erasing race: the story of Reena Virk," *Canadian Woman Studies*, York University, vol. 19, no. 3, pp. 178–84.

———. 2000, "The denial of race in the murder of Reena Virk," *Kinesis*, May.

Kadi, J. 1996, *Thinking class: sketches from a cultural worker*, Southend Press, Boston.

Lawson, G. 1999, "When no one is watching," *GQ* magazine, U.S., Feb., pp. 160–92.

Malette, L. & Chalouh, M. (eds) 1991, *The Montreal massacre*, Gynergy Books, Charlotte Town, Prince Edward Island, Canada.

Mama, A. 1997, "Sheroes and villains: conceptualizing colonial and contemporary violence against women in Africa," in J. Alexander & C.T. Mohanty (eds), *Feminist genealogies, colonial legacies, democratic futures*, Routledge, New York, pp. 46–62.

Meissner, D. 1999, "Pathologist tells grim details of Reena Virk's beating injuries," *Toronto Star*, Apr. 26, p. A6.

Morrison, T. 1992, *Playing in the dark, whiteness and the literary imagination*, Vintage Books, New York.

Perry, A. 1997, "Fair ones of a purer caste: white women and colonialism in nineteenth-century British Columbia," *Feminist Studies,* vol. 23, no. 3, pp. 501–24.

Purvis, A. 1997, "Fury of her peers," *Time Magazine,* Dec. 8, p. 68.

Rafael, V. L. 1995, "Colonial domesticity: white women and United States rule in the Philippines," *American Literature,* vol. 67, no. 4, pp. 639–66.

Rafiq, F. 1991, *Towards equal access: a handbook for service providers,* Education Wife Assault, Toronto.

Razack, S. 1994, "What is to be gained by looking white people in the eye? Culture, race, and gender in cases of sexual violence," *Signs,* no. 19, Summer, pp. 894–923.

———. 1998a, "Race, space, and prostitution: the making of the bourgeois subject," *Canadian Journal of Women and the Law,* no. 10, pp. 338–76.

———. 1998b, *Looking white people in the eye: gender, race, and culture in courtrooms and classrooms,* University of Toronto Press, Toronto.

Stoler, L. A. 1995, *Race and the education of desire: Foucault's history of sexuality and the colonial order of things,* Duke University Press, Durham.

Tafler, S. 1998, "Who was Reena Virk?," *Saturday Night magazine,* April, p. 15.

Webster, P. 2000, "France keeps a hold on Black Venus," *The Observer,* London, Apr. 2, p. 26.

Yegenoglu, M. 1998, *Colonial fantasies, towards a feminist reading of Orientalism,* Cambridge University Press, New York.

Chapter Five

Turbulent Talk: Girls' Making Sense of Violence

Michele Burman

In recent years, the researching and analysis of interpersonal violence has taken many forms (see, for example, Bradby 1996; Felson & Tedeschi 1993; Kappeler 1995; Newburn & Stanko 1994; Schwartz 1997). In the context of a perceived increase in violence involving young people, much recent research has been concerned with "violent youth," specifically young men. With a couple of exceptions in Britain (e.g., Cawson et al., 2000; Toon 2000) there has been little empirical examination of the meaning and effects of violence for young people, and specifically how it figures in their everyday lives. This is particularly so for girls.[1] Despite the rarity of female violence, there have been an increasing number of media accounts portraying violence by young women as a *new and growing* phenomena. These include reports of "girl gangs" roving the streets and attacking innocent victims and startling court cases where girls have been reported as "torturing" and maiming other girls. Although girls experience a wide range of different forms of violent victimization and, increasingly, are reputed to be engaging in more physical violence,[2] the voices of girls and young women themselves are rarely heard. Ideas about female violence have tended to be constructed out of existing theories premised upon male experience, and we have a limited theoretical and analytical vocabulary of violence that is not grounded in male behavior (Artz 1998). In our current work,[3] we have been investigating teenage girls' views and experiences of violence in order to grasp how violence is understood by them and how it is both encountered and mobilized in their daily lives. We have been doing this by drawing on girls' personal accounts of their own involvement in, and avoidance of, violence and conflict situations.[4] This was not conceived of as a study specifically of "violent girls"; rather, it focused on the everyday understandings, conceptualizations, and experiences of "ordinary" girls.

We conducted this research by means of self-report questionnaires (conducted with 671 girls), a series of discussions with small groups consisting of between four and ten girls (eighteen groups, eighty-nine girls), and individual interviews (twelve girls). Most girls were aged between thirteen years and sixteen years and were accessed through a variety of means, via schools, residential homes, youth groups, youth outreach workers, voluntary organizations, leisure clubs, and through snowball sampling. As such, girls were located largely through their membership in established groups and clubs and contacts with other girls. Only a very small number of "hard to reach" girls with more chaotic lifestyles took part in the research; they were recruited through other girls. Girls were drawn from a range of socioeconomic backgrounds and diverse communities—inner-city, small town, and rural areas—across Scotland, UK. Ours was not a representative study—rather, we aimed to include a cross-section of girls from different backgrounds in order to tap into a wide range of possible experiences and so, for the most part, the girls were not in the juvenile justice system[5] or part of an identifiable gang.

Talking with Girls as a Research Strategy

Although we asked girls to fill in a self-report questionnaire to provide personal, demographic, and attitudinal data, our central research strategy was talking with girls. One of the ways we examined girls' perspectives on violence was through the ways in which they speak about it. Our qualitative research encounters, the small group discussions and interviews, were rarely "one-off" meetings and contact with some girls spanned over two years (Burman, Batchelor, & Brown 2001).

We took a decision to move away from single direct questions and answers, and instead chose to conduct open "conversations" with the girls. Sometimes talking with the young women took the form of quiet chats; sometimes it also involved eating and drinking and "having a laugh." Our intention was to be responsive to their concerns, letting them talk their own way into, and about, what they considered important, although we did have some common issues and questions that we sought to raise in all groups and interviews. Our style of talking with girls, and our analytic method, was partly influenced by the voice-centered feminist approach (Brown & Gilligan 1992; Gilligan, Ward, & Taylor 1988), which entails listening to girls and women as authorities about their own experiences and representing their voices in text, rather than imposing irrefutable theoretical interpretations on what they say.

We paid special attention to the ways in which different groups and individual girls spoke about violence, the words they used, their tone of voice, the degree of emphasis placed upon certain words or remarks, the laughter, the euphemisms, the circumlocutions, and the silences in the "violence talk." We were particularly interested in the "violence stories" told to us by girls, and the ways in which girls recounted such stories and their role in them, as bystanders, protagonists, or victims. As Plummer (1995) eloquently points out, stories can be seen as issues to be investigated in their own right, as topics to be investigated rather than merely resources to draw on, as well as mechanisms for understanding human meaning. Violence stories are powerful vehicles conveying information about girls' views and normative beliefs concerning violence. In telling such stories, girls draw on their personal and emotional experiences, and their wider cultural and social life, to convey feelings of both powerlessness and empowerment. Heavily laden with both moral and cultural understandings, such stories also offer a way of allowing us to locate girls' views on the social uses of violence. Examining how girls *speak* about violence allows us to trace the multiplicity of ways in which it connects with and impacts upon other areas of their (gendered) lives, and enables us to see the ways in which actual and threatened violence structures daily social interactions.

Having said that, one needs to be cognizant of the context in which girls' talk of violence is produced. Despite our efforts to alleviate interviewer effects and maintain nonhierarchical power relations, girls' talk about violence is inevitably a situationally specific production. Our research encounters, in which we encouraged the deliberation of violence, provided a particular context within which such talk took place. We initiated such talk by asking girls to give their views and tell us their violence stories, and they responded to our questions and prompting. Whilst we were mindful of predefining the "problem" of violence, the word itself acted as a powerful catalyst.[6] Indeed, we were often surprised at the readiness with which many girls spoke about many forms of violence and its impact on their lives, and their feelings about being subjected to or using violence. These self-narratives, however, were not constructed by individual girls alone, but by the group (including the researchers) in conversation. Group dynamics shaped the flow of the discussions in different ways. At times, talk became turbulent as meanings were disputed, interpretations of shared experiences were challenged and arguments (and sometimes physical fights) broke out. Similarly, we (as researchers) had to be careful that we were not inadvertently leading girls to give responses they thought we were anticipating. Whilst we can neither presume that we have really grasped the meanings that violence holds for those who took part in the study, nor guarantee the accuracy of our interpretations of their talk, investigating girls' understandings about violence in this way is one means of rendering its complex, pervasive, and mundane nature more visible. In this chapter, I will be reporting some aspects of our conversations about violence, focusing on the main recurrent themes, as well as the gaps and silences that occurred in the violent talk.

What's in a Word?

Violence is a volatile, evocative, and compelling subject, and a difficult and complex topic to research. First, the word in itself is problematic. As a term, "violence" is at once both generic and highly contested. There are a range of competing discourses defining and conceptualizing it, but using the word *violence* also implies that we share a common understanding of what it means. "Violence" nevertheless means different things to different people. A key aim was to ground our study in girls' own conceptualizations, to prioritize their views, and use their words (which often conflicted with our "adult," "politicized," and "feminist" ideas) about what "counts" as violence. When we told girls that we wanted their views and experiences of violence, they responded by talking about many different forms of behavior that took place in a variety of contexts. When asked to define violence in the abstract, most girls, unsurprisingly, offered a normative—if somewhat restricted—conception of intentionally harmful physical behavior, such as fighting, slapping, punching, kicking, and the use of weapons, etc. to hurt another individual. But when recounting their *own* experiences of using, witnessing, or being on the receiving end of violence, girls told of a multitude of ways in which subtle and more blatant forms of violence are experienced in their everyday lives. They talked about a much broader array of diverse behaviors and incidents, including stalking, boxing, sexual assault, playground fighting, tormenting, verbal threats, stabbing, racial harassment, self-harm, offensive name calling, bullying, and intimidation, as well as vandalism, fire-raising, and cruelty to animals. In offering their opinions and relaying their violent stories to us each drew on their own particular discourses of experience. In these self-narratives, the term *violence* was interpreted much more widely and loosely as girls chose it to describe and categorize a range of incidents and experiences, very many of which did not correspond to the normative definition of violence they gave earlier.

Perhaps the strongest message conveyed to us by girls was that a sole focus on *physical* violence in an investigation such as ours would be misguided, as it obscures and detracts from other forms of intentionally harmful violating behavior that girls both engage in and experience as violence. Most also consistently maintained that they experience verbally abusive behavior (threats, name calling, taunting, etc.) as more hurtful and damaging than physical violence. This is particularly the case when verbal conflicts emanate from within an existing friendship. Falling-out with friends invariably involves the continued use of various forms of verbal abuse and intimidation, taunts and teasing, and in this the study confirms other research findings concerning the intensity of girls' friendships and the potential for hostility when they break up (e.g., Lees 1993; Fillion 1996; Hey 1997). In the self-report study, being the target for malicious gossip, particularly by ex-friends, emerged as the greatest overall fear for girls, and more than half said they were worried about being verbally bullied or threatened. In response to a question about the effects of verbal bullying and gossip, one group of younger girls (aged thirteen and fourteen years) who lived on farms and villages in a predominantly rural area but came together to attend a youth club had this to say:[7]

Kiki:	It can break up friendships and that, those that have been together for ages.
Anne:	And that hurts more than getting a punch in the face or something . . .
Jo:	. . . and I can tell you a lot about that. [laughter]
Kiki:	It depends who is punching.
Jenna:	I think that verbal stuff hurts you longer, physical violence, that is going to go away.
Anne:	Yeah.
Jo:	Verbal abuse is really gonna, it's really gonna be there forever. I think verbal abuse is actually worse than physical abuse.
Anne:	Some people are gonna shout at you though and you can't ignore it.

Researcher:	Does it matter if it is people that you know or those you don't know, or whether it is your family or friends?
Anne:	Yes, it's like if it is someone that you know, and they are constantly saying things to you . . .
Kiki:	. . . and they know it is getting to you.
Sue:	. . . yeah and they just keep on saying it, even when they know it is really hurting you. (Group 4)

Violent Talk

By far the most common conflict situation reported by girls from all backgrounds and situations and all ages concerned their own use and experience of what we came to term collectively as verbal abuse. It is important to stress however, that many girls in the study defined this as "violence." Included within the term is an array of abusive verbal tactics that girls report using, mainly toward other girls, often those who were once friends. Most of these encounters did not involve any physical blows between girls (at least initially) but were considered variously to be "worse," "more serious," "more damaging," "more effective" or "more harmful" than physical fights and so were seen, by girls, to warrant the label *violence*. Examples include offensive name calling—which can be personalized (e.g., "fat cunt," "smelly cow") or racialized (e.g., "Paki bastard," "fenian cow") as well as sexualized (e.g., "lezzie cow," "slag," "rabbit," "bicycle")—threats (e.g., "You're a lying cow and if you don't stop it I'm gonna kill you," "I'm gonna get you"), insults (e.g., calling someone a "pikey," a "sham," or a "ned"), ridicule (e.g., "Ya big ginger perm"), and intimidation by shouting or swearing. Whilst the subject of such insults are usually individual girls or sometimes groups of girls; often the abuse concerns a member of a girl's family, usually the mother (e.g., "your ma's a slag," "your ma's a druggie").

A key point about this type of abuse is that it is rarely a one-off altercation, but rather it is an ongoing verbal onslaught that can be kept up for long periods, whenever the "victim" is within earshot of the "abusers." Giving and taking such abuse can be a way of life, occurring on an everyday basis, rather than an isolated incident. The self-report data indicated that 91 percent of girls reported being verbally intimidated by offensive name calling, threats, taunts, or ridicule. This experience crosses economic, ethnic, and cultural divides, and affects all age groups. There are common themes to such abuse, such as body shape, demeanor, perceived sexuality, and, frequently, dress style (particularly where the style is distinctive or idiosyncratic or unfashionable (see Nilan 1992)). Verbal abuse is (cleverly) tailored toward individual girls' physical, familial, or racial characteristics (see also Lees 1993; Toon 2000) for maximum impact and effect.

The more time girls spent in the company of other girls, the more likely they were to have been shouted at, sworn at, or called names. Almost three-quarters (72 percent) reported being verbally abusive toward others. Girls reported that being on the receiving end of taunts, insults, slander, threats, and people spreading rumors and gossiping about them "behind their backs" were the most likely things to make them feel like crying or hurting themselves.[8] The routine trading of insults and abuse, and particularly when it involved ex-friends, was a topic that was raised spontaneously time and again in the small group discussions and interviews. Girls showed great awareness of the effectiveness of verbal abuse and intimidation as a means of self-assertion and of inflicting hurt on others. Some, particularly older girls in the fifteen to sixteen year age group, spoke of their pride in being "good at slagging" and knowing just what to say to cause the most embarrassment or damage. A group of white girls from relatively affluent backgrounds spoke authoritatively about the purpose of threats, slander, and ostracization of other girls:

Cara: [the purpose] is to undermine them.

Laura: . . . to get one up on them and show you are better. To make a point.

Cara: To get your own back.

Later, the discussion turned toward the importance of having an audience to witness the intimidation.

Laura: It depends on how nastily you would want to do it. If it is front of other people, it could be a comment that could hurt someone, and make other people laugh at them. Then you are getting the rest of the group to gang up on one person. (Group 12)

Within a group, girls can earn reputations and enhanced stature from being inventive and creative in their insults, especially if they are funny as well as cruel. It has been contended that females are criticized by other females if their talk is baldly aggressive and offensive (e.g., Campbell 1988) but, within the context of "slagging" this seems not to be the case as, within the group, the proficient "slagger" is celebrated. If one meaning of power is taken to be a relation of domination over others, then it may be argued that talking in this way can be construed as a means by which a particular (verbal) form of power is exerted. In assuming an openly confrontational style and orchestrating verbal disputes in this way, girls assert themselves at the expense of other girls. It has been argued that blunt antagonism is rare amongst girls, and that, even in conflict, girls' talk tends to be constructive and facilitative in that they use compromise, evasion, and acquiescence to achieve a particular goal (e.g., Sheldon 1992). However, on the basis of this and other research there are times when responsiveness to others is eschewed by girls in favor of a more harsh and injurious agenda.

Girls who described being the recipients of such hostility recalled feelings of humiliation, anger, and powerlessness at being the object of ridicule and criticism. Recent research into racist victimization in Britain (Chahal and Julienne 1999) concluded that racist violence occurs at an everyday, routine level of harassment, and not at an extraordinary level revolving around a particular incident. Such findings have a resonance for understanding girls' experiences of the types of verbal intimidation and harassment outlined above, in that it is rarely expressed as a discrete, single, or one-off event, but rather as a process, ongoing and cumulative, that pervades their everyday life.

Although a range of diverse behaviors were categorized as violent, conversely, many girls chose not to apply the term to other sorts of actions and conflict situations that are commonly labeled so. One example of this concerned physical violence between siblings within the home. Sibling fights were frequent occurrences; in the self-report study, 59 percent of girls cited regular involvement in such fights. For most, no matter how vicious or injurious these fights, they are considered not to count as violence, and as "not serious." Rather, they are conceived as "natural" occurrences, a normal and unremarkable facet of home life. Although the intention may very well be to cause harm, inflict injury, exert force, and assume dominance, the context and relationship together mitigate against seriousness. The following excerpt, from a discussion between girls from a local authority housing scheme in an inner-city area, is typical:

Emily: I think it's natural to fight with your brother and sisters.

Stacey: I know. It is not as serious as if you are fighting with somebody outside or something.

Ann: I always fight with my sister. (Group 16)

During the course of the research, we were told about, and witnessed, girls engaging in "rumbles" or play-fights with each other. Typically, they began as pokes and jabs and pushes between two or three girls in a friendship group, usually accompanied by laughter. Gradually, other girls joined in, and the prods and thrusts became more forceful. Sometimes it appeared as if the group turned on one or two individuals, subjecting them to hard blows, punches, and kicks. On a couple of occasions, some girls were obviously hurt. It seemed to us that these "play-fights" had escalated into something more serious and intentionally harmful. Frequently taking place in a public arena, outwardly they had all the characteristics of a violent encounter. In the following example, a group of fourteen year olds gleefully describe (and demonstrate) a "rumble":

Debbie: Aye, we "ken how no to go too hard and anything.

Melanie: Like we wouldn't like, pull each other's hair . . .

Debbie
[interjecting]: We'll no slap and punch hard, we'll just jump about mad on each other.

Christine: We do pull hair, we do punch, we do slap, we'll be just like wrestling with each other.

Debbie: Tripping up and throwing over and everything. But boys really punch you and kick you and elbow you and kick you. (Group 7)

These encounters look like intentional fights. Given girls' increasing mobility and on-street presence, to the casual observer this may present a picture of rowdy, out of control, and threatening behavior, fueling perceptions of dangerous girls and violent girl gangs. Informal discussions with police suggest that this type of behavior informs their perception of the rise in "troublesome" girls.

Initially, we were always assured by the girls that "rumbles" were "not violent" and not to be taken seriously, rather, they are normalized within a particular social context. They take place between groups of friends in the context of "having a laugh"—a very important and pervasive aspect of girls' socializing (Hey 1997). As Laura, a sixteen year old from a middle-class background said "When you are play-fighting there is not really a purpose. It is just for enjoyment or out of boredom or something like that" (Group 12). Yet as the study progressed, it became clear both from our own observation and the insights afforded to us by girls that, in some circumstances, "rumbles" do have a function beyond "having a laugh." They can provide a strategic mechanism for the acting out of particular antagonisms and a (relatively structured) means by which particular hierarchies of social relations within friendship groups are maintained. Quite simply, in the context of the "play-fight" individual girls are able to control other girls. This behavior is cross-gender; as in some boys' groups, such tests of strength and endurance are key indicators of physical dominance and can be a means of instilling respect or fear and gaining power.

Clearly, the context in which particular incidents take place is of key significance, as is the relationship between those involved. The importance of social context for understanding violence is well established (e.g., Newburn & Stanko 1994; Messerschmidt 1997; Edgar and Martin 2001; Stanko, 2001). Unsurprisingly, girls' definitions of violence revolve around what they see as appropriate behavior in particular social-situational and spatial contexts. This has implications for the shifting meanings of violence in girls' lives. All those involved in a particular event—whether as actors socially engaged in it or as witnesses to it (such as us as researchers)—have an influence on the meaning of that event. Using the example of the "rumble," for those taking part in it the particular configuration of context (having a laugh) and relationship (friends) is crucial for defining its meaning as "not violent." Without knowing the social context within which certain behavior occurs or, crucially, its relational aspect, we cannot understand the process of what is taking place or what those involved are trying to accomplish, nor indeed anticipate the outcome.

Silences

There were also profound silences in the conversations about violence, and these silences also offer some insight into the way violence is conceptualized. Of the recognized forms and sites of violence that girls did not spontaneously speak about, a striking omission concerns violence that takes place within the home or domestic sphere, and particularly that which takes place between family members. I have already mentioned the persistent view that fights between brothers and sisters do not "count" as violence. Girls did not often spontaneously talk about "domestic violence." This is not to say that domestic violence is not considered violent, but rather it is not spoken about in the same register as other forms of more public violence. This reticence was not unexpected; in research settings, and for many reasons, private violence often remains unsaid. However, there is another point about girls' conceptualizations of domestic violence that is worth reporting here. When discussion turned to domestic violence, almost always initiated by researchers, girls often revealed their confusion both about the common usage of the term itself (does it cover only physical violence or would arguments also count? does it cover violence between adults only or that perpetrated on children?) and about the legitimacy of the behavior, although there was some variation in understanding according to age, with older girls having a clearer grasp of the ambit of the term. In many ways this is not an unsurprising finding, and it mirrors other recent research, which revealed that young people—boys as well as girls—are fairly ambivalent about what sort of behavior counts as domestic violence (Mullender et al. 1999). It also reiterates the importance of social context. Girls' associations of violence, and those forms which they spoke about more readily, were very much centered on violent events that took place *outside* the home with people who were not family members. Family relationships and the home form a context within which violence is often either denied or simply not recognized as such.

In much the same way (and for much the same reasons) that girls were silent about domestic violence, they were not always forthcoming about their experiences of sexual encounters with boys known to them where they may have been coerced into having sex. Moreover, this is an area where the term *violence* to describe such situations seemed inappropriate to girls, and is an example of a disjuncture between what adults may term violence and what young people understand by the term. Girls' reticence about coercive sexual encounters with boys known to them contrasts markedly with the openness with which they discussed their fears of sexual violence. Girls' worries and fears tend to be expressed in terms of safety issues. The possibility of being sexually attacked *by a stranger* was spoken about as a major source of anxiety and vulnerability for many girls (in the self-report study, 58 percent reported being worried about being sexually attacked in this way). Other forms (of sexualized) harassment and threatening behavior *by strangers* (being watched, followed, on the receiving end of suggestive comments, and so on) was also expressed as a concern. Again, this suggests an association of violence with the public, rather than the private sphere, reflecting particular discourses about sites and forms of violence. Girls' safety concerns included being verbally bullied or threatened, being beaten up by other young people, and being out alone at night. Their fears of sexual assault from strangers should not be underestimated. In the self-report study, sexual assault was considered by far the worst thing that could happen. Fozia's view is typical. A seventeen-year-old South Asian living in an inner-city area, she was describing how she defended herself against a racial attack some weeks earlier. She could not find the words to adequately describe her horror of sexual assault, maintaining that she would rather experience racial violence than sexual assault:

| Fozia: | Actually I was attacked just a couple of weeks ago. I beat a guy up [laughter]. He was saying stuff to me, and there were four of them. And this was going on and on and on. He chucked me to the ground and battered me and said: "Get back to your country" blah, blah, blah. And I got hold of his cardigan, and beat him up. That happens, but you cannae avoid it. But I think a sexual attack would be more . . . more . . . I dunno. . . . I'd prefer it to be a racial attack I think than a sexual attack. (Group 15) |

For Fozia and the other Asian girls in her group, racial victimization is part of everyday life; it is familiar, knowable, and in some ways predictable, and contrasts markedly with the unknown, mysterious prospect of sexual attack.

For girls in the study who had experienced some form of sexual assault, the experience had shaped their lives in a different way. Violence is not separate from the rest of life, but is bound up with life. In the following excerpt, Lorna and Louisa, two fifteen year olds from an affluent suburban area, discuss what they consider to be the long-term effects of sexual assault:

| Lorna: | If you get physically attacked, it's all just scrapes and bruises but if you've been raped you will always think about things. If you get raped when you're younger and then you met a guy when you're older and you want to settle down, but say he touches you or something, then you're always going to be jumpy. |

| Louisa: | If you get a doing from people, then you will be conscious of walking about yourself. But if you get sexually assaulted then you wouldn't go out at all. |

Lorna: If you get a severe doing then you might not get
                one as bad as that again. But if you get raped then
                you're gonna go through it again and again, like if
                you meet someone that you pure love and that,
                it's gonna bring back memories. (Group 18)

Physical Violence as a "Bad" Thing

A key aim of the study was to examine girls' views about physical violence, is it a "good" or a "bad" thing? Does it have any uses? When
might it be justified? This was not straightforward; the nature of girls'
moral discourses on violence is often complex and contradictory. At the
outset, most girls voiced an outright condemnation of physical violence, denouncing it variously as pointless, stupid, disgusting, futile,
improper, wrong, a sign of immaturity and/or mental defectiveness, of
brutishness and ignorance, and, commonly, a waste of time. As fifteen-
year-old Jackie, who hung out with a group of girls from an inner-city
area with very high local street presence and had a local reputation for
violence, maintained in an interview: "I don't see the point in it 'cos you
don't get a Blue Peter badge or nothing, just don't see the point in it. It's
just 'I battered him and I battered her' and there just isn't any point"
(Interview 5).

In their condemnation of violence, girls told stories of incidents
they had witnessed (some undoubtedly true, some fictionalized, some
possibly apocryphal) involving what was considered to be wholly unacceptable types of violence. These included, for example, violence toward animals, smaller children, disabled people, those with learning
difficulties, the elderly, or others considered "defenseless"; racist and
sectarian violence; that involving weapons; and adult violence perpetrated on children or young people. Unprovoked violence directed toward a vulnerable target attracted the most censure. On the whole,
girls tended to be very judgmental of those individuals who were considered violent, and there was a strong focus on apportioning blame
and responsibility.

Yet, as discussion continued, and violent incidents were dissected
more closely in the retelling, the strong line of moral condemnation
often wavered as individual girls began to offer tentative explanations
for the violent action. Talk often became more turbulent and disagree-
ments broke out, with some girls condemning and others condoning violence in certain situations. Anna, a fifteen-year-old from an affluent
background who attended a youth group for physically disabled girls
maintained that violence could be used to stop violence:

Anna: Most of the time violence is a bad thing, except, I
             don't know, like wars and stuff, although that is
             started by violence it's always stopped by vio-
             lence as well. So mainly I would say, yeah, it is a
             bad thing but sometimes if it is to stop something
             that is getting out of hand . . . then you sometimes
             need to be violent to stop it. But I wouldn't say
             that for all the time, mainly yes. . . . But if you
             were getting bullied I wouldn't go "Go and punch
             that person's face." I wouldn't say that was the
             way to go, but sometimes, when it reaches the
             breaking point, you maybe need to. (Group 17)

The instrumental use of violence as a means to stop "things getting
out of hand," from wars to falling out with friends, was a recurrent
theme in many conversations.

Melanie: I think violence can be alright sometimes, ken. It
             depends. Like . . . like if you are having fights over
             stupid little things or things that you could sit and
             talk over or make better without fighting . . . but if
             it's something that has happened for ages and
             gone on and on and on then that's the only way
             you are going tae be able tae stop it. Cos, like,
             you've tried talking tae the person but they dinna'
             listen.

Christine: Aye, then it's alright. (Group 7)

Similarly, the idea of using violence as a resource for stopping, or
preventing, bullying was put forward, mainly by girls of school-going
age. A group of girls who lived in a low-income and environmentally
deprived inner-city area and who attended the same school had this
to say:

Researcher: Would you say that physical violence is always a
             bad thing?

Emily: I think sometimes it is needed.

Researcher: It's needed ?

Emily: Not all the time, but sometimes. Sometimes people
             need a good kick up the bum. [Laughter]

Sara: If you let them [insult you] at the end of the day, folk will just keep on doing it.

Emily: You read stories about bullying in magazines. It tells you to always tell somebody about it, but it is not that easy to tell somebody because you will just be classed as a grass. If you walk by, you are just going to get it worse, so . . . (Group 16)

According to Emily, using violence to stop bullying is both more effective and (amongst peers) more socially acceptable than telling a teacher or other adult and risking "being classed as a grass." In the next example, Jolene, who earlier described herself as "a pacifist," describes how she was unwillingly drawn into fighting with a girl in a last-ditch effort to stop being treated "like a daftie." In doing so she was sticking up for herself:

Jolene: The last time I fought was months and months ago. And I was dead, dead . . . I was pure scared of the lassie, and I tried to talk my way out of it, but it got to the stage where she was treating me like a pure . . . treating me like a daftie and I just flew off the handle and I ended up battering her. And I near shat myself, and I was like "what's that for? what's this for?" . . . See when people start shouting at you, "You're a cow. You're a slut and you're a tart" and all that. And that's what gets you pure angry. (Group 14)

Initially and rather as one might expect, girls were hesitant and, at times, embarrassed to talk about violent incidents they had been involved in. In the main, however, girls of all age groups spoke about their own potential for using violence, "if the situation warranted it," and some relayed instances of when they felt "forced" into using violence. On the whole, girls are not quick to use violence, and when they are violent, it is usually as a last resort. But what sorts of situations warrant it? As the last two examples show, retaliating to verbal attacks as a means of preventing continued harassment or bullying by other young people, was given frequently as an example of acceptable violence. Indeed, gossip, talking "behind backs" and "slagging" were cited among the main causes of conflict between girls. Contrary to its literal meaning "talking behind backs" is often done in the presence of the "victim" and, as such, is construed as an overtly challenging expression of aggression. It is often accompanied by gestures and posturing, such as prolonged staring, furtive whispering, and sarcastic laughter. Such behavior is perceived as highly provocative, generating the need to strike back in self-defense.

> Fozia: When I was in school I was always in fights. There was not one day when I wasn't in a fight. Most of it was because a guy would say something about my brother or cousin or someone and I would beat them up [laughter]. Or someone would call me a black bitch, or you black this or black that. Or just stupid things. . . . It was mostly racial but. (Group 15)

Earlier, Fozia and her friends, four Pakistani girls who attended an Asian youth club, had condemned physical violence in the strongest terms. They stuck closely to the cultural mandate of not appearing to be violent, claiming that Asian girls never get involved in violence with other Asian girls, and rarely get involved in violence with white girls. Yet, as they talked more, it emerged from the input of individual members of the group that three of them had been physically violent on several occasions toward white boys who shouted racial abuse at them. The incident recounted by Fozia, above, was seen as a perfectly justifiable retaliation to racist slurs that took place within the school environment.

Jackie, who earlier had condemned violence as puerile and pointless went on to modify what she had said, singling out the deserving victim as a justification for violence:

> Jackie: Sometimes, sometimes people deserve it, like a doing, 'cos of the loud mouth and that on them. Sometimes it's a shame for people, I think it's a shame cause they get a doing and that. (Interview 5)

Not all justifications focused solely on "victim precipitation," however. Other common justifications for hitting someone were "if they hit you first," in retaliation for "stealing a boyfriend," and to "stick up" for yourself, your family, or friends, either jumping in to assist in a fight in which they are involved or in order to protect their reputation. In the self-report questionnaire, half of the girls described the ability of "sticking up" for themselves (or for friends or family) in violent and/or verbally abusive situations as "extremely important." In these situations, physical violence could always be justified. These types of rationales for violence point toward broader motivational factors, such as frustration, disaffection, anger, and humiliation, which are often overlooked in accounts of girls' aggression. More often associated with boys, these kinds of incentives for violence point to the need to move beyond a conceptualization of girls' violence purely as a response to gendered forms of victimization, and a need to (re)consider the role of female moral agency in violent encounters. The following exchange took place within a group of younger girls from one of the small Scottish islands (referred to earlier). It arose in the course of a conversation sparked by a newspaper account of the "rising tide of female violence," which depicted girls as the "new lads."

Gerri:	Oh God. That's annoying. It is as though you have to be really girlie all the time. And petite and brilliant. It is really annoying because it is the real world and it is not Barbie dolls stuff, you have got to fight for yourself.
Jan:	Girls can be violent if they want to.
Gerri:	If you get attacked or something you are going to have to be able to fight back, you can't just sit there and take it. I am glad I am quite violent. I am never really going to get hurt because I can hit back.
Researcher:	Would you consider yourself a violent person?
Gerri:	It depends on who annoys me and what they do. I am not going to stand up and batter everybody, but . . .
Elsa [interjecting]:	It is more that you shout at people when you get annoyed, don't you?
Gerri:	When I get really angry I shout. I have got a bad, bad temper. I think that is what it is. It just flares up. (Group 9)

Alana, a sixteen-year-old from a working-class background who attended a group for young mothers spoke of the absolute necessity of sticking by friends when they get into trouble, even when they have precipitated the dispute: "Like if you're in a night-club and one of your mates is, ken, one of your mates, 'cos of drink or whatever, starts wi' somebody else, ken. You're bound to help your friend, ken. You stick up for your friend" (Group 6).

In a similar vein, two close friends, Debbie and Melanie, jointly recall a recent incident when Melanie hit another girl who ridiculed her disabled brother.

Debbie:	Aye, like, 'cos not long ago somebody says, like, ken, that her brother looked like Forrest Gump, and she went up and she battered the quine. And the quine's standing there denying that she says it. But she did say it. She just says, she shouted, "Run, Forrest, run," ken, to her brother. And her brother can hardly walk. And she's shouting, "Run, Forrest, run."
Melanie:	And that's how I battered that other quine, because she was speaking about my brother at the time. She was saying that she was'nae, that she did'nae say anything, but I says, "Aye, but you repeated it and you should'nae be going around repeating stuff like that." And she admitted repeating it to other people and I says, "You should'nae have repeated it." And I did take it personally.

As previously mentioned, only a small number of girls spontaneously included domestic violence in their definitions and stories about violence and, of these, a handful spoke of incidents that took place within their own homes where they had leapt to the defense of their mothers. Such descriptions were often graphic and startling, but the violence that emanated from sticking up for their mothers was regarded as wholly acceptable and justifiable. In the following excerpt, Tanya, a thirteen-year-old from an inner-city housing scheme who had earlier described herself as violent and as having an explosive temper, spoke about her attempt to protect her mother:

Tanya:	My dad hit me. He was going to hit my mum, so I was trying to protect my mum, so he hit me and I hit him back. No one hits me or my mum. [silence for six seconds]. He swerved right in front of mum and hit me and he broke my nose and the place was covered in glass as well because he was throwing porcelain dolls about . . . smashed all the

TV up. He threw the phone out of the window and the window smashed. And this was when my wee brothers and sisters were in their bed.

Researcher: So that was pretty dangerous, with lots of glass and things flying through the air.

Tanya: Yes, and I gave him a black eye. And that's with one punch. I've got a strong punch. Even Doug [friend] says that. And he's got these big muscles and I just went like that [demonstrates punching] and I broke his nose once. (Group 1)

For most girls however, violence tends to be a last resort, to be used in self-defense or when all other attempts (to avoid, to placate, to defuse) fail. Only a very small number portrayed themselves as "violent."[9] In discussion, these girls showed a readiness to use violence as a solution to problems and conflict. They described routine involvement in fights with other young people, reported antagonistic encounters with a range of adults (parents, teachers and police), and, on the whole, viewed interpersonal violence positively. Visibly excited and intensely involved when telling their stories, they spoke of their excitement when using violence. In addition to using violence in the types of situations outlined above, many, like Mel in the following example, described starting fights "for a laugh":

Mel: I admit I've been in a hyper mood, and I've been totally hyper. I'm maturer than a lot mair people my age. Other people will tell ye that. But see other times I can be really immature and get really hyper and just dae stupid things just for the sake of a laugh. I'll go and start on somebody just for the sake of doing it. Do something so they will say something to me. Or I've been really in a mood or something and somebody will try to be nice to me and say "What's wrong?" and I'll shout "It has got nothing to do with you!" and just snap and I'll end up hitting them or something. (Interview 4)

Although violence for fun is relatively rare, at the emotional level, many of those who described themselves as violent spoke about feelings of empowerment when using violence. This prompts the need to consider the significance of violence, for some girls, in terms of the rewards that it brings.

In some instances, girls spoke of their guilt, shame, and contrition following an incidence of violence. This has been remarked upon by other researchers of violence (e.g., Artz 1998; Campbell 1993). At a rational cognitive level, physical violence was regarded by the vast majority of girls as morally repugnant. Yet, when girls recounted violent incidents (their stories) that they had either been directly involved in or were aware of, a much more pragmatic stance was adopted. The ways in which disputes were interpreted were again dependent on context and relationship. Some technique of neutralization was utilized in the telling of the violent incident, most commonly that the violence was used in self-defense or in retaliation to some verbal provocation. They tended to become violent in reaction to a perceived slight or insult or challenge to their control of a particular situation. Feelings of being belittled, derided, and demeaned can spark retaliation. One way of understanding these acts of physical violence is that they take place in particular contexts when various factors combine: resentment, anger, humiliation, and a need to "stand up" for themselves or others close to them.

Gradually, then, a more contradictory nature of girls' moral discourses was revealed. There appeared to be two interlinked elements in operation. On the one hand, the strong line of moral censure condemning violence shows a strict concern with laying the blame on individuals or certain groups but, on the other hand, this is mitigated by some kind of explanation for the behavior—by which the acts of the violent individuals or groups can be better understood. Here, again, social context is key, as the girls, in what might be argued to be an effort to make sense of the violence, contextualize blame and culpability within the frameworks of particular social circumstances or social relationships and begin to offer justifications.

Critical to the girls' discussions about violence is the tension between, on the one hand, *blaming* individuals and, on the other, *explaining* their actions by means of an appeal to social context. Although there is an intense preoccupation with identifying culpability and laying blame, once these moral judgments are placed in a social context they become explicable. Girls' talk of violence is intertwined with talk about interpersonal relationships and social context; this is the framework within which girls make sense of violence.

Violence occurs in both subtle and explicit ways and girls from all socioeconomic, cultural, and geographical groups are affected by its multiple forms. Although violence is a common occurrence in their everyday lives, at once mundane and commonplace, talking about violence is difficult given its amorphous and insidious nature. Not all forms of violence are named or recognized as such and, in certain contexts, some of the behaviors which it encompasses are seen as acceptable. Nevertheless, efforts to understand the nature of violence in girls' lives elicited many responses. Overall, the girls who participated in this research shared a range of experiences, some that evoked fear and intimidation and eroded their self-confidence and others that instilled in them a sense of power and resistance. A common thread linking girls from all backgrounds and experiences concerned the multifaceted nature of violence and its pervasiveness in girls' everyday lives.

Notes

1. Use of the term *girl* might be deemed to be problematic insofar as it demeans young women and homogenizes identities. However, I use the term as the girls themselves use it.

2. See Batchelor, S. (forthcoming 2001) "The Myth of Girl Gangs" in *Criminal Justice Matters* for a description of the media preoccupation with "violent girls."

3. This research project, "A View From The Girls: Exploring Violence and Violent Behaviour," was funded by the Economic and Social Research Council (ESRC) Award No: L133251018.

4. The data collection and analysis for this study was undertaken at the University of Glasgow by Jane Brown, Susan Batchelor, Kay Tisdall, and myself.

5. This is the Children's Hearing System in Scotland.

6. The capacity for violence research to stir up aggressive tendencies and inflame already existing tensions amongst respondents is further explored in M. Burman, S. Batchelor, & J. Brown (2001), "Researching girls and violence: facing the dilemmas of fieldwork."

7. All names of participants have been changed.

8. The link between being the subject of verbal abuse and inflicting self-harm was very striking, and is the subject of further investigation.

9. Ten percent of those who completed the questionnaire reported using a wide range of different types of physically violent acts against another person (e.g., punching, kicking, cutting, hitting someone with some type of object). Ten percent of respondents also self-defined themselves as "violent." The group of girls that had committed seven or more physically violent acts *and* also described themselves as violent made up 5 percent of the total sample (n = 30). This was the measure that we have adopted to identify this group of girls—that is, those who routinely deploy a range of physically violent acts and who also describe themselves as being violent.

References

Alderson, P. 1995, *Listening to children: children, ethics, and social research*, Barnardos, London.

Alldred, P. 1998, "Ethnography and discourse analysis: dilemmas in representing the voices of children," in R. Edwards and J. Ribbens (eds), *Feminist dilemmas in qualitative research: public knowledge and private lives*, Sage, London, pp. 147–170.

Artz, S. 1998, *Sex, power, and the violent schoolgirl*, Trifolium Books, Toronto.

Barker, C. 1999, "'Cindy's a slut': moral identities and moral responsibility in the 'soap talk' of British Asian girls," *Sociology*, vol. 32, pp. 65–81.

Batchelor, S. 2001, "The myth of girl gangs," *Criminal Justice Matters* (Special Issue on Crime and the Media), no. 43, pp. 26–27.

Bradby, H. 1996, *Defining violence: understanding the causes and effects of violence*, Avebury, Aldershot.

Brown, L. M. & Gilligan, C. 1992, *Meeting at the crossroads: women's psychology and girls' development*, Harvard University Press, Cambridge.

Burman, M., Batchelor, S. & Brown, J. 2001, "Researching girls and violence: facing the dilemmas of fieldwork," *British Journal of Criminology*, vol. 41, no. 3 Special edition, "Methodological dilemmas in research," pp. 453–59.

Campbell. A. 1993, *Out of control: men, women, and aggression*, Pandora, London.

Campbell, K. 1988, "Woman and speaker: a conflict in roles," in S. Brehm (ed), *Seeing female: social roles and personal lives*, Greenwood Press, New York.

Cawson, P., Berridge, D., Barter, C. & Renold, E. 2000, *Physical and sexual violence amongst children in residential settings: exploring experiences and perspectives*, Economic and Social Research Council, Violence Research Programme, Summary Report, London, http://wwwl.rhul.ac.uk/sociopolitical-science/vrp/Findings/Findings.htm (accessed 08/03/02).

Chahal, K. & Julienne, L. 1999, "We can't all be white! *Racist victimisation in the U.K.*," Joseph Rowntree Foundation, Research Report Ref 679, York Publishing Services.

Edgar, K. & Martin, C. 2001, "The social context of prison violence," *Criminal Justice Matters*, no. 42, pp. 24–25.

Felson, R. B. & Tedeschi, J. T. (eds), 1993, *Aggression and violence: social interactionist perspectives*, American Psychological Association, Washington, D.C.

Fillion, K. 1996, *Lip service: the myth of female virtue in love, sex, and friendship*, Pandora, London.

Gilligan, C., Ward, J., & Taylor, J. (eds) 1988, *Mapping the moral domain: A contribution of women's thinking to psychological theory and education*, Harvard University Press, Cambridge.

Hey, V. 1997, *The company she keeps: an ethnography of girls' friendships*, Open University Press, Buckingham.

Kappeler, S. 1995, *The will to violence: the politics of personal behaviour*, Polity Press, Cambridge.

Lees, S. 1993, *Sugar and spice: sexuality and adolescent girls,* Penguin, Harmondsworth.

Messerschmidt, J. 1997, *Crime as structured action: gender, race, class, and crime in the making,* Sage, London.

Mullender, A., Kelly, L. Hague, G., Malos, E. & Imam, U. 1999, *Children's needs, coping strategies and understandings of woman abuse,* Economic and Social Research Council, Research Briefing No. 12.

Newburn, T. & Stanko, E. (eds) 1994, *Just boys doing business? Men, masculinities, and crime,* Routledge, London.

Nilan, P. 1992, "Kazzies, DBTs, and Tryhards—categorisations of style in adolescent girls' talk," *British Journal of Sociology of Education,* vol. 13, no. 2, pp. 201–14.

Plummer, K. 1995, *Telling sexual stories: power, change, and social worlds,* Routledge, London.

Schwartz, M. D. (ed) 1997, *Researching violence against women; methodological and personal perspectives,* Sage, London.

Sheldon, A. 1992, "Conflict talk: sociolinguistic challenges to self-assertion and how young girls meet them," *Merrill-Palmer Quarterly,* vol. 38, no. 1, pp. 95–117.

Stanko, E. 2001, "Murder and moral outrage: understanding violence," *Criminal Justice Matters,* no. 42, Winter 2000/2001.

Toon, I. 2000, "Girls, race, and place," paper presented at Challenges of Violence in the Lives of Girls and Young Women conference, Glasgow, Sept. 2000.

Chapter Six

Capturing Girls' Experiences of "Community Violence" in the United States

Laurie Schaffner

Elizabeth Martin,[1] a bright, blonde, sixteen-year-old "Valley girl" from suburban Northern California, was detained in a juvenile probation facility when I met her. She gave the following explanation for her current condition:

> I was in detention in Oakland and my Dad came to pick me up from there. On the way home, I told my Dad, "Give me the cell phone—I gotta call my boyfriend." He's all, "No way—you are in big trouble." So all I did was kind of show him this little knife on my key chain and he goes all ballistic and when we got home, he calls the police and now I'm in here for assault with a deadly weapon or brandishing a knife or something like that! (Elizabeth Martin, sixteen years old).

Martin's father "always criticized her mother." Gradually, Martin revealed that her father was physically violent toward her and her mother in the home, and that she had to be hospitalized after one of her father's beatings. She preferred living at her boyfriend's house (he was nineteen years old), because "he really helped me after I tried to kill myself."

Since the 1970s, I have had an interest in understanding young women in trouble with the law. In 1992, I began conducting a study drawing upon data from ethnographic observations, focus groups, and in-depth interviews with female juvenile offenders in juvenile "correctional" systems in four states: California, Illinois, Colorado, and Massachusetts. I met with young women in various settings, including detention facilities and psychiatric wards, and with adults who work with them. Much of my work revolves around the real-life experiences of girls such as Elizabeth Martin and others whose stories will be recounted and explored in the following pages.

Fifteen-year-old Alegra Johnson, a young woman from downtown Los Angeles, was in detention for assault with a deadly weapon, or "ADW." Johnson was tall, heavy, light-skinned—articulate, bright-eyed, and fast-talking. She said her father was "a one-night stand for [her] mother." She confided that she had been "touched sexually" when she was twelve years old by a "friend of [her] mom's." Johnson explained the circumstances surrounding the offense for which she was detained, saying, "I didn't want to go to that probation school! It was like forty guys and one girl. And they harass me! I knew I was gonna go off on them!"

Johnson was placed in detention because she "cracked a boy's head because he was trying to grab [her] tits." These events occurred in a special school for troubled youths that Johnson had been ordered to attend as part of her probation for a prior offense. In a moment of self-awareness, Johnson observed: "You know, I used to be sweet, but I became sour."

Seventeen-year-old Norma Guzman grew up with her great aunt in the Mission district of San Francisco because her mother was "strung out on dope [crack cocaine]." Guzman was Salvadoran-American, with wide, round, features and a soft way about her. When Guzman was fourteen years old, her great aunt passed away. Guzman went to live with a cousin, and a year later, that cousin was killed in street violence on her block.

During our conversation in a drab, institutional, interview room in the detention facility, Guzman explained that she was "stressed and depressed." Guzman was charged with assault after a fight in Dolores Park, where she and her (twenty-two-year-old) boyfriend had been "kickin' it in the park [hanging out and talking; passing time]." Another girl approached her and pulled her hair. As Guzman explained, "My hair is long and curly and that little bitch was jealous 'cause her hair was short and stringy."

This chapter focuses on the plight of young women in the United States' juvenile justice system and their unique life experiences.[2] Young women in U.S. corrections tend to be, but are not exclusively, from no-income, low-income, and working-class families (Owen & Bloom 1998).

Middle-class girls and girls from wealthy families tend to be diverted from adjudication early on in the public court process (Girls Incorporated and OJJDP 1996). African American and Latina/Hispanic girls are disproportionately represented in juvenile detention (Snyder and Sickmund 1999). In addition, lesbian, bisexual, queer, and questioning girls' needs and situations are ignored, rendering them practically invisible.

In general, criminologists have forwarded biological, psychological, political, cultural, or economic explanations for the etiology of criminal behavior. Some scholars suggest evolutionary survival strategies for understanding violent criminal behaviors (Rowe 1996). Commentators even discuss whether there is a "tough new breed" of young criminals, or if "kids' DNA has changed." (Butterfield 1998; DiIulio 1992; Zimring 1998). None of these reasons is sufficient to explain, or more importantly, understand the violent acts initiated by American girls today.

By noting changes in the *quality* of girls' offenses, rather than focusing solely on the overall increase, it becomes evident that some girls' aggressive responses are reflective of the violence they experience in everyday life. This violence has become part of the contemporary dominant mainstream and youth cultures in the United States. For example, a nationwide survey of high school students found that almost 36 percent had been in a physical fight during the last year (CDC 2001). Half the people arrested in 1991 for murder in the United States were under the age of twenty-five (Charles Stewart Mott 1994; Butterfield 1998). Large numbers of youth are both victims and perpetrators: between 1985 and 1994, the number of persons arrested for murder and non-negligent manslaughter increased by 150 percent for persons under eighteen years of age, while for persons eighteen years or older, the increase was only 11 percent (Federal Bureau of Investigation 1995; see also Levine & Rosich 1996; Garbarino 1992). According to the World Health Organization, few countries are as violent as the United States (Elliot et al. 1997).

Anthropologist Nancy Scheper-Hughes, studying everyday violence in Brazil, warned that a lived daily environment of violence may lead to a routinization of suffering. People "fail to see or to recognize as problematic what is considered to be the norm (as well as normal, expectable)" (Scheper-Hughes 1992). It is not that Americans consider violence "normal" or "usual," but that violence has become so widespread that we find ourselves adjusting, accepting, and adapting to it (Chalk 1994). We even coin terms, such as "date rape," "drive-by," "carjack," "road rage," and "air rage" for our new violent trends. It is my contention that young women in the United States grow up to live in, reflect, and reproduce this increasingly violent culture, just as we all do, in some measure.

The mission of this chapter is to expand our definition and identification of "violence" in young women's lives and to explore the etiology of girls' "violent offenses." This essay is not an attempt to solve juvenile detention problems per se or offer solutions or alternatives to girls' detainment. Instead, it proposes a revamping of the juvenile justice framework traditionally used to study "youth violence" and offers suggestions for areas of research that may better address the experiences and needs of girls in correctional systems for violent offenses (see Poulin 1996). The following section focuses on the juvenile justice system's shift away from penalizing the sexual girl to penalizing the violent girl. The discussion then shifts to the presentation of an argument that our understanding of the contexts in which girls' violent acts occur must broaden to include the current realities of the lives of some urban American young women. I suggest that we extend our traditional definitions of "community violence" and "youth violence" to include unique ways in which young women experience and perpetrate trauma in a context of witnessing violence, misogyny, and homophobia. Identifying the kinds of behaviors we punish, and exploring the real threats to public safety, will sharpen our interpretations of violent acts committed by young women.

From Sex to Violence? Punishing Gender Transgressions

Historically, the law focused on the "sexy" bad girl. The original goal at the founding of the juvenile court system in 1899 was to improve girls' morality and reform their sexual behavior (Odem 1995; Platt 1969; McNamee 1999; Abrams & Curran 2000a). In the first decades of the 1900s, Jane Addams (1909) wrote of the immoral temptations of working girls in the dance halls, and the Gluecks (Glueck & Glueck 1934) referred to the "illicit" sexual indulgences of "defectives" and delinquent women (See also Platt 1969; Breckinridge & Abbot 1912). Up until quite recently, the *femme fatale* and Marilyn Monroe–type sex kittens symbolized the sexually tantalizing and whore-like "bad girl" (see also D'Emilio & Freedman 1988). The idea of a "new female delinquent" arose out of seminal feminist analyses of female offenders in the 1970s (Adler 1975; Simon 1975). Criminologists speculated that the new female delinquent was more active, agential, and physical compared to her pre–women's liberation counterpart (Ward 1980). Scholars have since turned away from citing women's liberation as responsible for a new "masculine"-type female offender (Curran 1984; James & Thornton

1980; Datesman & Scarpetti 1980; Klein 1973). However, changes in gender norms do explain, at least to some extent, why society chooses to punish specific juvenile behaviors at specific times. Today, many scholars, feminists, and criminologists agree that although young women comprise a very small proportion of the total number of arrests for violent juvenile offenses, the rise in girls' arrest rates for violent crime requires critical analyses in order to be understood (Wing & Willis 1997; Tracy & Shelden 1992).

Gender norms, specifically regarding sexuality, have shifted in the last century. The 1960s "free love movement" and the 1980s Madonnaization of popular culture influenced a sexualization of young women's concerns, resulting in "even" middle-class, bare-midriffed, belly-button-ringed GapGirls exhibiting a kind of overt sexiness. Formerly understood as troublesome, and characterized as reserved for working-class "wayward" and "slutty" girls, this sexiness is now routine, accepted, and normalized. This shift is evidenced in popular magazines such as *Cosmo, Seventeen,* or *YM Magazine,* which target a youthful female readership and are full of photos of barely-clad females and advice on sexual mores. What is sexually and morally transgressive to mainstream American popular culture has changed (Nathanson 1991; Vance 1992; Snitow et al. 1983). While still under political attack, certain behaviors, such as illegitimate pregnancy, extramarital sex, and prostitution, are less alarming today than one hundred years ago, both to the public and to the law (D'Emilio & Freedman 1988; Gordon 1990; Maglin & Perry 1996; Alan Guttmacher Institute 1994; Nagle 1997).

Teenage girls now increasingly come to the attention of juvenile authorities for assault or other violent behavior (Snyder & Sickmund 1999; Peters & Peters 1998). This shift reflects two trends: girls *are* expressing themselves with more aggression and anger, and authorities and the media now focus on violent behavior more than on sexually related offenses, such as prostitution. For example, U. S. television and print media offer news magazine segments on girls in gangs, and talk shows, such as *The Jerry Springer Show,* feature physical fights among girls. One ABC News Prime Time show in 1998 was titled "Girls in the Hood: An Unprecedented Look at Gang Life from the Inside," and aired with a big fanfare about the new violent teenage girl delinquent.

The problem with sensationalizing the accounts of the few young women arrested for violent offenses is that it shifts the focus onto individual frightening youths, and invites the media audience to generalize to the whole teen population. Some youths, disproportionately youths of color, can then be represented as young people whose heinous crimes make them adults. From 1992 through 1995, forty-one states passed legislation making it easier for juveniles to be tried as adults (OJJDP 1997a). More than 90 percent of youths waived to adult court are males, indicating a gendered construction of adulthood (De-Frances & Strom 1997). Furthermore, panics about "youth and violent crime" shift the public gaze away from social, cultural, and economic inequalities, and deemphasize the losses resulting from large-scale environmental and elite, white-collar crime (Males 1998; Bailey & Hale 1998). As one scholar explains:

> "Youth" serves as a metaphor for key indicators of the state of a nation, shifts in cultural values over sexuality, morals, and family. The treatment and management of youth is expected to provide solutions to a nation's problems: drug abuse, gangs, violence, teen pregnancy, inner-city riots. The everyday operations of multinational capitalism or patriarchal power relations are seldom represented as the source of social problems. The "young" are assumed to hold the key to a nation's future. If problems such as unemployment or violence can be attributed to "problem youth," then respectable fears can be allayed and dealt with by focusing on "bad youth." (Griffin 1993)

So it is important that we not discuss girls' experiences of violence as sensational. Actually, we need to begin to see it as it really is: a "normal" part of living in a twenty-first century global economy.

Not only has girls' behavior shifted away from traditional gender norms, but also norms have shifted for girls' behaviors. Juvenile correction officers and the general public now fear that one of the worst social problems is violent crime, not the decline of sexual values. A study of U.S. youth in 1996 found that almost one-quarter of students report that "crime/violence" is the most important problem facing the nation, higher than the 15 percent who stated that the most important problem facing America was the "decline of moral and social values" (Horatio Alger Association 1996; Shuster 1998; Males 1998).

When adults were asked in a 1998 survey about the most serious problems facing children today, 24 percent mentioned "crime," while only 2 percent mentioned "sexual freedom" (Maguire & Pastore 1998). When teenagers were asked about the biggest problem facing people their own age, 9 percent replied "violence and crime" while only 3 percent mentioned "sex" (Maguire & Pastore 1998). I am not arguing that this is good news. I simply suggest that, whether it is a result of "progress," "social construction," or media hype, we are witnessing a shift in our cultural and political framing of the "bad" girl and the "good" girl.

Both historically and now, violent behavior is linked to males and perceived as masculine. Some scholars claim that gender socialization is the single strongest predictor of violence (Elliot et al. 1997). Between 1976 and 1991, nine in ten juvenile murderers were male—boys were ten times more likely to commit homicide than girls (Snyder & Sickmund 1995). One longitudinal study of eight hundred children compared boys' and girls' early aggressive behavior: early aggression was associated with preventing later educational attainment and aiding social failure more for girls than for boys. The authors offer this explanation:

Society is more tolerant of aggressive behavior in young males than in young females. Thus, when a girl responds aggressively, she is marked as deviant, and it is more likely to interfere with educational and social attainment. For boys, who are characteristically more aggressive, however, prosocial behavior that can mitigate the effects of aggression becomes the more important predictor of educational and social success regardless of early aggression. (Eron & Huesmann 1984)

One scholar notes that we may be asking the wrong questions about the popular notion that "boys will be boys":

With understandable frustration, some . . . have reacted to the violence data with the question: What is it about male sexuality that makes men that way? . . . Rather we should be asking, what is it about the construction of masculinity in different cultures that promotes aggressive sexual behavior by men? And what is it about the construction of femininity and the structure of economic and social power relations in societies that permits this behavior to continue? (Heise 1997)

A deeply nuanced gender theory that frames forms of aggression and violence as part of normalized "traditional" masculine socialization explains the prevailing idea among some juvenile court personnel that "girls are acting like males" and should be punished even more harshly for these transgressions (Newburn & Stanko 1994).

In general, juvenile court proceedings reflect and reinforce these social myths regarding gender and crime: males are violent and aggressive, females are sexy and relational (Schur 1983; Kimmel 1996; Kaufman 1997). Therefore, the current focus on female offenders who commit violent offenses, as opposed to sex-related misconduct, seems paradoxical at first. How can we square our dominant gender myths with the facts that assault is a more common reason for arrest for girls than for boys and more males than females are arrested for juvenile prostitution? (Girls Inc and OJJDP 1996). Perhaps these statistics reflect a trend that our cultural myths about gender prevent us from seeing: the state punishes gender transgressions.

Many of the girls who now come to the attention of juvenile corrections and the media are those who adopt a "masculine gender strategy" of violence, assault, and aggression. A "gender strategy" is "a plan of action through which a person tries to solve problems at hand, given the cultural notions of gender at play" (Hochschild 1989). Here, I am using the idea of gender strategies to suggest that traditionally, juvenile authorities could have seen "being sexy" as a "feminine" gender survival strategy, even though it was criminalized. "Being aggressive" has traditionally been the domain of "masculine" gender strategic behavior, which, in its extreme forms, was criminalized as well. Scholars rightfully caution against binary and reductionist conflations of social and physical ideas about sex and gender: young women can and do "choose" to be both "sexy" and "aggressive" (see Klein 1973). Nevertheless, certain forms of contemporary delinquency can be framed as gender transgressions: we punish when boys are "feminine" (prostitutes, homo/sexual) and when girls are "masculine" (aggressive, a/sexual). For example, San Francisco City and County rarely prosecutes girls for solicitation any more; instead officials cite female sex workers for "public nuisance," "loitering," or "jaywalking" offenses, in accordance with the recommendations of the 1996 Final Report of the San Francisco Task Force on Prostitution (Bernstein 1999).

Historically, young women have been sanctioned both formally and informally when they deviated from mainstream ideals for sexual behavior. However, due to changes in sexual mores, much behavior that would have been punished severely in the past no longer gives rise to criminal liability or social sanctions. Contemporary mainstream culture and law focus more and more on girls who commit assaults. Officials and researchers often explain this behavior as "girls acting like boys." In a sense, these comments are astute: we punish girls who use boys' gender-linked responses for addressing conflicts. However, the situation is more complex. Girls who respond violently respond to different pressures in different ways than do boys who respond with violence. Girls' aggression cannot be understood or "rehabilitated" without an awareness of the ways in which their life experiences differ from those of boys. Even if only a small number of girls are being arrested for committing violent offenses, the mission of this chapter is to contextualize the social logic that affects their choices so that we may better intervene, protect, and sanction them.

The Invisibility of Girls' Experiences: Broadening Definitions of Violence

Adults who work with girls in juvenile corrections commonly attribute girls' violent behavior to shifts in gender roles. They use a kind of short-cut way to describe what they see by claiming that girls who become assaultive are "acting like boys." As discussed in the prior section, to a certain extent these comments are insightful—laws punish girls when they use conventional male-type survival strategies that involve aggression. However, girls are doing something different than "acting like boys." Contextualizing female offending behaviors in the realities of girls' lives reveals that violence by girls is intimately related to the violence that girls witness and are victims of, in increasing numbers and in new ways. Not taking a careful, critical look at the contexts of their experiences does a disservice to young women who are in desperate need of emotional, educational, psychological, and economic assistance and nurturing. In my research, young women made repeated requests for "help with my anger."

Scholars and policy makers analyze youth violence in the context of "community violence." However, analyses often focus on youths and gangs, meaning *male* youths in gangs (Howell 1998; Sanchez-Jankowski 1991; Hagedorn 1998). Juvenile delinquency literature generally assumes that the "serious and habitual offender" is a male offender who belongs to a gang, fights with weapons, assaults, carjacks, and commits arson or robbery. Much of the history of—and theories about—youths in trouble were based on studies of the male experience. The history of female juvenile delinquency, however, is a history of state interventions in the sexual behavior of mostly working-class women of color in urban settings (Odem 1995; Devlin 1997; Tappan 1969; Abrams & Curran 2000b). Many textbooks, ethnographies, and theoretical overviews about delinquency include only one chapter (if that) on "gender"—meaning girls (Shoemaker 2000; Bourgois 1995; Pinderhughes 1997; Howell 1998). Many reports and studies of delinquency and violence focus mainly on either boys alone, or girls in gangs (Cohen 1955; Humes 1996; Harris 1988; Campbell 1991; Miller 2001). Thus, our current theories about youth and violence do not adequately explain the new rising rate of violence in which young women are involved—sometimes as witnesses, sometimes as victims, and sometimes as perpetrators. Nor do the current theories account for the uniquely gendered sexual experiences, which often lead to violence, or for the ways in which misogyny affects girls. Girls experience community violence differently than boys. First, the experiences of witnessing or being a victim of violence differ by gender. Second, domestic violence and wife beating in particular deeply affect all family members—especially daughters and sisters. Third, "girl hating" and girls' own misogyny increase the level of violence in girls' lives. Fourth, homophobia leads to violence against girls who are, or are perceived to be, lesbian, bisexual, queer, or questioning. Fifth, sexual harassment of girls in schools and on the streets is violence against them and often precedes their own assaultive behaviors. Contextualizing girls' offenses within their daily experiences may make the moral horizons of their choices more clear. This understanding may lead to the development of better, more effective interventions and prevention strategies. In the following sections I will briefly highlight these five undertheorized categories of community violence.

The Effects of Witnessing or Being a Victim of Violence

Criminologists generally correlate factors such as family violence, marital discord, parenting strategies, and the like with "at-risk youth" and delinquency (OJJDP 1994). Psychologists have long known that adolescents' exposure to community violence has serious consequences (Osofsky 1995; Garbarino et al. 1992; van der Kolk 1987). Studies show that exposure to violence in the media may result in young people (1) becoming less sensitive to the pain and suffering of others, (2) being more fearful of the world around them, and (3) possibly behaving in more aggressive or harmful ways toward others (APA 1995; Charles Stewart Mott Foundation 1994). Directly witnessing or being a victim of violence has even stronger effects (Baskin et al. 1993; van der Kolk 1987). But exposure to violence and abuse is a gendered experience (Finkelhor 1994).

Girls in juvenile corrections reveal that they witness an inordinate amount of violence on a regular, routine basis (Johnson 1998). In my sample, young women told me repeatedly about witnessing brothers, friends, cousins, fathers, and boyfriends being kicked, beaten, punched, knifed, shot, and killed. They witnessed their mothers being devalued and hurt physically by fathers, stepfathers, and boyfriends. I came to consider the young women in this population as unnoticed, mute witnesses of frontline violence in day-to-day urban life.

Girls are disproportionately victims of abuse. Young women are four times more likely than boys to be physically or verbally abused (Peters & Peters 1998). Three-fourths of children who are sexually abused are female (Greenfield 1997). Rape victims are disproportionately adolescent and female (Peters & Peters 1998; Greenfield 1997). In "date rape" cases, fourteen- to seventeen-year-old girls account for almost 40 percent of all cases (Peters & Peters 1998). Homicide is the second leading cause of death for African American females aged between fifteen and nineteen (Peters & Peters 1998). In a 1998 report on girls in the California juvenile correctional system, 92 percent reported experiencing sexual, physical or emotional abuse; many reported experiencing combinations of multiple forms of abuse and abuse on multiple occasions (Acoca & Dedel 1998). Probation departments and social service agencies are sending out a call for a collaborative and action-centered approach to this grave problem (Johnson 1998).

Girls in my study frequently lived in worlds tainted by aggression and assault.

I hit my brother. I'm tired of him slapping me around!

My brother accused me of threatening him with a golf-club and throwing a coffee can at his head. He was beating me up! He wants me to get sent to placement!

Many adolescents experience power struggles with siblings and parents. Such struggles constitute the context for the violence of some young women. As one young woman commented: "My mom called the police and turned me in for another thing. I did hit her, though." For the young women I interviewed, common household disputes such as not being able to see a boyfriend, use the telephone, or having a party became imbued with violence.

Girls' experiences such as these continue to remain invisible in studies and theories in the criminology literature. The short- and long-term effects of girls' exposure to violence is, with rare exceptions, undertheorized and untested. Factors such as witnessing and experiencing sexual and physical trauma are key when interpreting girls' violent offenses (Acoca & Dedel 1998; Owen & Bloom 1998; Herman 1992; van der Kolk & Greenberg 1987). It is essential to contextualize girls' perpetration of violence within the violence they experience: witnessing it, listening to it, watching it, suffering it. From my research, I find that a certain routinization of violence in girls' everyday lives appears to have a strong effect on their decision making.

Criminologist Jody Miller, in a study of adult female participation in violence, notes that women who experience extensive violence in everyday life "may be more likely than women who are situated differently to view violence as an appropriate or useful means of dealing with their environment" (Miller 1998; see also Simpson 1991). For some young women who are exposed to and who suffer violent

and/or sexual assaults, aggression itself may become a seemingly reasonable response (Herman 1992; van der Kolk & Greenberg 1987;
Tucker & Wolfe 1997). Instead of being "passive victims," these girls
are beginning to fight back and resist the onslaught of violence perpetrated upon them. This results in a theoretical and practical "tug-of-
war" for juvenile justice officials and theorists: is much of girls'
violence initiated aggressive assault or resistance and response to the
violence perpetrated against them (Gilligan et al. 1991; Tucker &
Wolfe 1997)? Understanding the context in which girls' experience
violence reveals that the latter view is more likely to be correct.

Domestic Violence and Woman-Battering

Children are born into families where they learn their culture and
family history, values, and how to love and work. Families can simultaneously offer girls and young women love, nurturance, and encour-
agement, and also violence, incest, neglect, homophobia, and abuse. In
my sample, many girls in trouble wander in empty and painful family
situations, with mothers and fathers absent because of divorce, over-
work, substance abuse, incarceration, or death. Troubled girls reported
feeling "passed around" to aunts and grandmothers, foster care, and
group homes.

One reason for family troubles is "domestic" or "intimate" violence. Witnessing woman-battering affects daughters deeply. One study
estimates that 3.3 million youths each year witness parental abuse,
ranging from batteries to fatal assaults involving knives and guns
(Charles Stewart Mott Foundation 1994). Other studies find that adolescents who grow up in homes characterized by violence are more
likely to report being violent (OJJDP 1994b; Fantuzzo & Wohr 1997).
Even though most children who grow up in homes where there is marital discord do not become violent, and many children who are exposed
to violence learn alternative ways to respond to problems, domestic violence remains an important area of study for those seeking to understand girls' violence (Saunders 1994; Penfold 1982; Cummings 1998).
One researcher notes that:

> It is critical to highlight the growing body of literature examin-
> ing the potentially deleterious effects of witnessing domestic vi-
> olence on the health and behavior of child witnesses. . . .
> Consequent disorders generally fall into two groups: "internal-
> ized problems such as withdrawn or anxious behaviors and

externalized problems such as aggression and delinquency." (Acoca 1998)

My own research suggests a link between witnessing wife beating and enacting violence in girls' own lives. One young woman in my sample explained, "I get drunk and beat my girlfriend the same way my dad gets drunk and beats my mom." Other accounts from girls reveal that young women in detention have witnessed or experienced an inordinate amount of family violence:

My dad is in jail for DV on my mom. It was a mess—I remember when the police came for him.

My dad was an abusive alcoholic and the divorce helped him straighten up. But since their divorce when I was eleven, all went downhill from there for me.

I called the police on my dad I don't know how many times! Fights: my dad taught me, "If someone hits you then hit them back!" I don't know how many times he's been in jail for assault and battery!

Elizabeth Martin, who watched her father hurt her mother and suffered physical abuse at his hands as well, sat in detention over a "fight with my Dad."

These kinds of experiences must come to the forefront of criminology literature if we are to understand girls' aggression and anger. The disciplines of psychology, sociology, and history literature contain some discussion of adolescent female experience with domestic violence and childhood abuse (notable works that theorize girls' anger include Brown 1998; Bernardez 1987; Jacobs 1993). However, while marital discord is consistently related to delinquency, no definitive criminological research has studied the ways in which girls who witness wife beating respond by being aggressive themselves (Spatz Widom 1989a; Spatz Widom 1989b). Family violence, especially wife beating, needs to be included explicitly in analyses of delinquency and of girls' involvement in violent crimes.

Girl-Hating and Misogyny

Girls absorb misogyny from a larger culture, particularly when they witness women being devalued (Ortner 1996). This harms them in two ways—it leads to girl-on-girl violence, and it prevents them from forming the friendships that might help them thrive in adolescence, or escape other violence in their lives.

Many young women in my study talked about witnessing their mothers and other women being debased. After seeing such events, girls may view women and other girls as worthy of less respect and interest in an attempt to "fit in" to a mainstream society that devalues women and girls (see also Ortner 1996; Bernardez 1987; Jacobs 1993). Young women also recounted stories about bloody fights, using weapons such as knives against other girls.

I got kicked out of school so many times for fighting, whatever. See these scars? This scratch? They're from fighting the other girls at school.

I have a temper—I fight back. Girls jump me. I get in so many fights because females hate me. I have so many enemies. All my life girls been pickin on me.

There was a girl at school and I gossiped about her behind her back. She beat me up. So I got a knife from the school kitchen and stabbed her twice in the back.

I saw this girl in a phone booth and she was lookin' at me funny. I hadda' jump her and I grabbed her gold chain around her neck. I don't like anyone frontin' me like that.

In our interviews, girls reported that they felt plagued by unresolved arguments and fights with other girls and rival groups, and that they often skipped school because it did not feel safe. Furthermore, violence on school property is now framed as a serious social problem (Devine 1996; OJJDP October 1998; Artz 1998). According to one recent study, almost 9 percent of female students nationwide had been in a physical fight on school property (CDC 1998).

In addition to causing girl-on-girl violence, girls' misogyny prevents them from forming beneficial friendships with other girls. As one social service provider explained:

These girls need to learn to come together and work together. Working together is how they will heal. The girls are so divided and male-identified. When they come together, especially survivors of childhood abuse, they see how they undermine their own success.

Working together is the healing—healing is the coming together. (Director, Girls Program, Massachusetts)

My interviews revealed that the friendships to which young women might potentially turn for help and nurturing seemed to be places of thinned-down care or worse. Unlike young women in other studies who seemed to "quarrel" and then work it out, the young women I met who were in trouble with the law had difficulty navigating friendships and camaraderie with each other (Griffiths 1995; Hey 1997; Eder 1990). Actually, young women in detention spoke much more about feeling disappointed by adult women and other girls (see also Ponton 1997; McLean Taylor et al. 1995; Thompson 1994). Girls in my study talked about how much they mistrusted other young women: "They talk all about your business behind your back." They repeatedly said that they preferred to hang out with males; they complained that "females are triflin'" and "I don't communicate a lot with girls because they talk too much and I have to beat them up."

Misogyny is prevalent in mainstream culture. Girls absorb it from the media, interactions with others, and most especially from other girls, which both leads them to commit violent acts against other girls and prevents them from forming healing friendships.

Homophobia as Violence

Reframing homophobia, the fear and hatred of homosexuality, as a form of community violence, demonstrates that it is a form of violence against and by girls (Dang 1997). Data regarding homophobia as violence against and by girls is extremely difficult to obtain: the experiences of queer girls are simply not tracked in national or public education, juvenile justice, or public health records. A 1984 survey by the National Gay Task Force found that 25 percent of females reported having been harassed or attacked in school because they were believed to be lesbian (Owens 1998: 96).

However, there is evidence that homophobia is on the rise in schools, and reports on gay bashing in the news are widespread (Ness 1998; D'Augelli & Dark 1995; Brooke 1998; Sullivan 1998; Kurwa 1998). In a recent poll of thousands of America's highest-achieving high school students, almost half admitted prejudice against gays and lesbians (Ness 1998). Ten percent of girls reported "being called lesbian" in a national survey of sexual harassment in schools (AAUW 1993).

Lesbian, bisexual, queer, and questioning girls suffer in silence and are hesitant to discuss their sexuality and identity issues freely (Dang 1997; D'Augelli 1998; Hunter 1996). Little is known about the numbers and experiences of lesbian, bisexual, queer, and questioning young women in the juvenile corrections system. Some agencies estimate that 40 percent of the runaway and street youth population surviving in the U. S. street economy may be gay or lesbian (NNRYS 1991). It appears that these young women may form a large, hidden population in crisis among girls in trouble.

Homophobia affects girls in juvenile corrections in different ways. One young woman testified that when she was locked in detention, she was "never given a roommate because she was a lesbian" and that "special showering arrangements were made to prevent her from showering with other girls" (Dang 1997). One girl told her story of living in a group home, saying, "I prepared myself to get in a fight when I went downstairs later that night for dinner" (Foster Care Youth United 1994). Findings from one Human Rights Commission hearing found that "many youth who enter the juvenile justice system for hate-related crimes have committed crimes against LGBTQQ people" (Dang 1997).

Approximately 35 percent of the girls in my sample mentioned involvement or interest in same-sex relationships, concerns about other girls "in here" being gay, and/or concerns about family members being gay. They also revealed that they had beaten up their girlfriends/lovers.

> I was involved with a hooker—she was bisexual. I was always buyin' her things but we fought a lot. I beat her up off crystal so I got an ADW off that.

> I beat my girl 'cause she ran away with Miguel. First we left him but then he started buggin' her. Then we fought. I beat her bad.

Lesbian, bisexual, queer, and questioning girls may be victimized by violence perpetrated either by boys and men or by other females. When girls are miseducated about lesbian and homosexual history, experience, desire, and practice, they may strike out in violence toward each other (Pastor et al. 1996; Way 1996). The effects of homophobia, both on the girls who are victims of violence and on the girls who perpetrate violence because of it, must be taken into account by those seeking to understand the environment of violence for female juveniles.

Sexual Harassment as Community Violence

Many girls, in my study, and in other national studies, report being sexually harassed in public, especially at school (AAUW 1993). Although they often are not able to fight back successfully, girls do attempt to do so (Wolfe & Tucker 1998). When this happens, officials who view the sexual harassment as inconsequential or untrue frequently label them violent offenders.

Girls are frequent victims of sexual harassment. An expert on the sexual harassment of girls at school states, "Whether it's the criminal version of sexual assault or the civil version of sexual harassment, school is a very violent place for girls" (Wellesley Centers 1998). School violence is often framed as a "gun" issue, not a "gender" issue (Devine 1996; OJJDP 1998; OJJDP 1997b). Yet being verbally abused by boys, being grabbed and fondled sexually, and even being shot at by boys were topics that girls brought up in their interviews with me and in other national reports regarding sexual harassment and school (Wolfe & Tucker 1998; AAUW 1993).

Girls' violent acts are often preceded by sexual harassment perpetrated against them by others. Many accounts from girls in detention about their school experiences were similar to the following: "I was suspended from school because this boy put his hands on me and I tried to hit him back." It is typical to meet young women in detention for not attending school because of fights involving self-defense from harassing males (Girls Inc and OJJDP 1996; AAUW 1993). Young women have somehow remained the invisible witnesses to and recipients of much school violence that is rarely characterized as sexual harassment, carrying the fear and responding by fighting and by dropping out.

More than half of the young women in my sample had already quit school. In 1998, more than half of all high school drop-outs were girls (CPS 1998). Truancy and not completing high school are linked to many problems for teenagers. National studies of girls in trouble with the law find that school problems are a significant factor in delinquency (Girls Inc and OJJDP 1996). Therefore, it is important to understand how to help this particular population of girls get on track with their academic tasks by making schools free of violence and sexual harassment against girls (Garry 1996; OJJP 1997b).

Juvenile justice reports on "school violence" rarely notice or link this violence to gendered forms of sexual harassment. That girls are targets and recipients of sexual harassment remains hidden in criminology reports about community violence. Without this knowledge, girls' violent acts appear unprovoked and aggressive. With this knowledge, the juvenile justice system could more effectively intervene in these situations and prevent such violent outcomes.

Conclusion

By taking a masculinist perspective on community violence and focusing only on guys, guns, and gangs, we learn little about young women's experiences. A routinization or normalization of violence in girls' everyday lives may result in righteous rage that they cannot express in safe, healthy ways (Brown 1998). The new "bad" girl is an angry girl, and the reasons for her frustrations are not acknowledged, perceived, or validated for her as reasonable concerns that would bring on justifiable anger. As one children's rights activist explained when I was interviewing her:

> Many young women in juvenile corrections have not yet healed from early childhood sexual injury, emotional neglect and loss, and are simply being re-injured by the system. (Staff member, Group home, California)

Not only do we need to expand the definition of "violence" to include girls' experiences, also we must conduct further research into the factors that contribute to punishing girls for gender transgressions. Girls expressing themselves violently are difficult for some to see and to analyze critically. Many adults who work with girls in group homes and detention facilities as counselors, social workers, and probation officers simply repeat the same refrain—"girls are harder to handle than boys" (Belknap et al. 1997). Girls are perceived to be more manipulative than boys, emotionally out of control, prone to outburst, constantly going AWOL and running away from placements, and violent in their responses to authority. However, these descriptions of girls' violent offenses do not place them in any structural or emotional framework that makes for clear interpretations of their actions.

The stories and experiences of Martin, Johnson, and Guzman are typical of young women in detention nationwide. They carry unhealed emotional wounds, are daughters of absent-hearted drug users and prison inmates, bear ungrieved deaths, suffer sexual violations, participate in self-soothing behavior with drugs and alcohol, receive insufficient nurturing attention from adults, and they sometimes strike out violently in anger and rage. These experiences provide the contexts for the moral horizons of girls in trouble.

A new focus in criminology needs to be developed that acknowledges the limitations of viewing juvenile violent behavior solely from a male-centered paradigm and that attempts to account for the different, especially sexual, life experiences girls encounter. The five areas I have highlighted as uniquely affecting girls contribute to this reworked definition of community violence and juvenile violent crime. We cannot begin to prevent, nor even interpret, the meanings of girls' violent behaviors without first recognizing that violence exists. Then we must formulate explanations of the social forces that influence *girls'* behavior, as opposed to "juveniles" as a unitary group, and move past the punishment of gender transgressions. Only after we grapple with these underlying causes can we hope to move toward a means of intervening and diverting girls from juvenile corrections. For intervention, prevention, or treatment programs to work, they must come to grips with the realities, meanings, and effects of troubled girls' experiences.

Notes

An earlier version of this essay appeared in *The Berkeley Women's Law Journal*, vol. 14, Spring 1999, 40–65, reprinted by permission of the University of Berkeley, California. I am deeply indebted to people I cannot name—the young women and professionals who granted me interviews and allowed me to spend time with them. My heartfelt appreciation goes out to my colleagues, friends, and family for intellectual and emotional support: Elizabeth Bernstein, Margaret Fiedler, Sara Hall, Kerwin Kay, Amanda Lewis, Beth Richie, and Richard Rountree Jr. Especialmente, quiero dar gracias por el trabajo experto de mi asistente, Lorena Diaz de Leon.

1. All names, identifying details, and case histories have been altered to protect the confidentiality of study participants. This research draws from a book manuscript under preparation, *Worlds of Girls in Trouble: Sex, Anger, and Violence in Everyday Life.*

2. The category "young women" is by no means a unitary category. Girls in U.S. correction systems are typically thirteen to seventeen years old. In this article, I use the terms *girls* and *young women* interchangeably (see also Girls Inc. and the Office of Juvenile Justice and Delinquency Prevention 1996).

References

Abrams, L. & Curran, L. 2000a, "Guardians of virtue: the social reformers and the 'girl problem,' 1890–1920," *Social Service Review,* vol. 74, no. 3, pp. 436–52.
———. 2000b, "Wayward girls and virtuous women: social workers and female juvenile delinquency in the progressive era," *Affilia,* vol. 15, no. 1, pp. 49–64.

Acoca, L. 1998, "Outside/Inside: the violation of American girls at home, on the streets, and in the juvenile justice system," *Crime and Delinquency,* vol. 44, no. 4, pp. 561–590.

Acoca, L. & Dedel, K. 1998, "No place to hide: understanding and meeting the needs of girls in the California juvenile justice system," National Council on Crime and Delinquency, San Francisco.

Addams, J. 1909, *The spirit of youth and the city streets.* MacMillan, New York.

Adler, F. 1975, *Sisters in crime: the rise of the new female criminal.* McGraw-Hill, New York.

Alan Guttmacher Institute 1994, *Sex and America's teenagers,* AGI, Washington, D.C.

American Association of University Women 1993, *Hostile hallways: the AAUW survey on sexual harassment in America's schools.*

Artz, S. 1998, *Sex, power, and the violent school girl,* Teachers College Press, New York.

Bailey, F. & Hale, D. C. 1998, *Popular culture, crime, and justice,* Wadsworth, Belmont, Cal.

Baskin, D., Sommers, I., & Fagan, J. 1993, "The political economy of street crime," *Fordham Urban Law Journal,* no. 20, pp. 401–18.

Bernardez, T. 1987, "Women and anger: cultural prohibitions and the feminine ideal," Stone Center, Wellesley, Mass.

Bernstein, E. 1999, "What's wrong with prostitution? What's right with sex-work? Comparing markets in female sexual labor," *Hastings Women's Law Journal,* vol. 10, no. 1, pp. 91–119.

Bourgois, P. 1995, *In search of respect: selling crack in El Barrio.* Cambridge University Press, New York.

Breckinridge, S. & Abbot, E. 1912, *The delinquent child and the home: a study of the delinquent wards of the juvenile court of Chicago,* Russell Sage Foundation Charities, New York.

Brooke, J. 1998, "Homophobia often found in schools, data shows," *New York Times,* Oct. 14, p. A19.

Brown, L. M. 1998, *Raising their voices: the politics of girls' anger,* Harvard University Press, Cambridge.

Butterfield, F. 1996, "Violent crime declines again—4th year in row, but experts say figures mask surge in teenage lawlessness," *San Francisco Chronicle,* May 6, p. A3.

———. 1998, "Guns blamed for rise in homicide by youths in 80s," *New York Times,* Dec. 10, p. A29.

Campbell, A. 1991, *Girls in the gang,* Blackwell, Cambridge.

Centers for Disease Control and Prevention 2000, *Youth risk behavior surveillance, United States, 1999,* 49/SS-5, U.S. Department of Health and Human Services, Atlanta.

Chalk, R. (ed) 1994, "Violence and the American family: report of a workshop," *Board on Children and Families,* National Academy Press, Washington, D.C.

Charles Stewart Mott Foundation 1994, *A fine line: losing American youth to violence.* CSFM, Flint, Mich.

Cohen, A. 1955, *Delinquent boys: the culture of the gang,* Free Press, Glencoe, Ill.

Cummings, M. 1998, "Children exposed to marital conflict and violence: conceptual and theoretical directions," in Holden, Geffner, & Jouriles (eds), *Children exposed to marital violence,* American Psychological Association, Washington D.C., pp. 55–94.

Curran, D. 1984, "The myth of the 'new' female delinquent," *Crime and Delinquency,* vol. 30, no. 3, July, pp. 386–99.

Dang, Q. H. 1997, "Investigation into the needs of lesbian, gay, bisexual, transgender, queer, and questioning youth," *A report by the Human Rights Commission City and County of San Francisco,* July 12.

Datesman, S. & Scarpitti, F. 1980, "The extent and nature of female crime," in Datesman & Scarpitti (eds), *Women, crime, and justice.* Oxford University Press, New York, pp. 3–64.

D'Augelli, A. & Dark, L. 1995, "Lesbian, gay, and bisexual youths," in Eron, Gentry, & Schlegel (eds), *Reason to hope: a psychosocial perspective on violence and youth,* American Psychological Association, Washington D.C., pp. 177–96.

DeFrances, C. & Strom, K. 1997, "Juveniles prosecuted in state criminal courts," U.S. Department of Justice, Bureau of Justice Statistics, Washington D.C.

D'Emilio, J. & Freedman, E. 1988, *Intimate matters: a history of sexuality in America,* Harper and Row, New York.

Devine, J. 1996, *Maximum security: the culture of violence in inner-city schools,* University of Chicago Press, Chicago.

Devlin, R. 1997, "Female juvenile delinquency and the problem of sexual authority in America, 1945–1965," *Yale Journal of Law and the Humanities,* no. 9, pp. 147–82.

DiIulio, J. J. 1992, " Rethinking the criminal justice system: toward a new paradigm," U.S. Dept. of Justice, Office of Justice Programs, Bureau of Justice Statistics, Washington, D.C.

Eder, D., with Evans, C., & Parker, S. 1997, *School talk: gender and adolescent culture.* Rutgers University Press, New Brunswick.

Elliot, D., Hagan, J., & McCord, J. 1997, *Youth violence: children at risk,* American Sociological Association, Washington D.C.

Eron, L. & Huesmann, R. 1984, "The relation of prosocial behavior to the development of aggression and psychopathology," *Aggressive Behavior,* no. 10, pp. 201–11.

Fantuzzo, J. & Mohr, W. 1999, "Prevalence and effects of child exposure to domestic violence," *The Future of Children,* vol. 9, no. 3, pp. 21–32.

Federal Bureau of Investigation 1995, *Uniform Crime Reports: crime in the U.S., 1994,* Department of Justice, Washington, D.C.

Finkelhor, D. 1994, "Current information on the scope and nature of child sexual abuse," *The Future of Children: Sexual Abuse of Children,* vol. 4, no. 2, pp. 31–53.

Foster Care Youth United 1994, "On the inside, looking out," Jan./Feb., Youth Communication, New York, pp. 2–4.

Garbarino, J., Dubrow, N., Kostelny, K., & Pardo, C. 1992, *Children in danger: coping with consequences of community violence,* Jossey-Bass, San Francisco.

Garry, E. M. 1996, "Truancy: first step to a lifetime of problems," Office of Juvenile Justice and Delinquency Prevention, U.S. Department of Justice, Washington, D.C.

Gilligan, C., Rogers, A., & Tolman, D. (eds) 1991, *Women, girls, and psychotherapy: reframing resistance.* The Haworth Press, New York.

Girls Incorporated and the Office of Juvenile Justice and Delinquency Prevention 1996, "Prevention and parity: girls in juvenile justice," U.S. Department of Justice, Washington D.C.

Glueck, S. & Glueck, E. 1934, *Five hundred delinquent women,* Knopf, New York.

Gordon, L. (ed) 1990, *Women, the state, and welfare,* University of Wisconsin Press, Madison.

Greenfield, L. 1997. "Sex offenses and offenders: an analysis of data on rape and sexual assault," U.S. Department of Justice, Bureau of Justice Statistics, Washington, D.C.

Griffin, C. 1993, *Representations of youth: the study of youth and adolescence in Britain and America,* Polity Press, Cambridge, Mass.

Griffiths, V. 1995, *Adolescent girls and their friends: a feminist ethnography.* Avebury, Aldershot.

Hagedorn, J. 1998, *People and folks: gangs, crime, and the underclass in a rustbelt city,* Lakeview Press, Chicago.

Harris, M. G. 1988, *Cholas: Latino girls and gangs,* AMS Press, New York.

Hawkins, J. D. (ed) 1996, *Delinquency and crime: current theories,* Cambridge University Press, New York.

Heise, L. 1997, "Violence, sexuality, and women's lives," in Lancaster & di Leonardo (eds), *The gender sexuality reader: culture, history, political economy,* Routledge, New York, pp. 411–33.

Herman, J. 1992, *Trauma and recovery,* BasicBooks, New York.

Hey, V. 1997, *The company she keeps: an ethnography of girls' friendship,* Open University Press, Milton Keynes.

Hochschild, A. 1989, *The second shift: working parents and the revolution at home,* Viking, New York.

Horatio Alger Association of Distinguished Americans, Inc. 1996, *The Mood of American youth 1996,* Alexandria, Va.

Howell, J. 1998, "Youth gangs: an overview," *Juvenile Justice Bulletin,* U.S. Department of Justice, Washington D.C.

Humes, E. 1996, *No matter how loud I shout: a year in the life of juvenile court,* Simon and Schuster, New York.

Hunter, J. 1996, "At the crossroads: lesbian youth," in K. Jay (ed), *Dyke life,* Basic Books, New York, pp. 50–60.

Jacobs, J. 1993, "Victimized daughters: sexual violence and the empathic female self," *Signs,* vol. 19, no. 1, pp. 126–45.

James, J. & Thornton, W. 1980, "Women's liberation and the female delinquent," *Journal of Research in Crime and Delinquency,* no. 20, pp. 230–44.

Johnson, S. 1998, "Girls are in trouble: do we care?" *Corrections Today* no. 60.

Kaufman, M. 1997, "The construction of masculinity and the triad of men's violence," in O'Toole & Schiffman, (eds), *Gender violence,* New York University Press, New York, pp. 30–51.

Kimmel, M. 1996, *Manhood in America: a cultural history,* Free Press, New York.

Klein, D. 1973, "The etiology of female crime: a review of the literature," *Issues in Criminology,* vol. 8, no. 2, pp. 3–30.

Kurwa, N. 1998, "Do schools condone harassment of gay students?" *San Francisco Examiner,* May 19, p. D-7.

Levine, F. & Rosich, K. 1996, *Social causes of violence: crafting a science agenda,* American Sociological Association, Washington D.C.

Maglin, N. B. & Perry, D. (eds) 1996, *"Bad girls"/"good girls": women, sex, and power in the nineties,* Rutgers University Press, New Brunswick.

Maguire, K. & Pastore, A. (eds) 1998, *Sourcebook of criminal justice statistics 1997,* Department of Justice, Washington, D.C.

Males, M. 1998, *Framing youth: ten myths about the next generation,* Common Courage Press, Monroe, Me.

McLean Taylor, J., Gilligan, C., & Sullivan, A. 1995, *Between voice and silence: women and girls, race and relationship.* Harvard University Press, Cambridge.

McNamee, G. H. (ed), 1999, *A noble experiment? The first 100 years of the cook county juvenile court, 1899–1999,* Chicago Bar Association, Chicago.

Miller, J. 1998, "Up it up: gender and the accomplishment of street robbery," *Criminology,* vol. 36, no. 1, pp. 37–66.

———. 2001, *One of the guys: girls, gangs, and gender.* Oxford University Press, New York.

Nagle, J. (ed) 1997, *Whores and other feminists,* Routledge, New York.

Nathanson, C. 1991, *Dangerous passage: the social control of sexuality in women's adolescence,* Temple University Press, Philadelphia.

National Network of Runaway and Youth Services 1991, "To whom do they belong? Runaway, homeless, and other youth in high-risk situations in the 1990's," The National Network, Washington D.C.

Ness, C. 1998, "Gay bias rising among top students," *San Francisco Examiner,* Nov. 12, p. A1.

Newburn, T. & Stanko, E. 1994, *Just boys doing business? Men, masculinities, and crime,* Routledge, New York.

Odem, M. 1995, *Delinquent daughters: protecting and policing adolescent female sexuality in the United States, 1885–1920,* University Press of North Carolina, Chapel Hill.

Office of Juvenile Justice and Delinquency Prevention 1994a, "Family strengthening in preventing delinquency," September, Department of Justice, Washington, D.C.

———. 1994b, "Violent families and youth violence," Fact Sheet #21, December, Department of Justice, Washington, D.C.

———. 1997a, "Juvenile offenders and victims: 1997 update on violence," Department of Justice, Washington, D.C.

Office of Juvenile Justice Programs 1997, "Keeping young people in school: community programs that work," Department of Justice, Washington, D.C.

Office of Juvenile Justice and Delinquency Programs 1998a, "Youth gangs: an overview," August, Department of Justice, Washington, D.C.

———. 1998b, "High school youths, weapons, and violence: a national survey," October, Department of Justice, Washington, D.C.

Ortner, S. 1996, "Is female to male as nature is to culture?" in Ortner (ed), *Making gender*, Beacon Press, Boston.

Osofsky, J. 1995, "The effects of exposure to violence on young children," *American Psychologist*, vol. 50, no. 9, pp. 782–88.

O'Toole, L. & Schiffman, J. (eds) 1997, *Gender violence: interdisciplinary perspectives*. New York University Press, New York.

Owen, B. & Bloom, B. 1998, "Modeling gender-specific services in juvenile justice: policy and program recommendations," Office of Criminal Justice Planning, Sacramento.

Owens, R. 1998, *Queer kids: the challenges and promise for lesbian, gay, and bisexual youth*, Harrington Park Press, New York.

Pastor, J., McCormick, J., & Fine, M. 1996, "Makin' homes: an urban girl thing," in Leadbeater & Way (eds), *Urban girls*, New York University Press, New York, pp. 15–34.

Penfold, S. 1982, "Children of battered women," *International Journal of Mental Health*, vol. 11, no. 1/2, pp. 108–14.

Peters, S. & Peters, S. 1998, "Violent adolescent females," *Corrections Today*, pp. 28–29.

Pinderhughes, H. 1997, *Race in the hood: conflict and violence among urban youth*, University of Minnesota Press, Minneapolis.

Platt, A. 1969, *The child savers: the invention of delinquency*, University of Chicago Press, Chicago.

Ponton, L. 1997, *The romance of risk: why teenagers do what they do*, Basic Books, New York.

Poulin, A. B. 1996, "Female delinquents: defining their place in the justice system," *Wisconsin Law Review*, pp. 549–51.

Rowe, D. 1996, "An adaptive strategy theory in crime and delinquency," in Hawkins (ed), *Delinquency and Crime*, pp. 268–324.

Sanchez-Jankowski, M. 1991, *Islands in the streets: gangs and American urban society*, University of California Press, Berkeley.

Saunders, D. 1994, "Child custody decisions in families experiencing woman abuse," *Social Work*, vol. 39, no. 1, pp. 51–59.

Scheper-Hughes, N. 1992, *Death without weeping: the violence of everyday life in Brazil*, University of California Press, Berkeley.

Schur, E. M. 1983, *Labeling women deviant: gender, stigma, and social control*, Temple University Press, Philadelphia.

Shoemaker, D. 2000, *Theories of delinquency: an examination of explanations of delinquent behavior*, 4th Edition, New York, Oxford University Press.

Shuster, B. 1998, "Contradiction in crime: as the numbers fall, fears keep rising," *San Francisco Sunday Examiner and Chronicle*, Aug. 23, p. A3.

Simon, R. 1975, *The contemporary woman and crime*, U.S. Government Printing Office, Washington, D.C.

Simpson, S. 1991, "Caste, class, and violent crime: explaining differences in female offending," *Criminology*, vol. 29, no. 1, pp. 115–35.

Snitow, A., Stansell, C. & Thompson, S. 1983, *Powers of desire: the politics of sexuality*, Monthly Review Press, New York.

Snyder, H. & Sickmund, M. 1995, "Juvenile offenders and victims: a focus on violence," Office of Juvenile Justice and Delinquency Prevention, Washington, D.C.

———. 1999, *Juvenile offenders and victims: 1999 National Report,* Office of Juvenile Justice and Delinquency Prevention, Washington, D.C.

Spatz, C. W. 1989a, "Does violence beget violence? A critical examination of the literature," *Psychological Bulletin,* vol. 106, no. 1, p. 3.

———. 1989b, "Child abuse, neglect, and violent criminal behavior," *Criminology,* vol. 27, no. 2, p. 251.

Sullivan, K. 1998, "Gay youths struggle in personal hell," *Sunday San Francisco Examiner and Chronicle,* July 26, pp. D1 and D4.

Tappan, P. 1969, *Delinquent girls in court: a study of the wayward minor court of New York,* Patterson Smith, Montclair, N.J.

The Wellesley Centers for Women 1998, "An interview with Nan Stein," in *Research Report From the Wellesley Centers,* Spring, Wellesley College, p. 12.

Thompson, S. 1994, "What friends are for: on girls' misogyny and romantic fusion," in J. Irvine (ed), *Sexual cultures and the construction of adolescent identities,* Temple University Press, Philadelphia, pp. 228–49.

Tracy, S. & Shelden, R. 1992, "The violent female juvenile offender: an ignored minority within the juvenile justice system," *Juvenile and Family Court Journal,* vol. 43, no. 3, pp. 33–40.

Tucker, J. & Wolfe, L. 1997, *Victims no more: girls fight back against male violence,* Center for Women Policy Studies, Washington, D.C.

van der Kolk, B. A. 1987, *Psychological trauma,* American Psychiatric Association, Washington, D.C.

van der Kolk, B. A. & Greenberg, M. 1987, "The psychobiology of the trauma response: hyperarousal, constriction, and addiction to traumatic re-exposure," van der Kolk (ed), *Psychological Trauma,* pp. 63–87.

Vance, C. (ed) 1992, *Pleasure and danger: exploring female sexuality,* Pandora, London.

Ward, D. Jackson, M., & Ward, R. 1980, "Crimes of violence by women," in *Women, crime, and justice,* Datesman & Scarpitti (eds), Oxford University Press, New York.

Way, N. 1996, "Between experiences of betrayal and desire: close friendships among urban adolescents," in *Urban Girls,* Leadbeater & Way (eds), 193–212.

Wing, A. & Willis, C. A. 1997, "Critical race feminism: black women and gangs," *Journal of Gender, Race, and Justice,* no. 1, pp. 141–76.

Wolfe, L. & Tucker, J. 1998, *Report of the summit on girls and violence,* Center for Women Policy Studies, Washington, D.C.

Zimring, F. 1998, *American youth violence,* Oxford University Press, New York.

Chapter Seven

Coming Out to Play? Young Women and Violence on the Street

Jenny J. Pearce

Smacks in the jaw between little girls are one thing, perhaps, but there were more formidable signs that all was not well with the gentle sex. . . . Elsewhere, three girls aged 15 and 16 year were bought to court for robbing a woman of 9s 2 1/2d after they had hustled her. Described by the police as a well—known gang of "expert pick-pockets," the news headlines identified them as "Girl hooligans."

—*South London Chronicle*, 13 August 1898
and 3 September 1898

Introduction

The fear of the violent "girl hooligan," of the girl doing "boy's things" out in "boys places," predates the twenty-first century; but as new stories appear in the press, usually in response to isolated incidents, concern reemerges that girls are acting more and more like boys (Clarke 1997). These moral panics about girls acting like boys in boy's spaces distract us from developing an understanding of how young women do spend their leisure time out-of-doors within their everyday routines. I draw on research material where young women talk of employing their local streets and estate stairways and landings in their day to day routines. I argue that it is through such use of the public domain that young women gain a detailed knowledge of the nature of violence within their environment. With this knowledge they develop useful strategies, sometimes choosing to participate in causing local disruption, more often facilitating their own safety. Based on my own research I show that it is through time spent inhabiting local streets and estate landings and stairways that young women learn how to coexist with violence and danger in their immediate environment. I conclude by arguing that, as a pathway between home and the outside world, there is at the other end of this same street a place used by young women who are running away from home. However, in this role as a place detached from an interconnected home life, the street has no protective walls, leaving the young women particularly vulnerable to violence and sexual exploitation.

Our Knowledge of Youth and Violence

We need to further our understanding of young women's negotiations with violence in the public domain. This is both in everyday activities, when locations such as the street represent a playground within which young people "hang around," and in the more exceptional circumstances when the outdoors becomes a sanctuary from intolerable indoor home circumstances. It is in these latter situations that vulnerability can be exploited through violence and emotional and sexual abuse. This juxtaposition of refuge and danger that is represented by the street for young women needs further exploration through research, policy, and practice interventions.

Gendered divisions between a feminized indoor, and a masculinized outdoor domain have dominated many studies of young people (Massey 1998). Inquiries into young people and violence have primarily focused on boys on the street, while girls are discussed as victims of sexual and domestic violence in the home (Anderson 1997; Walklate 1995). As complexities emerge within the debates about the cause and nature of violence and disorder, the simple dichotomies that position young women against young men and black youth against white have been challenged (Gilroy 1987; Small 1994; Mirza 1992; Cohen, Keith, & Back 1996). This has required exploring the meaning given to the term *violence* itself.

Should emotional intimidation, bullying, as well as racial and sexual harassment, all of which carry potential long-term damage to victims, be incorporated within discourses of violence (Stanko 1998; Brown, Burman, & Tisdall 2000)? As "commonsense" interpretations of aggression and violence have been contested (Stanko 1998) so too have studies of antiracist youth work raised awareness of the extent of harm that can be caused by racial harassment and abuse (Back 1990). As the concept of "violence" is questioned as a male preserve, issues regarding young people, race, and gender have similarly been addressed (Campbell 1991; Brown, Burman, & Tisdall 2000). Despite this, the long-standing expectation that violent crime and public disorder is something that boys do and that men research has continued relatively unchallenged (Newburn & Stanko 1994). This is not surprising as statistical evidence positions boys and men as perpetrators of the majority of violent crimes, and groups of boys as those most likely to generate fear of violence within a local community (Mirrlees-Black et al. 1998; Campbell 1993; Marlow & Pitts 1998; Crawford 1998, 1999).

While the data indicate that boys are responsible for the majority of violent offenses (Mirrlees-Black et al. 1998), only a small percentage of young men are persistent offenders: about 3 percent of offenders being responsible for approximately one-quarter of all offenses (Pease 1998). The statistical evidence creates a number of consequences. For example, policy interventions through youth justice and community safety strategies focus attention on boys (Pearce & Stanko 1999), and the face to face work attracts mostly male workers who invariably engage with the young men to enhance their own feelings of "street cred" (Hudson 1988). On the other hand, women and girls are commonly perceived to be victims of crime: invariably, private crimes taking place behind closed doors (Crawford 1998; Stanko 1998; Fitzgerald & Hale 1996; Mason & Palmer 1996).

Some of the studies that have aimed at "filling in the gaps" have focused on the complex ways that young women balance the demands of the domestic, indoor domain against the need to be out on the street, engaging with boys and their activities (Lees 1993; McRobbie 1994). Young women's "bedroom culture" has been explored, the bedroom being a meeting place for girls that either creates a site in opposition to the male occupation of the street, or the safe location within which femininity can be practiced and endorsed (McRobbie & Garber 1976; McRobbie 1991; Lees 1993). Subsequent studies have delved farther into the gendered nature of young people's use of space, challenging the division between two separated domains: the feminized indoor and the masculinized outdoor (Skelton & Valentine 1998; Watt & Stenson 1998; Massey 1998; Brown, Burman, & Tisdall 2000). This work is open to the possibility that young women may spend time on the street and that they have an awareness of danger, often violent danger, in the outdoor domain.

Working with a definition of violence that includes emotional as well as physical harm, I draw on research with young people from a school located within a complex of high crime, a multiracial inner-city estate. I look to young women's accounts of their use of the street and the estate stairways and landings. Through this regular contact with the outdoor, public domain the young women develop a knowledge base about violence within their area, a violence with which they sometimes participate but also learn to negotiate and to avoid.

Young Women and the Street: Situated Knowledge

The research, which took place between 1995 and 1999, involved 107 young people made up of 55 boys and 52 girls: 13 boys and 13 girls from year 7 (aged 11–12), 17 boys and 21 girls from year 10 (aged 14–15), and 25 boys and 18 girls from year 11 (aged 15–16). The area within which the school is based is renowned for petty crime, local disorder, and racial tension. Previous studies of crime and disorder have identified "pockets" of social and economic deprivation within inner-city areas where incidents of vandalism and repeat victimization have been high and where efforts to improve the environment have concentrated on the outdoor, public domain in attempts to "design out crime" (Clarke & Mayhew 1980). More recently, there has been additional focus placed on the key characteristics of communities faced with high levels of crime and social disorder, accompanied by similarly high levels of fear of crime. These characteristics include few economic resources, a dominance of poorly maintained rented accommodation and rapid demographic change, all of which can result in new communities competing against themselves, and against the residual indigenous population, for depleted community provision (Hope 1998; Pitts 1998; Evans 1998).

The estates surrounding the school held all these characteristics of deprivation. The school's local authority had seen rapid economic decline with the exodus of skilled labor leaving an indigenous white unskilled or semiskilled labor force to occupy mainly rented accommodation. Housing policies worked to accommodate first Bengali, and more recently Somali, populations who were moving, or being moved, into the area. The proportion of Bengali young people within the school rose from 18 percent to 54 percent during the 1980s to 1990s, with a corresponding fall in white pupils from 62 percent in 1981 to 30 percent in 1995 (Pearce 1996). Urban regeneration schemes have created "top down" changes to the area where "urban entrepreneurs" engage in commercial projects with income enhancement rather than community cohesion in mind (Zukin 1995). The new local shopping mall has become a protected space for commercial exchange and, in common with many such developments, is policed to exclude "undesirables" (such as young people) from "hanging around" within it (Sibley 1995: xi). The lack of sports facilities, of community-based youth club resources, and of shopping spaces to wander in quite literally throw the young people onto the street to fight over territory within which they can hang around.

To explore the young people's uses of the local spaces available to them I asked each to draw annotated maps of their local area and to chart the spaces they frequented, noting why and when they were used. It was acknowledged that the maps would vary in precision and presentation depending on drawing and writing skills, but that subsequent group discussions would help elaborate on the information and ideas provided. After analyzing the maps and charts I ran four discussion groups with year ten students: split into separate groups of white and Bengali young men and young women respectively.

The young people were assured that their confidentiality would be protected and their names changed in publication. I also explained that I did not intend to assume general "truths" from the work but was interested in hearing about different and specific relationships with violence in their everyday lives. As noted within crime prevention and youth work-studies, the credibility of self-report studies and the validity of oral accounts can be questioned (Cohen 1999). However, it is acknowledged (see for example Anderson, Kinsey, & Loader 1994) that while young people's accounts of witnessing crime may carry exaggerations they can also reflect fears about potentially dangerous people and places. Similarly, Holloway and Jefferson (2000) argue that narratives can provide accounts of different memories and perceptions that give insight into the images conjured by the speaker and the anxieties portrayed in the speech. These are useful for providing accounts of the speaker's inner and outer worlds. As such, I explained that any extracts selected within the research for discussion would provide "situated" rather than universal knowledge: offering insight into these young women's relationship with violence situated within their own geographical, social, and economic context (Haraway 1991: 111, 188).

Young Women: Coming Out to Play

Defying the general assumption that the street is a male preserve, the white young women talked of using the street as a place to meet, to hang around, and to be with friends. As such it is an extension of the indoor hallway providing a place for private activity within an apparently public domain. Thirty-two of the fifty-five young men and twenty-two of the fifty-two young women noted named streets on their charts, saying that streets were important places to meet friends and hang around. In their discussion groups, the young women noted that the street is "where we live," the year ten young women confirming that they are on the street all the time

Sue:	Yeah, all the time innit?
Jenny:	Is it all the time?
Mel:	Yeah, like when you get home from school you go out . . .
Jenny:	And is it safe, do you feel safe?
Sue:	What, on the street? Yeah, 'cos you know everyone. Like where you live and that.

The importance of getting out onto the street outweighs the importance of staying in and doing homework. Talking of the fear of missing out on local events Jane notes:

Jane: The thing is, I think partly you, you worry about what your mates think like, what did you do last night? "Oh, I stayed in, did my homework," "what did you . . ." "Oh we was all round there blah, blah, blah . . ." and you think to yourself, I was in doing me homework and they're all out. What am I doing?

And

Sue: If I was to do my homework, I'd come in about ten [P.M.] and then I'd, like, do it for an hour. I'd still be out but I'd do it later.

The street is the meeting place where, through hanging around, news and information is exchanged. Young women talked of games they play when they become bored on the street. Some of these would be understood as disruptive and threatening to targeted adults within the community. For example, playing "chase", a game where young people aggravate adults, is playing with the risk that the adult will lose their temper and try to chase the young people away.

Jane: Like if we're just having a laugh, like we just knock on people's doors and just run off, or do whatever, whatever we do. Like someone's being silly or something and some man gets the hump and comes after yer, or whatever . . .

The more serious the threat, the more fun the game.

Jane: Like that shop down there, Dave, he's always got this metal pole behind, and you say one word to him and he'll chase you out the fuckin' shop with it . . .

The young women playing chase are taking part in activities that could be perceived by local adults to be threatening. The young women describe "winding up" adults as a part of the daily fun on the estate. Jane later continued into a tirade about the boredom that, she says, is a result of the lack of facilities within the area:

Jane: Like people say, "Oh kids do this, kids do that," "kids take drugs." But what do they expect? They don't give us no clubs, and the clubs they have given us are closing down. Like you've got nothing for our age group . . . and they say we're all immature for our age. They should give us something to do for our age group, no matter what . . .

I understood that although Jane was going to say "no matter what we do" she decided to stop short of admitting further involvement with creating a public nuisance. Jane was threatened with being excluded from school for truanting and for being disruptive and intimidating to other pupils. She had also been convicted of minor offenses: petty theft and disturbing the peace. I understood her to be mindful of owning up to further misdemeanors. The essential part of her disclosure, however, was that chase is no more than a game, a game that relieves the boredom through playing with danger.

While the activities last throughout the year, the locations for hanging around change according to the weather. When it becomes too cold to hang around on the streets, they are replaced by the stairways of the local estates.

Jenny:	Are there other places like, that you would . . .
Sue:	On people's stairs, and things like that.
Sandra:	That's one of the most common places people go, especially in the winter, when it's cold.

The above gives extracts from white young women's discussions. The Bengali young women also talk of using the street, despite many being fearful of racist attack from white young men and of recrimination from their elders.

Jenny:	Are there places in the street where you would feel scared?
Shanaz:	Yes there is.
Aisha:	Yes sometimes.
Shanaz:	It 's like, we live in this area, it's like gangs of boys hanging about all the time.

And

Aisha:	I see like all the people, like, getting cussed by white people, like white kids walking down threw stones at them, but they [those being attacked] can't do nothing. They can't do nothing because if they touch them or anything, they could get, like, police on them or anything. They just walk away.

Implicit within this statement is the fact that these young women feel alone in coping with racist abuse and violence. They explained that they did not want to trouble their parents, giving them additional burdens to those they already carry, and that they had little confidence that telling the police would result in helpful intervention. Rather than using the streets, these young women talk of spending time outdoors on the estate stairways. This gives them a "private" meeting place outside from, but in close proximity to, their home. As well as being a place of their own for hanging around, having access to the outdoors also relieves pressure from the overcrowded conditions indoors, as experienced by many young people on the estate. The borough's own research notes that 68 percent of its population lived in local authority accommodation and that

> the majority of pupils lived in homes which had 3 or more children with just over 1 in 6 homes having 5 or more children. . . . [J]ust under half (46 percent) of children lived in houses where there were more children than bedrooms. (L.A. 1995: 40)

When the streets are too dangerous, the Bengali young women noted that they "do landing." Doing landing means hanging out on the estate landing where safety is enhanced by staying closer to home.

Sonia: Yes, you know we've got a lot of friends. I must have about five friends on one landing.

Despite feeling safer, there is still the worry that boys or older men may challenge their presence outdoors.

Sonia: Oh, we have friends on the landing so that we go to their house just to play . . . sometimes there's a lot of boys around and everything, and if you come on the landing, the men start talking, give you a bad reputation.

And later:

Shanaz: 'Cos like, a lot of girls don't go. That's why, you know, everybody is scared to go down the stairs by themselves, and because of some old men, we're not allowed to go outside . . .

Sonia: 'Cos like a lot of girls don't go out anymore because of that. Older men start talking to other people and say that we're bad like, erm attitude and everything.

Najma, however, challenges these fears of reprisal:

Najma: Yes, we only live once. We might as well make the most of it . . . we don't want to get cooped up in a room and stay there forever. If we want to go

out, then we go out. Like, me, if I want to go out,
I don't care what other people say. . . . They say
nasty things to me, only I'm a big mouth. I swear
at them, I say nasty things to them. If they say
anything to me, I'll shout back at them, I'll back
at them. You see, I don't let anyone get away
with doing something to me.

While there are clearly diverse ways that different young women
cope with the threat of abuse or violence, the regular use of the landing
and stairways provides an opportunity for them to warn each other
against possible danger. For example, the young women talk of a man
who spends time on the stairways:

Rehana: And he comes back, it was in the summer, and he
                 was like, he starts threatening girls, or like grabs
                 them and starts touching them up and all this
                 stuff . . . he tried to touch me up! Like after a few
                 days after my birthday. . . . He grabbed me and
                 started pushing me and I said . . . then I kicked
                 him and started running up the stairs and he
                 started running up, and I like got to my house.
                 And they did phone the police and the police
                 couldn't like . . . this happened to another girl . . . I
                 gave the same description as this Chinese girl.

Information is shared between the young women to keep track of
the man's whereabouts.

Rehana: He used to live round our area . . . but he got
                 kicked out . . . and he used to hang about on the
                 stairs and scare people. He used to live on the
                 stairs, then like . . . he went somewhere, and I
                 don't know where, and he always comes back
                 summers.

While many young women spoke of spending time on their local
streets, the year ten white young women also talked of negotiating their
way through potentially dangerous places to meet their boyfriends. The
young men's maps, charts, and discussion groups note that they rarely
moved out of their area for fear of straying onto territory belonging to
other groups. To move out of the area could result in violent fighting

between white and Bengali young men and is, in the main, avoided. As a result, the boys consider the girls to have more freedom of movement:

Danny: I think girls can really go anywhere, it's boys isn't it?

John: Yeah.

Danny: I think girls can go anywhere and they ain't going to get started on. Unless there's girls like telling them not to go there. But it's mainly boys. Because boys have to show how much of a man they are I suppose.

Pete: So you stay in your own area. Even if you don't live around the area, and you hang around the area. You still stay to your own area. Boys do, boys always stay in the same place but girls I hang about with, they can go anywhere really, they don't get any trouble.

The young women are consistently mindful of their safety and dispute the apparent ease young men attribute to girls for moving around. When talking of avoiding being on their own, the young women note that they try to travel in pairs:

Barbara: But if you are with a mate it's different, 'cos you know your mate, if it's a true mate, you know they're not going to stand there. It's a bit scary though, when like everyone goes home, and you're on your way home and you've gotta walk home on your own. Specially like, specially when you've got dark alley, dark street.

Jenny: So does that happen much?

Barbara: Yeah, every night.

They discussed the different ways that they each aim to protect themselves during night and day. Talking about carrying a knife as protection, they confirm that they see other young people carrying knives "plenty of times." Barbara notes that her "dad always told me before now to take a flick-knife out with me and keep it under wrap," while Mel notes that "If I carry anything, I'd carry like, erm, hairspray or something, to spray," while Louise says that, like her mother, she carries an alarm with her. The need for self-protection was generated through conversation about traveling between local areas at night. The discussion continued to note the possibility of fights between young women as they refuted the boy's comments that they would be safe. Talk of avoiding going to a particular nightclub prompted the young women to note that:

Barbara:	Yeah, I don't feel like getting my face sliced.
Mel:	No one wants to go there, no one.
Geri:	It's so dangerous, especially at night-time.
Louise:	Yeah, there's a lot of fights and a lot of trouble over there.
Geri:	If you keep yourself to yourself you still get done . . . even if you go round . . . they kept themselves to themselves and even Julia got. . . . All you have to do, right, is like, you're somewhere and all you have to do is look at someone and walk away and then . . . "Was you looking at me?" and it starts too much trouble.
Louise:	They still hit ya.

Talking of not being able to walk away from trouble Geri notes:

Geri:	And you don't really want to back down when all your mates are around 'cos it makes you look silly.

Asked whether the fights are promoted through racial tension Barbara confirms that it is "mostly whites against blacks," and is usually fights between smaller numbers of young women:

Barbara:	If there is girls I'd say it was two on one, or one on one on the streets.

I have argued above that the young women in my study who live within a complex of high crime inner-city estates make use of different outdoor areas to relieve the pressures generated within overcrowded indoor spaces. The streets, landings, and stairways become places where private activities take place: meeting friends and hanging about. This contradicts the proposition that the street is exclusively a male domain, a contestation supported by the young men in the study who argue that their female counterparts have more freedom to wander through different areas than they do themselves. Through such use of the streets, stairways, and landings young women develop knowledge of, and play a part in, everyday violence and disorder. In the main, this is a consequence of daily "run of the mill" activities on the estate. It could, however, highlight behavior that media coverage would identify as the property of the "girl hooligan": the "violent" girl rampaging the street. Each of these descriptions could be used to present a picture of an individual, isolated, and violent young woman causing a public nuisance. If the knife, carried as protection, did end up being used in self-defense one evening on the way to the night club; if the Bengali young woman speaking above of "backing" to abusers threw stones in retaliation rather than turned away; if the game of chase resulted in the iron bar being turned on the shopkeeper, the young women would be seen as committing a violent act. In fact these remain incidents of everyday life that fail to attract the attention of the public eye or pass unnoticed by the youth worker or researcher who is concentrating on conflicts between young men. Thus, the complex ways that young women on the estates negotiate through their everyday encounters with danger and violence is lost to view while isolated incidents focus attention on one or two individuals who are then regarded as "different" from their other female counterparts.

Young Women and the Street: Violence against the Vulnerable

I want now to look at situations when the balance is tipped and the street becomes the bedroom itself: the permanent escape from home. Young women who run from home, firstly for a night but then increasingly for longer periods of time, can find themselves living on the street, usually in unfamiliar territory. As noted above, many young women experience the street as local playground, a playground with which they develop a relationship over time. It is the depth of this relationship that gives them reliable knowledge of potential and actual dangers. By contrast, young women running from home move into unknown territory and will be poorly equipped to cope with potential danger and exploitation. In these situations the majority of young women fall off the tightrope between showing themselves to be capable of being a domestic object indoors (a "drag") on the one hand and a sexual object outdoors (a "slag") on the other (Lees 1993). As the

scope to be domestic within the home disappears, survival increasingly involves the risk of sexual exploitation and associated violence in
unfamiliar places outdoors.

While young people from all social, racial, and economic backgrounds may run from home at times in their childhood (Shaw et al.
1996; Patel 1994), it is predominantly those from homes with few economic or social resources to support them who develop consistent
"running careers," staying longer away from home each time until
eventually failing to return (Pitts 1997; Safe on the Street Research Team
1999). Centrepoint, a charity in London for homeless young people
notes that 39 percent of those children under sixteen years of age who
used their refuge had no income or money of their own, a further
48 percent only having up to £39 to their name (Centrepoint 1997: 6).
Faced with poverty and social marginalization, young women on the
street become particularly vulnerable to physical and sexual exploitation in return for accommodation, money, or drugs.

Awareness of the pressures facing these young people in general,
and young women in particular, is not new. Lee and O'Brien argued in
1995 that young people invariably swap sex for somewhere to stay,
something to eat, for drugs or other payment in kind. The young person
is introduced to prostitution as a means of surviving, often in a way that
reproduces previous histories of abuse from which they have run (Lee &
O'Brien 1995). Through recent research it has become apparent that
many women start the work, not only as a conscious effort to survive,
but as a result of persuasive coercion, often involving violence from the
very people on the street who claimed to be their friends. Retrospective
studies where women working in the sex industry have provided accounts of where and why they started selling sex, reveal that initial contact with "friends" on the street can lead to dependency and abuse. The
befriender encourages the young woman to become dependant upon
them, often as a boyfriend who claims to provide support, such as access
to accommodation, money, or gifts and drugs. This quickly shifts to a dependency, which is abused through violence, drug misuse, and sexual
exploitation (Melrose, Barrett, & Brodie 1999; Pitts 1997).

It has been widely documented that many women who are selling
sex started their work while young adults or children (Barrret 1997;
Green 1992; Jesson 1993; Lee & O'Brien 1995; Scrambler & Scrambler
1997). One study noted that thirty-two of a sample of forty-six women
and four men interviewed became involved in prostitution before they
were sixteen, three-quarters (twenty-four) of whom started when they
were fourteen or younger (Melrose et al. 1999: 25). Similarly, research
with forty-three women selling sex in a Northern English town showed

that 65 percent of the forty-three women interviewed were under seventeen years of age when they started selling sex, 27 percent of these being aged between thirteen and sixteen years old (Pearce & Roach 1997).

This same research also showed that younger women were particularly vulnerable to coercion from violent friends or partners, 46 percent of the women noting that they started working against their will, while 37 percent of them started because of pressure from partners and peers. As younger women they felt particularly vulnerable to violence and coercion, being less equipped to insist on practicing safe sex or to be aware of the potential threats to their safety. The older women noted that it is with time and experience that women learn how to "spot a dodgy client" and to gain confidence to avoid potentially violent situations, which were a reality of everyday life. Fifty-three percent noted experiences of violence on the street, defining violence as being hit, robbed, raped, kicked, and physically attacked. Twenty-one percent experienced violent attacks on a daily, 35 percent weekly, and 9 percent on a monthly basis. Fifty-seven percent of the women noted that the violence was perpetrated by people known to them, invariably this being their partner who would depend upon the women's work to fund their own drug habit (Pearce and Roache 1997: 44). Similarly, a more recent survey in Glasgow, Leeds, and Edinburgh showed that prostitutes working outdoors were younger than those working indoors and that more than 80 percent of the women selling sex on the street experienced violence while they were working. Thirty-seven percent of the women had been robbed, 24 percent threatened with a weapon, 25 percent held against their will, 20 percent having been kidnapped, 20 percent experienced strangulation, 22 percent experienced vaginal rape, and 17 percent forced to give the client oral sex (Church, Henderson, Barnard, & Hart 2001). It is the street where women experience most violence, and as young women under the age of eighteen are more likely to start selling sex on the street, rather than in saunas, they are particularly vulnerable to these violent attacks (McKeganey & Barnard 1996).

As noted in the earlier discussion of young people's use of the local streets, violence is not separate from other everyday events, but is integrated into the general experience of life on the street. While young women may aggravate adults for fun by playing chase on their local estates, it is invariably the younger women who take more risks "playing," or testing the boundaries, with punters. Young women are more likely to practice "clipping," where money that was to be paid in exchange for sex is snatched from the punter without a service being provided. Such actions can leave them at risk of violent recrimination (Crosby & Barrett 1999: 128). Reprimand and recrimination from clipping and from associated labels such as "prostitute" have been argued to attribute blame to young people who are vulnerable and needy.

This vulnerability is not only to violent attack but also to increased dependency on drugs. Young women who may initially have been encouraged to work to fund the drug habit of a friend or partner quickly become dependent themselves. Pearce and Roache noted that 43 percent of the forty-six women interviewed said that they started the work to pay for drugs, 39 percent doing so to pay for drugs for their partners. Once the women became dependant upon using drugs themselves, often as a means of enabling them to cope with the pressures of the work, 56 percent worked subsequently to pay for their own drug use (Pearce & Roache 1997: 37). Crosby and Barrett (1999) argue that the problems facing sexually exploited young people on the street must take due consideration of drug misuse. They note that it is generally accepted that women who work from the street, rather than other locations, are more likely to use drugs and that the work "can often lead to a rapid escalation in drug use which then necessitates them working longer hours and more frequently in order to make enough money to fund their habit" (Crosby & Barrett 1999: 128).

Yet it is younger women who are less likely to approach support services that may be able to provide some assistance. The fear of systems of care and control taking command of the (relative) freedom that they ran away to find, discourages many young people on the run from accessing police, outreach workers, and specialist support workers (Rees 1993; Kirby 1995; Hayes & Trafford 1997). The street provides a more secretive space where younger women can work according to their own time schedules, freer from the official regulations and inspections that preside over the running of saunas. However, as noted above, it is the younger women who become particularly susceptible to dangers on the street and who are often poorly equipped to cope.

While our understanding of the extent of violence against vulnerable young women on the street is developing, responses in policy and practice interventions remain limited (Barrett 1997; Safe on the Streets Research Team 1999). As we need further outreach work and research to understand young women's regular day to day use of their own local streets, so too do we need to assess the ways that, detached from a home, these same young women can be used and abused by street life. To facilitate this understanding, we need to acknowledge that young women are not hidden behind closed doors within private locations but are engaging in the public world. It is through such engagement that, with appropriate support, young women can develop the tactics and strategies that allow them to cope with violence they feel or experience and make independent, informed decisions about their transition into adulthood.

I argue that there is a continuum: between the more mundane, everyday experiences of young women's relationship with violence on the street; through the early stages of a "running career," where the street becomes a permanent pathway from a familiar area; to a situation where the young woman may be dislocated from home and potentially more vulnerable to dangerousness and sexual violence. Although not all young women who use the street as a place to play then run from home, or find themselves sexually exploited, we all too often fail to understand the complexities within such transitions. This can allow young women who play with violence on their local streets to be demonized for transgressing gender boundaries or can sexualize those who are vulnerable, making them into objects of intrigue and desire. Until we open the door to allow young women's part in the broader picture of the understanding of violence and the public domain to be explained, we limit both our knowledge and the support that could be made available to them.

References

Anderson, E. 1997, "Violence and the inner city street code" in J. McCord (ed), *Violence and childhood in the inner city*, Cambridge Criminology Series. Cambridge University Press, Cambridge, pp.1–30.

Anderson, S., Loader, I. & Kinsey, R. 1994, *Cautionary Tales*, Avebury, Aldershot.

Back, L. 1990, *Racist name calling and developing anti-racist initiatives in youth work*, Research paper in Ethnic Relations, No 14: ESRC. Warwick: Centre for research in Ethnic Relations.

Barrett, D. (ed) 1997, *Child prostitution in Britain: dilemmas and practical responses*, The Children's Society, London.

Brown, J., Burman, M. & Tisdall, K. 2000, "Just trying to be men? Violence, girls, and their social worlds," in J. Lawrence & P. Starkey (eds), *Child welfare and social action in the twentieth century*, Liverpool University Press, Liverpool.

Campbell, A. 1991, *The girls in the gang*, Blackwell, Cambridge.

Campbell, B. 1993, *Goliath: Britain's dangerous places*, Methuen, London.

Carpenter, V. & Young, K. 1986, *Coming in from the margins: youth work with girls and young women*, Spider Web, London.

CentrePoint 1997, *Centrepoint Annual Report 1996–1997: Getting young people out of boxes*, Centrepoint, London.

Church, S., Henderson, M., Barnard, M. & Hart, G. 2001, "Violence by clients towards female prostitutes in different work settings: questionnaire survey," *British Medical Journal*, vol. 322, 3 March 2001, pp. 524–25.

Clark, J. 1997, *Nightmare of the bully girls culture, The Daily Mail*, Thursday, June 5, p. 7.

Clarke, R. V. & Mayhew, P. (eds) 1980, *Designing out crime*, HMSO, London.

Cohen, P. (ed) 1999, *New ethnicities, old racisms*, Zed Books, London.

Cohen, P., Keith, M. & Back, L. 1996, *Issues of theory and method*, New Ethnicities Unit of East London, Centre for Urban and Community Research, Goldsmiths College, University of London, London.

Crawford, A. 1998, *Crime prevention and community safety*, Longman, London.

Crawford, A. 1999, *The local governance of crime: appeals to community partnerships*, Oxford University Press, Oxford.

Crosby, S. & Barrett, D. 1999, "Poverty, drugs, and youth prostitution: a case study," in A. Marlow & G. Pearson (eds), *Young People, Drugs, and Community Safety*, Russell House Publishing, Lyme Regis, pp. 127–34.

Evans, K.1998, "Community safety in high crime neighbourhoods: a view from the street," in A. Marlow & J. Pitts (eds), *Planning safer communities*, Russell House Publishing, Lyme Regis, pp. 181–89.

Fitzgerald, M. & Hale, C. 1996, *Ethnic minorities: victimisation and racial harassment*, Home Office Research Study 154. Home Office Research and Statistics Directorate, London.

Gilroy, P. 1987, *There ain't no black in the Union Jack*, Hutchinson, London.

Green, J. 1992, *It's no game*, National Youth Agency, Leicester.

Haraway, D. 1991, *Simians, cyborgs, and women*, Free Association Books, London.

Hayes, C. & Trafford, I. 1997, "Issues for voluntary sector detached work agencies," in D. Barrett (ed), *Child prostitution in Britain*, The Children's Society, London, pp. 59–76.

Holloway, W. & Jefferson, T. 2000, *Doing qualitative research differently: free association, narrative and the interview method*, Sage, London.

Hope, T. 1998, "Community safety, crime, and disorder," in A. Marlow & J. Pitts (eds), *Planning Safer Communities*, Russell House Publishing, Lyme Regis, pp. 168–81.

Hudson, A. 1988, "Boys will be boys: masculinism and the juvenile justice system," in *Critical Social Policy*, no. 21, pp. 30–48.

Jesson, J. 1993, "Understanding adolescent female prostitution: a literature review," in *British Journal of Social Work*, no. 23, pp. 517–30.

Kirby, P. 1995, *A word from the street: Young people who leave care and become homeless*, Centre point/Community Care/Reed Business publishing, London.

L. A. 1995, *Living in a London borough: A survey of the attitudes of secondary school pupils*, available from J. J. Pearce, Middlesex University.

Lee, M. & O'Brien, R. 1995, *The games up: redefining child prostitution*, The Children's Society, London.

Lees, S. 1993, *Sugar and spice: sexuality and adolescent girls*, Penguin Books, London.

Marlow, A. & Pitts, J. 1998, *Planning safer communities*, Russell House Publishing, Lyme Regis.

Mason, A. & Palmer, A. 1996, *Queer bashing: a national survey of hate crimes against lesbians and gays*, Stonewall, London.

Massey 1998, "The spatial construction of youth cultures," in T. Skelton & G. Valentine (eds), *Cool places: geographies of youth cultures*, Routledge, London, pp. 121–30.

McKeganey, N. & Barnard, M. 1996, *Sex work on the streets*, Open University Press, Buckingham, Pa.

McRobbie, A. & Garber, J. 1976, "Girls and sub-cultures," in S. Hall & T. Jefferson (eds), *Resistance through rituals: youth subcultures in post-war Britain*, Hutchinson and Co., London, pp. 209–23.

McRobbie, A. 1991, *Feminism and youth culture: from jackie to just seventeen*, Macmillan Education, Basingstoke.

———. 1994, *Postmodernism and popular culture*, Routledge, London.

Melrose, M., Barrett, D. & Brodie, I. 1999, *One way street: retrospectives on childhood prostitution*, The Children's Society, London.

Mirrlees Black, C., Budd, T., Partridge, S. & Mayhew, P. 1998, *The British crime survey: England and Wales*, Home Office, London.

Mirza, H. 1992, *Young, female, and black*, Routledge, London.

Newburn, T. & Stanko, E. 1994, *Just boys doing the business: men masculinities and crime*, Routledge, London.

Patel, G. 1994, *The Porth project: a study of homelessness and running away amongst vulnerable black people in Newport, Gwent*, The Children's Society, London.

Pearce, J. J. 1996, "Urban youth cultures: gender and spatial forms," in *Youth and Policy*, no. 52, pp. 1–12.

Pearce, J. & Roache, P. 1997, *Report into the links between prostitution, drugs, and violence*, Society of Voluntary Associates (SOVA), Sheffield.

Pearce, J. & Stanko, E. 1999, "Young women and community safety," in *Youth and Policy*, no. 66, pp. 1–19.

Pearson, G. 1983, *Hooligan: a history of respectable fears*, Macmillan, London.

Pease, K. 1998, *Repeat victimisation: taking stock*, Crime Prevention and Detection Series paper 90. Home Office Police Research Group, London.

Pitts, J. 1997, "Causes of youth prostitution, new forms of practice and political responses," in D. Barrett (ed), *Child prostitution in Britain: dilemmas and practical responses*, The Children's Society, London, pp. 139–58.

———. 1998, "Young people, crime, and citizenship," in Marlow, A. & Pitts, J. *Planning Safer Communities*, Russell House Publishing, Lyme Regis, pp. 84–98.

Rees, G. 1993, *Hidden truths: young people's experiences of running away*, The Children's Society, London.

Safe on The Street Research team 1999, *Still running: children on the streets in the UK*, The Children's Society, London.

Scrambler, G. & Scrambler, A. (eds) 1997, *"Rethinking prostitution: purchasing sex in the 1990's,"* Routledge, London.

Shaw, I., Butler, I., Crowley, A. & Patel, G. 1996, *Paying the price: young people and prostitution in South Glamorgan*, School of Social and Administrative Studies, University of Wales, College of Cardiff.

Sibley, D. 1995, *Geographies of exclusion*, Routledge, London.

Skelton, T. & Valentine, G. (eds) 1998, *Cool places: geographies of youth cultures*, Routledge, London.

Small, S. 1994, *Racialised barriers: the black experience in the United States and England in the 1980's*, Routledge, London.

Stanko, E. 1998, *Taking stock: what do we know about violence?* ESRC Violence Research Programme, Brunel University, Middlesex.

Walklate, S. 1995, *Gender and crime: an introduction*, Prentice-Hall, London.

Watt, P. & Stenson, K. 1998, "The street: 'It's a bit dodgy round there' safety, danger, ethnicity, and young people's use of public space," in T. Skelton & G. Valentine (eds), *Cool places: geographies of youth cultures*, Routledge, London, pp. 249–66.

Zukin, S. 1995, *The cultures of cities*, Blackwell, Oxford.

Chapter Eight

Violence in the Schoolyard: School Girls' Use of Violence

Sibylle Artz

Schoolyard violence became a serious concern in North America in the early 1990s as evidence from school systems across Canada and the United States showed that violence in schools was on the rise (Bibby & Posterski 1992; Hamilton 1993; Cameron, deBruijne, Kennedy, & Morin 1994; Mathews 1994; Ryan, Mathews, & Banner 1993; and Boothe, Bradley, Flick, Keough, & Kirk 1993). In particular, interest was sparked in a marked increase in the participation of girls in violent activities.

In research on this subject, schoolyard violence is often referred to as "bullying", a term that suffers from interpretative difficulties. *Webster's Ninth New Collegiate Dictionary* (1991) provides the following definitions: "1. *archaic* **a:** SWEETHEART **b:** a fine chap 2. **a:** a blustering browbeating fellow; *esp* . . . one habitually cruel to others weaker than himself; **b:** the protector of a prostitute: PIMP . . ." (187). The cruel abuse of power inherent in bullying is sometimes masked by the less threatening interpretations attributed to the term—protector, blusterer, or fine fellow. Especially confusing is the notion that a bully also protects those who adhere to him or her, as does a pimp. Bullies attract followings largely because they offer a sense of security, however false, even to those they exploit so long as they remain loyal and under the bully's control.

Researchers have defined bullying as "an interaction in which a dominant individual (the bully) repeatedly exhibits aggressive behavior intended to cause distress to a less dominant individual (the victim)" (Craig, Peters, & Konarski 1998: 1). Bullies gain power over their victims

151

Figure 8.1
Percentage of Canadian Students who bullied
others in school in 1993/94 and 1997/98

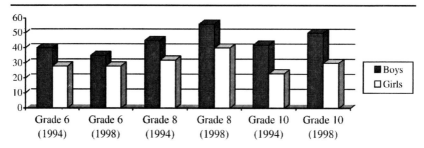

Source: Auditor General of British Columbia 2000, "Fostering a Safe Learning Environment: How the British Columbia Public School System is Doing," Office of the Auditor General of British Columbia, Victoria, B.C., p. 113.

through a variety of means: physical strength, status within the peer group, knowing another child's weaknesses, or recruiting the support of other children (Connolly, Pepler, Craig, & Taradash 2000).

Bullying is prevalent at similar frequency in Canadian, Australian, Scandinavian and English schools (Pepler & Connolly 2000; Connolly, Pepler, Craig, & Taradash 2000). It occurs once every seven minutes on school playgrounds and once every twenty-five minutes in classrooms (Craig and Pepler 1997). In school playground interactions, 68 percent of children have been observed in both the role of bully and the role of victim (Pepler & Sedighdeilami 1998).

In Canada the most recent national data available indicate a slight rise from 1993-94 to 1997-98 in the percentage of school girls who report bullying others and having been bullied (see Figures 8.1 and 8.2). Bullying was found to be most prevalent at ages twelve and thirteen (grades seven and eight), with 56 percent of boys and 40 percent of girls admitting that they had bullied someone in 1998 (Auditor General of British Columbia 2000).

Comparing Violent School Girls And Boys

Aggressive and violent girls, much like aggressive and violent boys, experience greater problems than nonaggressive and nonviolent girls in their families of origin (Pepler & Sedighdeilami 1998). Their family dynamics are characterized by parental and sibling strife and family

Figure 8.2
Percentage of Canadian students who were bullied
in school in 1993/94 and 1997/98

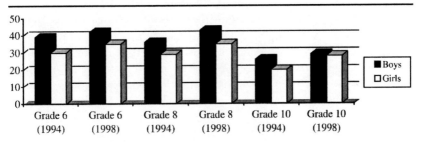

Source: Auditor General of British Columbia 2000, "Fostering a Safe Learning Environment: How the British Columbia Public School System is Doing." Office of the Auditor General of British Columbia, Victoria, B.C., p. 113.

violence grounded in fathers' use of intimidation and violence to dominate family members (Artz & Riecken 1994; Artz 1998; Artz, Riecken, MacIntyre, Lam, & Maczewski 1999; Artz, Blais, & Nicholson 2000; Artz 2000).

The influence of family on the development of aggression and violence in children has been well documented (literature reviews on the subject by Flowers 1990; Whithecomb 1997; Augimeri, Webster, Kogel, & Levene 1998). Family characteristics linked to youthful violence include: socioeconomic deprivation and poverty, harsh and inconsistent parenting, marital discord, spousal, parental, and sibling violence, poor parental mental health, physical and sexual abuse, and parental alcoholism, drug dependency, and other substance misuse.

Parents play a significant role in the development of aggressive behaviors among children. There is a strong relationship between such behavior in children and hostile parental interactions and inconsistent and harsh punishment practices (Craig, Peters, & Konarski 1998). Girls' aggression at home and with peers is significantly related with mothers' and fathers' verbal and physical aggression, negative parental communication styles, parental rejection, and low parental support (Leschied, Cummings, Van Brunschot, Cunningham, & Saunders 2000). Cavell (2000) suggests that social learning models explain the influence of parental practices on the development of childhood aggression. Such models propose that aggressive behavior is developed and maintained through the use of negative reinforcement and escape conditioning in parent-child interactions.

Violent schoolgirls and boys have a number of other things in common. They experience greater problems than their nonaggressive peers in their psychosocial domains, where they suffer from greater emotional problems, negative self-concepts, behavioral difficulties, and academic challenges (Pepler & Sedighdeilami 1998). Both violent schoolgirls and boys reported associating with the same peer groups and placing high importance on having the right kinds of clothes (that allowed them to fit in with their group or gang), on popularity, and on attending parties. At the same time, they reported similar rates of victimization by groups or gangs of kids (Artz & Riecken 1994; Artz, Riecken, Van Domselaar, & Laliberté 1994).

Violent schoolgirls and boys were also similar in their endorsement and participation in rule-breaking, deviant, and delinquent behaviors. They shared in the endorsement and use of direct and indirect violence at significantly higher levels than nonviolent youth. Further, they reported smoking without parents' permission, lying to parents, staying out all night without permission, skipping classes or school, stealing items that did not belong to them, stealing from stores, ruining something that belonged to their parents after an argument, drinking alcohol, smoking marijuana, and using other illegal drugs at rates that were significantly higher than those reported by nonviolent schoolgirls and boys (Artz & Riecken 1994; Artz 1998; Artz, Riecken, MacIntyre, Lam, & Maczewski 1999).

While violent schoolgirls and boys are similar on a number of dimensions, Canadian studies identify key differences in their relationships with mother, fear of and experience with physical and sexual abuse, social and interpersonal values and self-concept (in particular as evidence in food consumption) (Artz & Riecken 1994; Artz 1998). Girls who use violence reported enjoying their relationships with their mothers to a significantly lesser degree than all other groups: nonviolent girls and boys and violent boys (Artz & Riecken 1994; Artz 1998). This observation is echoed in another study that found that girls with high trait anger (i.e., higher base levels of anger) have low maternal attachment (Wright, Cameron, & Susman, under review). Similarly, other findings indicate that conflictual family interactions, especially between mothers and their daughters, can prompt and sustain aggressive behavior in girls (Pepler & Sedighdeilami 1998). In their study of the development and treatment of girlhood aggression, Levene, Madsen, and Pepler (in press) found that the parents of the girls (usually mothers, because fathers were largely absent) who participated in their study had trouble setting limits and engaged in coercive and escalating interactions that often culminated in physically punitive action on the part of mothers.

Additionally, the parent child-relationships often appeared enmeshed, with unclear boundaries about the roles of parents and children, while sibling relationships were described as fraught with conflict.

Violent girls also reported significantly higher levels of fear of being physically abused at home along with significantly greater levels of experiencing physical abuse at home than all boys and nonviolent girls. These girls also reported significantly higher rates of fear of sexual victimization (being talked into sex against their will by a boyfriend and experiencing sexual abuse) along with significantly higher rates of sexual victimization than all other groups (Artz & Riecken 1994; Artz 1998; Artz, Riecken, MacIntyre, Lam, & Maczewski 1999).

Girls, whether violent or nonviolent, endorsed the reciprocal values of respect for others, forgiveness, politeness, honesty, concern for others, and generosity at significantly higher levels than boys, violent or nonviolent. Violent girls and nonviolent schoolgirls also reported the same higher levels of social concern for AIDS, child abuse, racial discrimination, violence against women, teenage suicide, drug abuse, and youth gangs. Violent girls expressed significantly higher levels of concern than all other groups for the unequal treatment of women, and violence in schools. As well, all girls, violent and nonviolent, reported seeing themselves as less capable, less confident, and less attractive than all boys, violent and nonviolent, and all girls stopped themselves from eating significantly more often than all boys (Artz & Riecken 1994; Artz 1998; Artz, Riecken, MacIntyre, Lam, & Maczewski 1999).

While violent schoolgirls participated in similar rule-breaking, deviant, and delinquent behaviors as violent boys, at the same time they experienced greater levels of abuse and victimization than all other groups. Further, they retained pro-social values, and in that regard had more in common with nonviolent girls than they did with any boys, violent or nonviolent (Artz & Riecken 1994; Artz 1998).

Forms of Violence

Early research suggested that girl bullies tended to use indirect or relational aggression to manipulate social groups through the use of name calling, verbal abuse, gossip and rumor, and social exclusion and shunning (Craig & Pepler 1997). Jones (1998), in a study of twelve to eighteen-year-old girls' school students, found evidence of bullying through exclusion and harassment in chat rooms and via e-mail. More recently, an analysis of Canada's National Longitudinal Survey of Children and Youth (NLSCY) concludes that "girls have higher levels of indirect aggression at every age, and that indirect aggression increases with age for both boys and girls" (Tremblay 2000: 20).

Boys, on the other hand, were thought to be more consistently instrumental than girls, that is, more physically and outwardly oriented and focused on power and control directed at external events (Leschied, Cummings, Van Brunschot, Cunningham, & Saunders 2000, citing Crick & Dodge 1994), while girls were thought to be more interpersonally oriented and focused on controlling relationships. In contrast to such claims, Moretti and Odgers (in press) state,

> Some studies have found, for example, that girls and boys engage in relational aggression to the same extent (Crick & Grotpeter 1996; Rys & Bear 1997). Indeed in some studies (Craig 1998; Henington, Hughes, Cavell, & Thompson 1998; Roecker, Caprini, Dickerson, Parks, & Barton 1999; Wolke, Woods, Bloomfield, and Karstadt 2000) boys are found to engage in even higher levels of relational aggression than are girls. (8)

Findings of two surveys of school children conducted in Canada indicated no consistently greater use of indirect and relational aggression by girls than boys. When 143 ten to twelve-year-old school children (seventy boys, seventy-three girls) were asked how they would respond if they were angry with another student because that person had been saying hurtful things about them, significantly more boys than girls reported that they would, "start rumors about that person to get even" (Artz, Riecken, MacIntyre, Lam, & Maczewski 1998). In another study involving 338 youth (183 males, 155 females) aged thirteen to sixteen years, it was found that nonviolent boys engage in name calling more often than violent girls.

Violent girls reported greater involvement than nonviolent boys in damaging something that belongs to someone else, greater use of blackmail, spreading more rumors, and shunning someone. However, violent boys reported engaging in more name calling and roughhousing than violent girls and there were no statistically significant differences between violent girls and violent boys for shunning, spreading rumors, using homophobic put-downs, obscene language, blackmail, threats, and damaging something that belongs to someone else.

When such behaviors as acting up in school and damaging school property are included as forms of indirect violence, again boys consistently reported significantly higher levels of involvement than girls (Artz, Riecken, Van Domselaar, & Laliberté, 1994; Artz, Riecken, MacIntyre, Lam, & Maczewski 1999). Overall, these findings suggest that boys, violent and nonviolent, use name calling more than girls, and that violent boys use at least as much indirect and relational violence as violent girls and in some cases use more.

A further study examined the use of indirect and relational violence by school-age youth who were incarcerated for their use of violence and whose workers (male and female) had raised concerns that girls were harder to work with (Artz, Blaise, & Nicholson 2000). The workers maintained that girls were far more feared than boys and more manipulative, mean, and cruel than boys. One male worker explained:

> A lot of the time, girls will come in here and they'll be so afraid of the other girls that even if they're living in a different unit, they'll stay in their room, so if all these girls are living in the same unit. . . . What kind of meaner? They're very degrading to each other, like the real bad bully, like guys will say, "fuck you," or "you're an asshole," but the girls get right down to the nitty gritty, like they'll make up stories about each other about screwing the other guys—as dirty as they can get, that's how dirty they'll get. Girls are just way more degrading. The boys are more physical. People are way more concerned about girl-to-girl violence. (Quoted in Artz 2000: 50)

Workers' concerns were echoed by the male and female youth. One girl described the dynamic as:

> Girls are mean. Girls are like here for a week before, they'll do it [victimize] mentally. . . . Like it's totally about power. They'll victimize them [other girls] and then they'll like beat them up. With guys, they'll like throw everything that they're doing down and then like, "Let's go!" And they'll fight and it's over. With girls it's like weeks and weeks . . . (quoted in Artz, Blais, & Nicholson 2000: 29)

A boy stated emphatically,

> I don't see any victimization [from] guys to girls here, just girls-to-girls (quoted in Artz, Blais, & Nicholson 2000: 56).

While workers and youth were quite clear in their beliefs that females used far more indirect and relational violence than males and that females are so much "meaner," the evidence gathered through case studies pointed in a different direction. Girls were more often victimized by boys than by girls. These boy-to-girl victimizations most often took the form of sexual abuse and sexual harassment, as in the following examples:

> It's in certain programs. You can go to the bathroom. . . . One of the guys told me that they did that. Guys get away with all this crap, right? They stick their hands down a girl's pants in here, and then do whatever for a while. It's like, "Where do you guys do all that stuff?" (A girl's description of where and how victimization takes place. Quoted in Artz, Blais, & Nicholson 2000: 28)

Boys gave clear descriptions of well-developed techniques for indirect and relational violence towards girls:

> A guy might say "Look at that ugly thing" when [a girl] walks by. (An example of a male verbally victimizing a female in Artz, Blais, & Nicholson 2000: 56)

Boys also harassed other boys:

> Victims are those who are geeks based on their attitudes, their looks or even the style of their running shoes. (Male youth's description of the labeling of other males in Artz, Blais, & Nicholson 2000: 56).

> He calls him names, makes him feel like scum, pushes him around a little. (Male youth's description of the use of indirect violence in combination with direct violence during intimidation in Artz, Blais, & Nicholson 2000: 56)

Other examples of indirect violence described by youths, but largely overlooked by workers, included the clenching of teeth, making a fist, and selected hand signals (Artz, Blaise & Nicholson 2000).

Direct Violence

The Canadian surveys that generated findings (Figure 8.3) in relation to self-reported involvement in direct aggression (Artz, Riecken, Van Domselaar, & Laliberté 1994; Artz, Riecken, MacIntyre, Lam, & Maczewski 1999) indicated that boys and girls reported significantly different levels of involvement in such behaviors as beating up another kid and carrying a weapon. These studies were part of a five-year longitudinal study of male and female participation in school-based violence prevention that tracked reported school-related incidents of violence and showed that males consistently participated in such incidents at significantly higher rates than females (Table 8.1). However, the majority of workers in schools and the youth justice system persisted in their beliefs that "girls are so much worse" (Artz 2000; Artz, Blaise, & Nicholson 2000; Artz, Riecken, MacIntyre, Lam, & Maczewski 1999).

The self-report data captured in Figure 8.3, and the violence participation rates captured in Table 8.1 (provided by the schools that participated in the study), indicate that, indeed, males appear to be more active with regard to direct violence. It is, however, noteworthy, that in general, both groups show a decline in their participation in violence over the five-year period of the study. Nevertheless, caution is required in interpreting such data because of the difficulties involved in making sense of changes in percentage when comparisons are being made between groups where one group , in this case females, has such small numbers to begin.

Overall, research suggests that boys and girls both participate in a variety of forms of violence; therefore, given the possibility raised by the currently conflicting findings regarding especially indirect violence, it may be premature to conclude that there are definitive gender differences with regard to domains of violence. A more fruitful comparison may be the examination of gender differences in contexts of violence with a view

Figure 8.3
**Participation Rates in Violence: Males' and females'
self reports: 1993 and 1998**

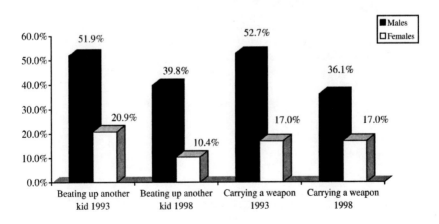

Source: Artz, Riecken, MacIntyre, Lam, & Maczewski 1999: 10

Table 8.1
Ratio Male - Female Incidents across all Participating Schools

	1994/95	1995/96	1996/97	1997/98	1998/99
Average male incidents per year	340.6	299.7	276.5	248	182.4
Average female incidents per year	133.6	116	104.9	78.5	85.9
Ratio male-female incidents	**2.5 : 1**	**2.6 : 1**	**2.6 : 1**	**3.2 : 1**	**2.1 : 1**

Source: Artz, Riecken, MacIntyre, Lam, & Maczewski 1999: 21

to better understanding the conditions under which girls and boys tend to use violence. In this chapter, given the focus of this book, the contexts of girls' use of violence will be examined. Boys' contexts will only briefly be referred to, thus leaving the door open for future work.

The Context of Girls' Use of Violence

Girls fight other girls largely to defend their sexual reputations or their connection to a boyfriend and describe themselves as competing for male attention on the "pretty power" hierarchy (Artz 2000). As one sixteen-year-old girl participating in an ongoing study on high risk girls explained,

> I hate girls, they're always in competition for boys, always calling each other sluts, whores and bitches, always worrying about how they look. (Artz, Nicholson, Lark, & Halsall, in progress)

Boys fight other boys to establish and maintain dominance within their group and territory and to display their masculinity and their adherence to the boy code. (Pollock 1998; Riecken 2000). As one seventeen-year-old boy explained,

> [Life is] hard, On the streets, it's just hard, 'cause everybody's always thinking of killing, selling drugs, violence this, violence that. . . . I answer violence with violence . . . toughness is what counts, [I] can't walk away from a fight.

Both girls and boys are ultimately seeking male approval and acceptance, girls however, are always second in line. Violent schoolgirls struggle with sexual objectification, mistrust, and misogyny and experience
relationships with other girls and even other boys, not so much as bonds
of friendship, but as alliances of power (Artz, in press). Violent school-
boys are concerned with maintaining a masculine image and resist engaging in any behavior that may make them vulnerable to accusations of
not being man enough (Garbarino 1999; Pollack 1998; Riecken 2000).

Tanenbaum (1999) suggests that when girls are confronted with
someone who does not fit their idea of the ways girls "should" act or
look, they grasp for a sexually insulting label. This reflects the extent to
which the systematic devaluation and sexual objectification of women
and girls is culturally embedded (Wolf 1997; Chesney-Lind & Shelden
1998). Of course, girls are not the only ones to use insulting labels to describe and control girls. Girls are subjected also to derogatory and de-
meaning sexual labeling by boys and on occasion by adults. For example,
a teacher in referring to the hairdo of a fourteen-year-old asked her, "Is
that little bun on your head meant to match the two on your chest?"
When challenged first by the student and later by the school principal the
teacher suggested that neither of them "could take a joke" (Artz 1997).

Among adolescents, the label "slut" is often used to single out a girl
who is viewed as deserving of aggression. The key informants in Artz
(1998) noted that in most, but not all cases, they beat up other girls primarily because they saw these girls as "sluts" who threatened their relationships with males. These key informants felt justified in attacking
"sluts" and saw them as deserving of being beaten because they were
sexually provocative or promiscuous. They also felt justified and honor-
bound in attacking those who attempted to attach this label to them.

Creighton and Farr (1999) in interviewing 133 non–high risk youth
(seventy-five female and fifty-eight males), also found clear indications
that indeed

> [t]he link between being labeled a slut and being targeted for sex-
> ualized violence is clearly demonstrated by some youth's beliefs.
> That is, some teens feel that guys are sexually "entitled" to certain
> girls and that these girls (labeled as sluts) have lost the right to say
> "no" or that they don't mean "no." The teens agreed that nobody
> deserves to be sexually assaulted, however many stated that sluts
> are "asking for it." (Creighton and Farr 1999: 4)

That insults directed toward girls by other girls and boys often
involve sexuality, reflects their perspective on the place of females

within our culture. In their research in schools, Sadker and Sadker (1994) found that girls generally had a higher awareness than boys of forms of gender discrimination and the way gender "works" in society. When girls "buy in" to being inferior and maintaining "their place" in deference to males, they often enact these beliefs in their aggression toward other girls, especially those that they perceive to be breaking gender "rules." The violent girls in Artz (1998, 2000) espoused beliefs that are similar to those that support male-to-female violence—patriarchal rights to control and dominate females. These girls tended to attack other girls in order to maintain alliances of power that enable them to attract males. Thus, violent girls' social interactions involve a constant battle for dominance of girls over girls in search of male attention.

Conclusion

Girls who endorse male dominance are more likely to use violence in their own lives (Bennett, Addams, & Fineran 1997). Further attitudes maintaining that a woman's body and sexuality are her only assets serve to perpetuate various forms of abuse of girls by both girls and boys (Jiwani 1998). Violent girls, in emulating boys' devaluation of girls and women, in joining them in similar rule-breaking, deviant, and delinquent behaviors and attitudes, and in attacking other girls in search of male attention, are demonstrating their limited access to alternative ways of understanding themselves and others, and are exhibiting classic oppressed group behavior (Freire 1984; Roberts 1983). Their worlds and self-concepts are being shaped by a dominant group, in this case males, who determine their value. Boys, in enacting violence, assert their power, girls in enacting violence, because of their subservience to male acceptance and male attention, subvert their power and perpetuate the sexual double standard.

The challenge for theorists, researchers, and all those who seek to understand and assist violent girls is helping them to break free from what Diane Fuss (1992) calls the "homospectatorial" gaze, that is, viewing themselves and the world through the hegemonic male gaze that includes a continual referencing of their worth and their range of choice against the standards set by males. Ultimately, as long as girls are locked in to "a way of looking that is being looked upon" and through this way of looking frame their actions, they are, as Mary Gergen (2001) points out, "in some sense blind" (147). As long as girls are thus blinded, their choices are foreclosed and they are not free in any real way to choose and be held fully accountable for their choices. Under such circumstances, not even their violence is truly their own.

References

Artz, S. 1998, *Sex, power, and the violent school girl*, Trifolium. Toronto.

———. 2000, "Considering adolescent girls" use of violence: a researcher's reflections on her inquiry," *The B.C. Counsellor*, vol. 22, no. 1.

———. (in press), "The guys here degrade you: youth perspectives on sex." *Journal of Child and Youth Care*.

Artz, S., Blais, M. & Nicholson, D. 2000, "Developing girls' custody units," unpublished Report, Justice Canada.

Artz, S., Nicholson, D., Larke, S. & Halsall, E. (in progress). "Developing a gender-sensitive community needs assessment tool for supporting at-risk girls and young women," National Crime Prevention Centre, Ottawa.

Artz, S. & Riecken, T. 1994, "A study of violence among adolescent female students in a suburban school district," unpublished Report, British Columbia Ministry of Education, Victoria, B.C.

Artz, S., Riecken, T., Van Domselaar, T. & Laliberté, P. 1994, "A study of violence among adolescent female students in a suburban school district: Phase I: A survey of student life," unpublished Report, British Columbia Ministry of Education, Victoria, B.C.

Artz, S., Riecken, T., MacIntyre, B., Lam, E. & Maczewski, M. 1998, "A community-based violence prevention project, University of Victoria and School District 62 at Sooke," BC Health Research Foundation Fifth Quarter Report, August 16, 1997-January 21, 1998, BC Health Research Foundation, Vancouver, B.C.

———. 1999, "A community-based violence prevention project," BC Health Research Foundation, Final Report, September 1999, BC Health Research Foundation, Vancouver, B.C.

Auditor General of British Columbia, 2000, "Fostering a safe learning environment: how the British Columbia public school system is faring," Office of the Auditor General of British Columbia, Victoria, B.C.

Augimeri, L., Webster, C., Koegl, C. & Levene, K. 1998, "EARL-20B: Early Assessment Risk List for Boys, Version 1, consultation edition." Earlscourt Family Centre, Toronto.

Bennett, L., Addams, J. & Fineran, S. 1997, "Sexual and severe physical violence of high school students: power beliefs, gender, and relationship." Paper presented at the 74th Annual meeting of the American Orthopsychiatric Association, Toronto, March 1997.

Bibby, R. W., & Posterski, D. C. 1992, *Teen trends*, Stoddart, Toronto.

Boothe, J., Bradley, L., Flick, M., Keough, K. & Kirk, S. 1993, "The violence at your door," *The Executive Educator*, February 1993, pp. 16–21.

Cameron, E., deBruijne, L., Kennedy, K. & Morin, J. 1994, "British Columbia Teachers' Federation Task Force on Violence in Schools, Final Report," British Columbia Teachers' Federation, Vancouver, B.C.

Cavell, T. 2000, *Working with parents of aggressive children: a practitioners guide,* American Psychological Association, Washington, D.C.

Chesney-Lind, M. & Shelden, R. 1992, *Girls, delinquency, and juvenile justice,* Brooks/Cole, Pacific Grove, Cal.

———. 1998, *Girls, delinquency and juvenile justice,* 2nd edition, West/Wadsworth, Belmont, Cal.

Connolly, J., Pepler, D., Craig, W. & Taradash, A. 2000, "Dating experiences of bullies in early adolescence," *Child Maltreatment*, vol. 5, no. 4, pp. 299–310.

Craig, W. 1998, "The relationship among bullying, victimization, depression, anxiety, and aggression in elementary school children," *Personality and Individual Differences,* no. 24, pp. 123–30.

Craig, W., Peters, R. & Konarski, R. 1998, "Bullying and victimization among Canadian school children," paper presented at Investing in Children: A National Research Conference, Ottawa.

Craig, W. & Pepler, D. 1997, "Naturalistic observations of bullying and victimization on the playground," unpublished Report, LaMarsh Research Centre on Violence and Conflict Resolution, York University.

Creighton, G. & Farr R. 1999, "Sexpectations: youths perceptions of sexual assault Report 2," unpublished Report, Victoria Women's Sexual Assault Centre, Victoria, B.C.

Crick, N. & Dodge, K. 1994, "A review and reformulation of social information-processing mechanisms in children's social maladjustment," *Psychological Bulletin*, no. 115, pp. 74–101.

Crick, N. & Grotpeter, J. 1996, "Children's treatment by peers: victims of relational and overt aggression," *Development and Psychology,* vol. 8, pp. 367–380.

Flowers, R. 1990, *The adolescent criminal: an examination of today's juvenile offender,* McFarland & Company, Jefferson, N.C.

Freire, P. 1984, *Pedagogy of the oppressed,* Continuum, New York.

Fuss, D. 1992, "Fashion and The Homospectatorial Look," in Gates Jr. & K. Appiah (eds), 1995, *Criticism in identity literature.* University of Chicago Press, Chicago.

Garbarino, J. 1999, *Lost boys: why our sons turn violent and how we can save them,* The Free Press, New York.

Gergen, M. 2001, *Gaze and the naked maja,* Sage Publications, Thousand Oaks, Cal.

Hamilton, J. 1993, "It's a jungle out there," In *Leading the way to violence free schools*, Conference Handbook, British Columbia School Trustees Association/British Columbia Teachers' Federation Conference, BCSTA, Vancouver, B.C.

Henington, C., Hughes, J., Cavell, T. & Thompson, B. 1998, "The role of relational aggression in identifying aggressive boys and girls," *Journal of School Psychology*, no. 36, pp. 457–77.

Jiwani, J. 1998, *Trafficking and sexual exploitation of girls and young women*, BC/ Yukon Feminist Research, Education, Development and Action (FREDA) Centre, Vancouver, B.C.

Jones, C. 1998, "New-age bullies use cyberspace to harass peers," *www.theage. com.au/daily/981006/news/news15.html*

Leschied, A., Cummings, A., Van Brunschot, M., Cunningham, A. & Saunders, A. 2000, "Female adolescent aggression: a review of the literature and the correlates of aggression (User Report No. 2000-04)," Solicitor General Canada, Ottawa.

Levene, K., Madsen, K. & Pepler, D. (in press), "Girls growing up angry: a qualitative study," in D. Pepler, K. Madsen, K. Levene and C. Webster (eds), *Girlhood aggression*, Erlebaum, Toronto.

Mathews, F. 1994, *Youth on youth gangs*, Solicitor General Canada publication, Toronto & Ottawa.

Merten, D. 1997, "The meaning of meanness: popularity, competition and conflict among junior high school girls," *Sociology of Education*, no. 70, pp. 175–91.

Moretti, M. & Odgers, C. (in press), "Aggressive and violent girls: prevalence, profiles, and contributing factors," in, R. Corrado, R. Roesch & S. Hart (eds), *Multi-problem and violent youth: a foundation for comparative research*, IOS Press, Amsterdam.

Pepler, D. & Connolly, J. 2000, *Bullying and victimization: the problems and solutions for school-aged children*, National Crime Prevention Council, *Fact Sheet*, Ottawa.

Pepler, D. & Sedighdeilami, F. 1998, *Aggressive girls in Canada*, Human Resources Development Canada, Ottawa.

Pollack, W. 1998, *Real boys: rescuing our sons from the myths of boyhood*, Henry Holt, New York.

Rhys, G. & Bear, G. 1997, "Relational aggression and peer relations: gender and developmental issues," *Merrill-Palmer Quarterly*, no. 42, pp. 87-106.

Riecken, T. 2000, "'What's your problem, man?' (and how can I help?): redesigning the landscape of boyhood," *B.C. Counsellor*, vol. 22, no. 1.

Roberts, S. 1983, "Oppressed group behavior: implications for nursing," *Advances in Nursing Science*, July 1983, pp. 22–30.

Roecker, C. E., Caprini, J., Dickerson, J., Parks, E. & Barton, A. 1999, "Children's responses to overt and relational aggression, " paper presented at the Biennial Meeting of the Society for Research in Child Development, Albuquerque, N.M., March 1999.

Ryan, C., Mathews, F. & Banner, J. 1993, *Student perceptions of violence*, Central Toronto Youth Services, Toronto.

Sadker, M. & Sadker, D. 1994, *Failing at fairness: how our schools cheat girls*, Touchstone, New York.

Tanenbaum, L. 1999, *Slut!: growing up female with a bad reputation*, Seven Stories Press, New York.

Tremblay, R. 2000, "The origins of youth violence," *Isuma,* vol. 1, no. 2, pp. 19–24.

Webster 1991, *Webster's Ninth New Collegiate Dictionary,* Thomas Allen & Sons, Markham, ON.

Whithecomb, J. 1997, "Causes of violence in children," *Journal of Mental Health,* vol. 6, no. 5, pp. 433–42.

Wolf, N. 1997, *Promiscuities: the secret struggle for womanhood,* Random House Canada Ltd, Toronto.

Wolke, D., Woods, S., Bloomfield, L. & Karstadt, L. 2000, "The association between direct and relational bullying and behavior problems among primary school children," *Journal of Child Psychology and Psychiatry,* no. 41, pp. 989–1002.

Wright, J., Cameron, C. A. & Susman, E. (under review), "Cortisol stress responses of angry girls," unpublished article, Fredricton, N.B.: Department of New Brunswick.

Chapter Nine

Situational Effects of Gender Inequality on Girls' Participation in Violence

Jody Miller and Norman A. White

The labeling of girls as increasingly violent is widespread. In the United States, "violent girls" are often characterized as an urban, racial minority, and most probably members of street gangs (see Chesney-Lind, this volume). However, few scholars outside of feminist circles have taken charge of challenging these labels and building a sophisticated understanding of girls' violence. In particular, there has not been sufficient effort to examine how girls' violence is produced within social contexts of inequality, and how it is shaped specifically by gender inequality.

Those who would seem best in a position to understand girls' violence—who have shown theoretical sensitivity and sophistication when explaining violence by young men—continue to fall short. Even the most lauded recent ethnographies of street violence fail to address girls' use of violence. For example, Anderson's (1999) *Code of the Streets,* heralded as one of the best contemporary works on inner-city violence, frames urban young women primarily as girlfriends, sexual partners, and teen mothers. In part this is a result of the peripheral space allotted to girls on the streets, which remain a male-dominated terrain (see Maher 1997; Miller 2001). But it is also a reflection of Anderson's and other ethnographers' failure to bring a sophisticated gendered lens to their investigations, and instead to view girls primarily through traditional frameworks.

Feminist scholars insist upon a critical gendered inquiry, emphasizing the ways gender is produced and reproduced through social institutions and social interaction (see Daly 1998). Moreover, it is important to recognize that manifestations of gender and gender inequality are quite varied, and shaped by the organization and situational contexts of any given setting or environment (see Messerschmidt 2000; Thorne 1993). In this chapter we suggest that girls' use of violence cannot be understood fully unless it is examined in the context of the situational enactment of gender inequality. Recognition of the significance of unequal power relations between women and men—and girls and boys—helps to explain quite a bit about girls' violence. This includes when and how girls choose to adopt violent strategies of interaction but also when and how girls respond to situations without resorting to violence or by attempting to diffuse potentially violent situations.

Our approach here is to examine girls' *gendered violence:* the contexts and qualities of their use of violence, and the social organization of these actions.[1] We highlight three theoretical issues necessary to understand girls' violence: (1) cultural definitions of masculinity and femininity and their impact on girls' behavior; (2) power differentials between males and females and how these regulate and constrain girls' use of violence; and (3) the impact of group and situational gender composition in shaping violence. We begin by discussing each of these issues separately, but will show how they are interrelated with regard to the why and how of girls' violence.

Cultural Definitions of Masculinity and Femininity

Feminist criminologists often examine "gendered crime" by utilizing sociological theory on gender as situated accomplishment (West and Zimmerman 1987; West and Fenstermaker 1995). According to this perspective, gender is "much more than a role or an individual characteristic: it is a mechanism whereby situated social action contributes to the reproduction of social structure" (West and Fenstermaker 1995: 21). Women and men "do gender" in response to normative beliefs about femininity and masculinity. These actions are "the interactional scaffolding of social structure" (West and Zimmerman 1987: 147), such that the performance of gender is both an indication of and a reproduction of gendered social hierarchies.

This approach has been incorporated into feminist accounts of crime as a means of explaining differences in women's and men's offending (Messerschmidt 1995, 2000; Simpson & Elis 1995). Here, violence is described as "a 'resource' for accomplishing gender—for demonstrating masculinity within a given context or situation" (Simpson & Elis

1995: 50). Though the concept of gender as situated accomplishment has primarily been brought to bear on male offending and constructions of masculinity, feminist theorists recently have attempted to account for female crime based on the same framework. Messerschmidt (1995: 172), for example, suggests that "'doing gender' renders social action accountable in terms of normative conceptions, attitudes and activities appropriate to one's sex category in the specific social situation in which one acts."

Theorizing about young women in gangs, Messerschmidt argues that girls engage in gang activities, including violence, with the goal of enacting normatively appropriate femininity:

> For girls in the gang, doing femininity means occasionally, and in appropriate circumstances, doing violence. However, because participation in violence varies depending upon the setting, girls are assessed and held accountable as "bad girls" differently. Given that gang girls realize that their behavior is accountable to other girls and boys in the gang, they construct their actions in relation to how those actions will be interpreted by others in the same social context. (Messershmidt 1995:183)

Thus, Messerschmidt suggests that males and females make decisions to engage in particular acts of lawbreaking as a means of enacting masculinity or femininity. Their decision making is guided by how their actions will be read by others around them, who have the ability to sanction or approve their success in "doing gender."

Gendered Power Differentials

It is also important to recognize that cultural definitions of masculinity and femininity are asymmetrical. They are "based on an organizing principle of men's superiority and social and political-economic dominance over women" (Daly & Chesney-Lind 1988: 504). When analyzing the relationship between "doing gender" and "doing violence," this means it is also necessary to examine the ways that power imbalances between males and females constrain and regulate girls' ability to use violence. Beyond particular forms of violence being read or sanctioned as "unfeminine," girls must gear their actions toward what they can safely accomplish or get away with in the context of male-dominated settings such as the streets. Thus, gender definitions are brought to bear on social practices in multiple ways.

For instance, in some situations violence may be used as a resource for accomplishing gender. In other situations the converse may be true—gender may be used as a resource for accomplishing or avoiding violence. Several recent studies examining women's participation in drug sales, for example, have shown that women often draw from cultural beliefs about gender to successfully sell drugs (Jacobs & Miller 1998; Lauderback, Hansen, & Waldorf 1992; Miller 2001). The police perceive the typical drug seller to be male, operating on street corners, and dressed in flashy clothing (see Jacobs 1999). Women in these studies used such stereotypes to their advantage. For example, dressing in a mundane way, selling from more out-of-the-way locations, and even using decoys such as bags of groceries or their children as a means of legitimizing their presence on the streets and deflecting attention away from their activities. As we will show, girls sometimes employ similar gender strategies with regard to violence.

One of the most important situational factors guiding young women's decisions about whether and how to engage in violence is gender stratification within criminal and street networks. There is compelling evidence that gender inequality remains a salient feature of the urban street scene. Street-level networks have a male-dominated institutional structure, and are highly gender segregated and gender-typed (Maher 1997). Prominent stereotypes of women characterize them as physically and emotionally weak, unreliable, and untrustworthy. Research has documented how gendered status hierarchies structure both women's and men's participation in street crime—including the exclusion of women from drug-selling networks (Bourgois 1995; Maher 1997) and of female gang members from serious forms of gang crime (Bowker, Gross, & Klein 1980; Miller & Brunson 2000). To understand girls' violence, we must take into account the impact of these features of their environments. This means examining how young women negotiate within gender-stratified settings, and how they accommodate and adapt to gender inequality in their commission of violence (see Kandiyoti 1988).

Importantly, this approach also allows scholars to avoid the reification of gender differences. For example, even when crime or violence is recognizably gendered, it is not necessarily the case that this results from differences in the morals, norms, or beliefs of males and females. Even when girls' and boys' goals or motives are similar, because their decision making occurs within the context of gender stratification, their actions are likely to remain gendered. Thus, when gender differences are uncovered—as they most often are—it remains necessary to also examine the *sources* of these differences, which likely are multiple and varied.

Gender Composition of Groups

Scholars in the sociology of organizations have long recognized gender composition as a key feature shaping interactional dynamics within groups (Blau 1977; Kanter 1977). In fact, Kanter (1977) notes that often conclusions drawn about differences between males and females and attributed to "gender roles" or cultural differences between women and men are in fact more appropriately attributable to situational or structural factors such as the gender composition of groups. For example, she suggests that female tokens in primarily male groups typically adopt two strategies of action: overachievement according to the "masculine" standards of the group; and attempting to become "socially invisible"—to "minimize their sexual attributes so as to blend unnoticeably into the predominant male culture" (Kanter 1977: 974; see also Konrad et al. 1992). As a consequence, their patterns of behavior are more likely to be "masculine" than the behavior of females in groups with more gender-balanced membership.

Recent research in the field of gang studies suggests that one of the sources of variation in gang girls' use of violence results from the gender composition of their gangs (Joe-Laidler & Hunt 1997; Miller & Brunson 2000; Peterson, Miller, & Esbensen 2001). Prior to this research, various studies uncovered what appeared to be discrepant findings. For instance, some scholars suggested that girls' use of violence in gangs was limited due to exclusionary practices of male gang members (Bowker et al. 1980), while others suggested it resulted from differences in the norms and values of girls and boys (Campbell 1993; Joe & Chesney-Lind 1995). Still other scholars challenged the image of nonviolent, noncriminal gang girls, documenting young women's active participation in gang delinquency and violence (Lauderback et al. 1992; Taylor 1993). Finally, several scholars reported greater variation in young women's participation in delinquent activities than young men's (Fagan 1990; Miller 2001).

In fact, it appears that differences in gang girls' participation in violence, and the normative salience of violence for girls, is influenced by the gender organization of their gangs. Comparing all-male, majority male, gender balanced, and all/majority female gangs, Peterson et al. (2001) found significant differences across gang types with regard to members' levels of participation in delinquency. Males and females in majority male gangs had the highest rates of delinquency. In fact, girls in majority male gangs had *higher* rates of delinquency than males in all-male gangs, while girls in all/majority female gangs had the lowest rates of delinquency.

Similarly, Joe-Laidler and Hunt (1997) report differences in young women's exposure to violence across gang types. Young women from Joe-Laidler and Hunt's study who were members of an all-female gang described violence occurring in three types of situations: violence associated with the drug trade, fights with girls in other gangs (over both men and turf), and intimate partner violence committed by their boyfriends. In contrast, young women in "auxiliary" gangs were subject to more violence-prone situations, many of which were tied to their associations with young men. These included violence in the context of gang initiations, conflicts with rival gang members—both male and female[2]—conflicts *among* homegirls in the same gang (over reputation, respect, jealousies over males, and fights instigated by males), as well as intimate partner violence at the hands of boyfriends. As these studies suggest, gender plays a complicated role in girls' gang participation, including their involvement in delinquency and exposure to violence. It is a structural determinant of girls' experiences rather than simply a result of differences between males and females. Later in this chapter, we suggest that in addition to the gender composition of girls' groups, the gender makeup of individuals involved in interpersonal conflicts also influences whether and how girls use violence.

The Studies

To further illustrate the theoretical concepts we have just outlined we draw from several recent qualitative studies undertaken by one or both of the authors. In each case, young women were interviewed at length about their involvement in violence.[3] The first study (Miller 1998; see also Wright and Decker 1997) is drawn from interviews with ten young women actively involved in street robbery, along with a comparative sample of male robbers.[4] These interviews focused on situational motivations, target selection, and the accomplishment of robbery. The second (Miller 2001; Miller & Brunson 2000) is based on interviews with forty-eight young women who are members of street gangs, as well as interviews with thirty-one male gang members. In these interviews we specifically explored girls' participation in gang conflict and violence. The third study (Like, Miller, & White 2000) is an investigation of the situational contexts shaping violence against urban African American girls. Interviews conducted with thirty-five young women include discussions about the nature of conflicts between girls as compared to girl-boy conflicts in schools. This facet of the study is the focus of our analysis here.

In each of the three projects, we utilized in-depth interview techniques for data collection. The strength of in-depth interviewing is that it provides a means of understanding the social world from the points of view of respondents, highlighting the meanings individuals attribute to their experiences (Glassner & Loughlin 1987; Miller & Glassner 1997). In addition, in-depth interviews provide detailed descriptive information about the nature and situational contexts of girls' violence. In these studies, our particular concern was to understand the social situations in which violence emerges, variations in its enactment, and the meanings of violence in young women's lives. Combined, the three studies provide us with the opportunity to compare girls' violence across several types of situations—violence utilized for instrumental goals (e.g., robberies), symbolic violence associated with intergroup (gang) conflicts, and violence occurring in the context of more routine interpersonal conflicts.

The vast majority of interviews we draw from in this chapter were conducted with girls living in central city neighborhoods in St. Louis, Missouri.[5] This site is particularly well suited for exploring the problem of street violence, as St. Louis has comparatively high rates of violent crime. In fact, it consistently ranks among the five U.S. cities with the highest annual rates of homicide (Rosenfeld, Bray, & Egley 1999). Researchers link the city's high crime rates to socioeconomic trends and urban distress. Like many other Midwestern cities in the United States, St. Louis has been negatively affected by substantial deindustrialization and population loss in the last several decades (see Decker & Van Winkle 1996). These problems are linked to extreme racial inequality and segregation. In fact, St. Louis is one of the ten most racially segregated cities in the United States, with considerable gaps between African Americans and whites in income, poverty, and unemployment rates[6] (Rusk 1995).

At the outset, we should also highlight the unique populations of which these samples (especially the robbery and gang samples) are illustrative. Young women involved in street-level violence are an exceptional group, rather than typical of most girls or most girls in urban communities. As detailed throughout this volume, the rush to assume that girls are becoming more violent—or that certain groups of girls (such as girls of color) are especially violent—is highly problematic, and linked to contemporary stereotypes and fears about race, gender, and adolescence.

Street robbery, for instance, is one of the most gender-differentiated serious crimes in the United States. According to the FBI's Uniform Crime Report for 1995, females accounted for only 9.3 percent of robbery arrestees (Federal Bureau of Investigation 1996). Young women's participation in street robberies, thus, is a rare phenomenon. Likewise for girls' participation in street gangs and gang violence: despite the growth in gangs throughout the United States since the 1980s (see Klein 1995), studies that gauge the prevalence of gang participation have found that only a small percentage of young people are gang members. For example, results from the Gang Resistance Education and Training Program, based on a school-based sample of youth from six U.S. cities, show prevalence rates of only 3 percent of youths (Esbensen 2000). Estimates suggest that females account for anywhere from 20 to 46 percent of gang members (see Esbensen & Winfree 1998). Even among those girls in street gangs, there is great variation in their participation in violence. Studies show that most gang girls are involved primarily in sporadic and minor offending, while just a minority participates routinely in violent crimes (Fagan 1990; Miller 2001).

The young women in the final study we discuss report experiences more typical of a broader range of girls in urban communities. Unlike in the case of the robbery and gang studies, these girls were not selected for interviews because they had committed robberies or joined gangs. Instead, we targeted girls at risk for negative life consequences by virtue of their living in dangerous neighborhoods and having problems in school or in the family. Some were involved in delinquency and violence; others were not. Nonetheless, all of them had experienced some kind of conflicts in school with other girls and/or boys, and these conflicts are the basis of our analysis here.

It is important to keep these issues in mind in the discussion that follows in order to understand young women's use of violence within its broader contexts. Young women who commit street robberies and girls in gangs do not represent typical urban girls or typical female offenders, nor are they representative of a so-called "new violent female offender" whose participation in serious and violent crime has escalated in recent years (see Chesney-Lind, Shelden, & Joe 1996). Nonetheless, these girls have something significant to teach us about how gender shapes the use of violence, including when it is seen as an appropriate method of interaction and how it is enacted.

Young Women and Violence

As noted above, our goal in this chapter is to examine the situational aspects of girls' decision-making processes with regard to the use of violence in the context of gender inequality and gender-stratified networks and groups. Our specific emphasis is on how girls accommodate and adapt to these inequities in their decisions about whether and how to engage in violence. Kandiyoti (1988) coined the phrase "bargaining with patriarchy" to highlight how women's strategies of action occur within particular sets of gendered constraints. She notes: "Different forms of patriarchy present women with distinct 'rules of the game' and call for different strategies to maximize security and optimize life options with varying potential for active or passive resistance in the face of oppression" (Kandiyoti 1988: 274).

Our interest here is to compare girls' "gender strategies" regarding violence across situations with different types of origins: instrumental violence in the form of street robbery, gang violence, and female/female versus male/female conflicts arising from interpersonal disputes in schools. As we illustrate, girls' use of violence varies across circumstances, and is shaped by motives and goals, by the gender of other parties involved, and by the situations in which it occurs. Combined, the studies highlight the salience of gender inequality and imbalanced power relations between males and females in shaping girls' violence.

Young Women's Participation in Street Robbery

We begin by examining young women's involvement in street robbery. To understand how gender shapes the commission of robbery, we must first examine the motivations guiding decisions to commit robbery. As noted, this study benefited by having a comparative sample of males and females who participate in robbery (Miller 1998). In fact, one striking feature of the robbery study was that males' and females' discussions of the reasons they committed robbery was more a case of gender similarities than differences. For both, motives were primarily economic—to get money, jewelry, and other status-conferring goods—but also included elements of thrill seeking, attempting to overcome boredom, and revenge. Most striking was the continuity across gender in respondents' accounts of their motives for committing robbery.

Describing the mix of economic and sensual (see Katz 1988) rewards of robbery, Ne-Ne explained: "I don't know if it's the money, the power or just the feeling that I know that I can just go up and just take somebody's stuff. It's just a whole bunch of mixture type thing." Likewise, CMW said she commits robberies "out of the blue, just something to do. Bored at the time and just want to find some action." She explained, "I be sitting on the porch and we'll get to talking and stuff. See people going around and they be flashing in they fancy cars, walking down the street with that jewelry on, thinking they all bad, and we just go get 'em." Despite similarities in motivation, there were clear differences in how young women versus men actually accomplished robberies. These differences result from young women's strategic choices in the context of gender-stratified environments.

The young men in the sample described committing robberies in a strikingly uniform manner—using physical violence or its threat and most often a gun placed on or at close proximity to the victim in a confrontational manner. In male robberies, in fact, physical violence could sometimes be avoided because of the compliance achieved from the presence of a firearm. This method was employed regardless of whether men robbed male or female victims, though the former were more common targets than the latter. In contrast, young women's techniques for committing robberies varied considerably depending upon whether they were targeting male or female victims, and if they were working with or without male accomplices.

When young women robbed other females, they did so either alone or with female accomplices, but not with male accomplices. Young women's robberies of other females were physical confrontations that typically involved no weapon (or occasionally a knife). They described targeting female victims because they were seen as less likely to resist than males. CMW explained, "See, women, they won't really do nothing. They say, 'oh, oh, ok, here take this.' A dude, he might try to put up a fight." The use of weapons in these robberies was often deemed unnecessary, though other forms of physical violence were quite common. According to Janet Outlaw, "We push 'em and tell them to up their shit, pushing 'em in the head. Couple of times we had to knock the girls down and took the stuff off of them."

In contrast, young women's robberies of men nearly always involved guns, and did not involve physical contact. Janet Outlaw described a great deal of physical contact in her robberies of other young women, but described her robberies of men in much different terms. "If we waste time touching men there is a possibility that they can get the gun off of us, while we wasting time touching them they could do anything. So we just keep the gun straight on them. No touching, no moving, just straight gun at you." The circumstances surrounding female-on-male robberies differed as well. Young women's strategy for robbing men involved pretending to be sexually interested in their male victims. When the man dropped his guard, this provided the opportunity for the robbery to take place. Young women played upon men's beliefs about women in order to accomplish these robberies. These include the assumption that women won't be armed, won't attempt to rob men, and can be taken advantage of sexually. Quick explained:

They don't suspect that a girl gonna try to get 'em. You know what I'm saying? So it's kind of easier 'cause they like, she looks innocent, she ain't gonna do this, but that's how I get 'em. They put they guard down to a woman. . . . Most of the time when girls get high they think they can take advantage of us so they always [say] let's go to a hotel or my crib or something.

Men's actions, and their attitudes about women, thus made them vulnerable targets.

Finally, when young women committed street robberies in tandem with male accomplices they described using the same techniques that men routinely employ—physical contact that involved the display and placement of a gun on the victim. Young women said it was because they had male accomplices that they were able to avoid the struggle likely to occur if they used the same technique on a male victim by themselves. Only one young woman described employing this technique without the presence of a male accomplice. Ne-Ne explicitly indicated that she was able to complete the robbery because the victim did not know a female was robbing him. Describing herself as physically large, Ne-Ne said she dressed and adopted mannerisms that masked her gender. She wore a baseball cap "pulled down over my face and I just went to the back and upped him. Put the gun up to his head. . . . He don't know right now to this day if it was a girl or a dude."

Thus, while young women's and young men's motivations to commit robbery were similar, when they actually commit robbery their actions are strikingly different. These differences highlight the clear gender hierarchy that exists on the streets. Young women are participating in a male-dominated environment, and their actions reflect an understanding of this. In some cases they target female victims, believing they are easily intimidated and thus easy to rob. In other cases, they draw upon similar gender beliefs—that women are weak, sexually available, and easily manipulated—to turn the tables in order to rob men. Unlike young women's robberies of other females, these tend not to involve physical contact but do involve the use of guns. Because they recognize men's perceptions of women, they also recognize that men are more likely to resist being robbed by a female, and thus they commit these robberies in ways that minimize their risk of losing control and maximize their ability to show that they're "for real." Only with the backup of male accomplices—or in Ne-Ne's case by concealing her gender—did young women safely accomplish robberies in the traditional "masculine" style. These variations reflect practical choices made in the context of a gender-stratified environment—one in which, on the whole, males are perceived as strong and females as weak.

Girls, Gender, and Gang Violence

Unlike in the case of street robbery, girls' motives for joining gangs rarely have much to do with instrumental desires such as getting money. Instead they are linked to living in impoverished, dangerous neighborhoods where gangs are a visible presence, often coupled with family problems and the desire to meet social and emotional needs through group membership and identity (Miller 2001). Gang membership itself does not guarantee that young women will be involved extensively in violence. Instead, as noted above, research documents that most girls in gangs are involved in delinquency and violence rather sporadically, while a minority—around one-quarter to one-third—participate routinely in these gang activities (Fagan 1990; Miller 2001).

Gangs have a facilitation effect on violence. Gang norms, group processes, and gang youths' associations with violent peers encourage them to engage in these activities (Battin et al. 1998; Thornberry 1997). In fact, Klein (1995) suggests that violence, especially intergang conflict, is more than just an outcome of gang membership. Instead it serves as a source of group cohesion for its members. Challenging and fighting rival gangs is an important element of gang life. It is often through these antagonisms that youths stake out the identity of their gang, because having common enemies facilitates members' perceptions of themselves as a unified group (see Decker & Van Winkle 1996). Thus, gang involvement "may directly facilitate violence by virtue of the public and participatory nature of gang conflicts" (Rosenfeld, Bray, & Egley 1999: 514).

What is notable about gangs, however, is that the most serious forms of gang violence, including gun use and homicide, are almost the exclusive purview of *male* gang members. For example, in a recent analysis of gang homicides in St. Louis from 1990 to 1996, *none* of the 229 gang homicides committed during that period were attributed to a female gang member (Miller & Decker 2001). Thus, an important question that arises in studying girls' use of violence in gangs is to explain why most girls are not frequently involved in serious violent altercations, particularly since violence is a normative feature of most youth gangs.

As we described earlier, to address this question it is first necessary to examine the nature of gang girls' groups. The vast majority of girls in the current study were in gangs with both male and female member-ship, but the groups were clearly male-dominated. There were distinct gender hierarchies in these gangs that included male leadership, a dou-ble standard with regard to sexual activity, and the sexual exploitation of some young women (see Miller 2001). Moreover, girls and boys re-ported that male gang members often excluded most females from par-ticipation in serious gang crime, particularly drive-by shootings. As Sheila noted, "The dudes think they run it all."

Likewise, young men suggested that girls were less reliable than boys and thus couldn't be counted on to be "down" when the gang re-ally needed them (see Miller & Brunson 2000). Mike explained, "We don't want to take a chance of them getting soft for real." Lamont con-curred, "Females really can't handle drama. . . . A female can't fight. I can't say all females can't fight males but you just don't want to take that chance." To account for the handful of girls that participated in se-rious gang conflicts, young men typically characterized these girls as atypical and as "one of the guys." For instance, Robert explained: "Tia's not a regular girl, she like a boy for real. She act like a boy and work around the boys. Other girls, I don't think they should be in no gang, they soft for real."

In fact, because of the male-dominated nature of their groups, many young women described adopting a gender identity as "one of the guys" (see Miller 2001). They heavily identified with the young men in their gangs and characterized these groups as masculine enterprises. Ironically, even though most girls described themselves as "one of the guys," they also highlighted gender differences within their gangs, and drew from beliefs about gender to justify their limited participation in violence. Thus, male exclusion of female participation in serious gang violence doesn't fully account for young women's limited involvement in serious violent confrontations. Instead, young women engaged in ac-tive decision making to participate in particular kinds of gang conflicts and avoid others.

Young women's accounts of gang-related conflict shed some light on these issues. While girls are involved in altercations with rival gangs, they rarely escalate to serious violence involving weapons. Opposition to rival gangs is a central theme in the cultural imagery and symbolism that gang youths adopt. Confrontations with rivals are often a conse-quence of these displays, particularly in conjunction with the defense of territorial boundaries. For instance, Crystal explained, "if a Blood come on our set [turf] and we Crips, as long as they come on our set saying, 'what's up Blood,' they . . . just gonna start a fight. 'Cause they diss [dis-respect] us by coming on our set and saying 'what's up Blood.' There ain't nobody no Blood over there." Vashelle concurred: "A dude [from a rival gang] come over [to our neighborhood], he know what kind of 'hood it is to begin with. Any dude that come over there from a gang and know that's a Blood hood, you try to come over there Cripped out [donning Crips symbolism], you know you gonna eventually have it some way."

The vast majority of confrontations girls were engaged in involved fists, occasionally knives, but not guns. However, most young women said when they encountered rivals, as long as they weren't met with a direct challenge, they were willing to tolerate their presence rather than escalate into a fight. Pam explained:

> We going to the show or skating, to the mall. We be seeing some of our enemies too when we do those things, clubs and stuff, we be seeing a lot of our enemies. [If] they don't say nothing to us, we don't say nothing to them. They say something to us, we say something to them. So that way everybody just go they own little way if they don't want nothing to happen.

Many young women echoed Pam's account. While violence and confrontations with rivals were normative features of their gangs, and actions gang girls placed value on, they were often content to leave such activities to young men. Girls' discussions of status hierarchies in their gangs, and their descriptions of gang members they looked up to, show that violence was a normative feature of their groups. They especially admired individuals who "did dirt" for the gang by committing gang-motivated assaults and participating in the confrontation of rivals. Status emerged in part from having proven oneself on these grounds. That girls described looking up to members who had such qualities is an indication of their acceptance of these gang norms. For example, Diane described a highly respected female member in her set as follows:

> People look up to Janeen just 'cause she's so crazy. People just look up to her 'cause she don't care about nothin'. She don't even care about makin' money. Her, her thing is, "Oh, you're a Slob [Blood]? You're a Slob? You talkin' to me? You talkin' shit to me?" Pow, pow! And that's it. That's it.

Nonetheless, most girls saw males as the members most likely to carry these activities to their most extreme conclusion. Young women held males and females to different standards based on their perceptions of what "femaleness" or "maleness" brought to their interactions and behaviors, and some girls used this as a basis for limiting their participation in serious gang violence, particularly gun violence. As Tonya exclaimed, "We ain't no supercommando girls!" Crystal noted, "Girls don't be up there shooting unless they really have to." And Keisha explained, "Guys is more rougher. We have our G's [fellow gang member's] back but, it ain't gonna be like the guys, they just don't give a fuck. They gonna shoot you in a minute." Pam suggested that girls don't use guns because "we ladies, we not dudes for real . . . we don't got to be rowdy, all we do is fight."

As Pam's comments suggest, it's not just that gang girls participated in or avoided certain crimes as a means of enacting femininity. Rather, they also used norms about gender to temper their involvement in serious and dangerous gang violence—because they are girls, they "don't got to" engage in serious violence. Girls could gain status in the gang by engaging in those violent activities that mark members as "hard" and "true" to the set. But many young women drew on the gender inequalities that permeated status hierarchies and expectations about member behavior in order to avoid such activities.

In addition, as we saw with female robbers, gang girls also played on beliefs about gender in other circumstances, using their presence to shield suspicion from the actions of their gang. For instance, Tonya described:

> Like when we in a car, if a girl and a dude in a car, the police tend not to trip off of it. When they look to see if a car been stolen, police just don't trip off of it. But if they see three or four niggers in that car, the police stop you automatically, boom. . . . [Girls have] little ways that we got to get them out of stuff sometimes, we can get them out of stuff that dudes couldn't do, you know what I'm saying.

Thus, gender—and gender stereotypes—were often resources that young women drew from to both negotiate and limit their involvement in gang violence, and to facilitate the success of gang members' crimes.

Interpersonal Violence: Girl/Girl Versus Girl/Boy Conflicts

Robbery primarily involves the instrumental use of violence—violence enacted to successfully obtain an individual's money or property. Gang violence, on the other hand, is often symbolic and its goal is to protect and promote the gang's name, territory, and reputation. Violence can also result from interpersonal conflicts between individuals. Here we compare girls' descriptions of such conflicts, comparing fights between girls with conflicts that arise with boys. As Artz (1998) documented in her study of violent girls, girls' descriptions of interpersonal conflict show that they typically see others as the instigating parties, and themselves as the target of others' ill deeds or words. Their descriptions of altercations are thus framed with regard to how they respond to such actions.

Research on the situational dynamics shaping interpersonal violence among young men highlights how violence emerges in response to a perception of being "disrespected," and the need to retaliate in order to maintain respect and reputation (Anderson 1999; Bourgois 1995). On the other hand, girls' interpersonal conflicts are typically framed as petty events that most often emerge from fights over boys. In fact, young women themselves often frame girls' fights in such a trivializing manner. Yolanda described conflicts between girls as "silly girl fights [over] he say-she say stuff, or over boyfriends, stupid stuff." Shantay said fights between girls are "stupid. If a girl look at another girl, it's a fight. If a girl say something to a girl it's a fight. Over boys, stupid little stuff, girls'll fight over anything." Likewise, Vashelle commented that girls "fight over stupid stuff." She elaborated, "I mean the gals over there banging [fighting] over a dude. You all over here banging over him but he probably ain't even exist for you right now." Vashelle's frustration stemmed from the fact that girls often fight one another over boys who actually care little for the girls involved.

However, when these conflicts are recognized as also being disputes about respect, they begin to make more sense and seem less "silly." Power imbalances between males and females manifest themselves through a sexual double standard that includes a wide range of acceptable sexual practices for males. For instance, within street gangs there are rare instances in which girls are initiated into the gang by having sex with multiple male gang members. Girls who undergo this form of initiation are extremely stigmatized by other gang members while the male members' behavior is viewed as acceptable (see Miller 2001). Likewise, young men are rarely held accountable for their indiscretions when they cheat on their girlfriends. As Artz (1998: 177) notes, girls often view this behavior as part and parcel of being male, and as something they have little power to challenge or change.

Consequently, girls often have to rely on the good will of other girls to respect the boundaries of their relationships with boys and be willing to take a hands-off approach to their boyfriends. When young women violate this code and become sexually involved with another girl's boyfriend, their actions are read as disrespect. For example, Keisha had a boyfriend in her gang who cheated on her with another girl in the gang. When this happened, her hostility was not directed toward her boyfriend, but toward the other girl. She explained, "That's disrespect, that's real disrespect. . . . We ain't cool no more. For the simple fact she did it to my boyfriend." In some instances, disrespect may even be the goal of girls' actions. Yvette described fighting with a young woman who had previously been a good friend of hers when the other girl "talk[ed] about my man, like 'I'll take her man' . . . and said a couple of other things about me."

Because of the sexual double standard and girls' requisite need to protect their reputation, disputes also emerge among girls when one challenges the sexual reputation of another or spreads rumors about her sexual activities. Sometimes these conflicts remain verbal duels, but they can escalate to physical fights as well. For example, DaWanna found out through her nephew that a girl at her school had been spreading rumors about her. She confronted the girl, asking "why was she lyin' to my nephew." In response, the girl "got a little attitude." Explaining the conflict that ensued, she said, "She got attitude and junk, and talkin' 'bout she gonna kick my butt after school and stuff. So we got into it after school." Asked if the conflict escalated to physical violence, DaWanna responded, "Oh yeah!"

Likewise, conflicts among girls sometimes escalated into fights as a result of other kinds of rumors and name calling, and often were instigated by third parties. Sharmi described a conflict that ensued after her sister and a friend told her that another friend had called her "ugly" and "a bitch." She said girls fight one another over "everything—he say-she say stuff, lookin' at you the wrong way, *anything*." Likewise, of a recent fight she witnessed, Sheron said, "One girl went outside and she was like, 'I heard you said this,' and the girl was like, 'I ain't say that.' And she just hit her for no reason and the other girl hit her back and they just, just one big ol' fight." Janelle said what typically happens is that:

> Somebody will run back and forth, like the instigator. "So and so said this." And then they'll tell one person, "Well this person said this," and they'll go back and tell the other person. That's mostly how most of the fights get started. . . . It always starts out verbal, you know, sometimes it will get real heavy and go into physical fighting.

While girls' fights with one another are routinely defined as "stupid" and trivial, like conflicts between males they are primarily the result of individuals responding to situations in which they feel they have

been disrespected. That this disrespect often results from girls' involvement with other girls' boyfriends or spreading sexual rumors is indicative of the impact of differential power between boys and girls, and the
negative consequences of the sexual double standard that is a feature of
adolescent peer culture. Rather than acting against a culture that they
have little chance of changing, girls frequently participate in the mis-
treatment of other girls within the boundaries of these cultural norms
(see also Artz 1998; Miller 2001).

Girls' descriptions of their conflicts with boys offer further evidence
of the deleterious effects of these types of gender inequalities. The vast
majority of girl-boy conflicts recounted by young women result from
boy's sexual harassment and misconduct. As Artz (1998: 177) describes,
"Everyday life for [girls] mean[s] running a gauntlet of staring eyes,
groping hands, and derogatory comments about their bodies." Yvonne
described the routine harassment of girls by boys at school: "[They be]
just like touching and stuff. Trying to touch on your boobie or your
breasts or whatever. How they come at you, you know what I'm saying,
it ain't cool." She illustrated with the story of an altercation she was
involved in at school:

> Once in the classroom with this dude, he sitting in a chair, I was
> at a desk, he was in a chair. I had on a blue-jean skirt. And he kept
> rubbing my thigh or whatever and I was like, "Why don't you
> move?" and I pushed him and then he pushed me in my head and
> I got up in it because nigger you touching me, you know what I'm
> saying. So I stood up or whatever and I pushed his chair to the
> side. And he hopped up like he was gonna hit me or whatever.
> But the teacher came over there, which was a dude or whatever.
> He took my side and I like told him. We don't talk no more. We
> used to be real cool, but we don't talk no more after that.

In order to preserve their reputation and minimize sexual harassment, girls must respond in a negative way to boys' actions. Otherwise,
not only is the harassment likely to continue and escalate, but they will
be held accountable for it and their sexual reputations damaged as a
result. Jackie explained:

> You might be walking down the hallway and they just come up
> behind you and touch your butt. And everybody be standing right
> there and you just look around feeling embarrassed. [If you don't
> take action, others say,] "You let that boy do that and you ain't
> goin' do nothing about it?"

But girls are also in a double bind about *how* to respond: if they come on too strong in their rebuff of a boy's advances and he feels as though he's been disrespected, his recourse may be violent. Sometimes girls choose a confrontational verbal response, avoiding physical contact they recognize as likely to draw a violent response. For instance, Shantay said once when a young man was being inappropriate with her, "I got up in his face talking stuff. I knew I couldn't beat him up or nothing so I was just loud and in his face." Likewise, LaToya witnessed a similar conflict between a boy and a girl:

> They was loud and everybody was in the hallway and stuff, and she was mad and stuff. . . . She was just frontin' 'cause she wasn't goin' to hit him and stuff. 'Cause he the type he'll hit her back or whatever, like that. So they was just goin' at it back and forth like.

Girls also described instances in which their reactions did result in violent responses. Most often this occurred when their response to the harassment became physical. Shantay said once at school "a boy was jon'in' on a girl and he pushed her pant and she got up and pushed him, and he pushed her back, he pushed her real hard."

Interviewer: She pushed him first?

Shantay: Yeah, to tell him don't touch her. . . . He got angry, pushed her real hard.

In fact, Shantay had a similar experience herself:

> He kept coming over and he kept hitting me like that [touching her breasts] and I tell him to "quit playing with me, quit playing with me." He was like, "I don't have to quit playing with you." He was trying to show off in front of his friends or whatever. So I went over there and I kicked him in, you know what I'm saying, his thing or whatever. And um, that's when he got, he started choking me or whatever.

Thus, the decision of how to respond to boys' sexually harassing behavior is a daunting one. If young women are not vigilant enough they are viewed as encouraging and accepting sexual advances that label them as loose and sexually available. If they are too aggressive in their response, the conflict is likely to escalate into a physical battle that the young man is most likely to win. While many girls are willing to fight other girls when they have been disrespected in some way, they are more cautious in bringing challenges with males to a head because they believe young men's greater physical strength guarantees a lost battle.[7] Here girls are in a lose-lose situation unless they develop acute verbal confrontation skills sufficient to end the harassing behavior without disrespecting the harasser too blatantly.

Conclusion

For girls, gender stratification and power imbalances between males and females—along with their requisite stereotypes of women as weak, unreliable, and sexually available—are situational contexts that must be confronted in their decision-making processes about whether and how to use violence. Our comparative approach here highlights the significance of the role of asymmetrical cultural definitions of masculinity and femininity, gender inequality, and the gender compositions of both groups and conflicting dyads in shaping girls' use of violence. As we have described, in each case, girls' gendered techniques and actions represent practical choices they make while taking into account the gendered nature of their environments.

In the case of young women who commit robberies, while their motives are similar to young men's, at all levels of the robbery event they enact the crime differently than young men. They are physically aggressive with other girls but find it unnecessary to use weapons, while they avoid physical aggression with males and instead use guns. They both buy into the stereotypes of girls as weak and easily intimidated—thus forgo guns as unnecessary—and use these stereotypes in order to place men in vulnerable positions that allow them to be robbed. Gun use is deemed quite necessary with men, as guns level the playing field and force males to take their female aggressor seriously.

Gender also shapes and limits girls' use of violence in street gangs. Consistent with other evidence of gender stratification in offender networks, boys' perceptions of most girls as weak and unreliable led to the exclusion of females from serious gang violence. But girls also actively negotiated their roles and activities in their gangs. They themselves held young women and young men to different standards of conduct based on beliefs about gender. Despite sometimes describing themselves as "one of the guys," girls used gender as a resource both to temper their involvement in violence and sometimes to successfully accomplish gang crime. The nature of their groups—mixed gender but masculine in orientation—facilitated girls' enactment of gang violence in these limited ways.

Finally, we compared interpersonal conflicts between girls and between girls and boys. Here again, our findings highlight the significance of gender inequality—particularly the impact of the sexual double standard—in shaping both girl-girl and girl-boy conflicts. Rather than viewing girls' conflicts with other girls as trivial and "stupid," they can best be seen as contests over respect in an environment in which girls are severely disadvantaged vis-à-vis young men. The double bind girls face when confronted by sexually harassing behavior by young men further highlights the deleterious effects of the sexual double standard. Young men feel entitled to comment, touch and grope on girls in sexually explicit ways; young women's responses must be aggressive enough to send the message that they are not asking for it, but not so aggressive as to result in violent retaliation.

As these findings suggest, rather than simply labeling girls as "violent," it is necessary to examine and understand the social contexts in which violence emerges as a strategy for young women. Girls' violence is produced within social contexts of extreme gender inequality. How and when girls choose to adopt violent strategies, as well as when and how girls negotiate within potentially violent situations—each of these is best understood by recognizing the significance of the contextual construction of unequal power relations and gender asymmetries.

Notes

1. Daly (1998: 94–99) outlines four areas of inquiry for contemporary feminist criminology: examination of the gender ratio of offending, gendered pathways into crime, gendered crime, and gendered lives. Here we focus on one of these areas—gendered crime, specifically violence.

2. In fact, Joe-Laidler and Hunt note that fights between rival girls were often instigated by males, who reportedly enjoyed watching females fight. Though they describe rules excluding girls from fighting males from rival gangs, young women sometimes got caught in these conflicts.

3. For detailed descriptions of the study methodologies, see Miller 1998, 2001; Like, Miller, & White 2000.

4. The original study (Miller 1998) included fourteen female robbers, including four adult women (aged twenty-five and over). Two of the adults committed robberies to support drug habits; the other two robbed clients in the context of prostitution. They have been excluded from the discussion here. One additional caveat: while the ten young women from this project ranged in

age from sixteen to twenty-two, girls interviewed for the other projects were younger, on average, including a few girls as young as twelve.

5. This is the case with all of the robbery and school violence interviews. The study of girls in gangs was a two-city comparison of St. Louis and Columbus, Ohio. While there were notable differences across the two sites (see Miller 2001), there was a great deal of consistency across St. Louis and Columbus with regard to the topic of interest here—gender, gang conflict, and violence.

6. A note on how St. Louis and Columbus compare with regard to these problems: based on city-level indicators, Columbus is one of the few Midwestern cities to thrive during the deindustrialization of the last decades, as it has experienced continuous economic and population growth during this period. However, there are substantial pockets of impoverished neighborhoods with high concentrations of African Americans in Columbus, and income, poverty, and unemployment disparities remain pronounced (see Miller 2001).

7. One additional solution that some girls employ is to rely on other boys—brothers, cousins, boyfriends, or friends—to retaliate for a boy's misdeeds. Girls most often reported using this form of informal or "street justice" for more serious assaults such as rape, but occasionally responded to sexual harassment or resulting violent confrontations in this fashion.

References

Anderson, E. 1999, *Code of the street*, W.W. Norton & Co, New York.

Artz, S. 1998, *Sex, power, and the violent school girl*, Trifolium Books, Toronto.

Battin, S. R., Hill, K. G., Abbott, R. D., Catalano, R. F., & Hawkins, J. D. 1998, "The contribution of gang membership to delinquency beyond delinquent friends," *Criminology*, vol. 36, pp. 93–115.

Blau, P. M. 1977, Inequality and heterogeneity: a primitive theory of social structure, The Free Press, New York.

Bourgois, P. 1995, *In search of respect: selling crack in el barrio*, Cambridge University Press, Cambridge.

Bowker, L. H., Gross, H. S., & Klein, M. W. 1980, "Female participation in delinquent gang activities," *Adolescence*, vol. 15, pp. 509–19.

Campbell, A. 1993, *Men, women, and aggression*, Basic Books, New York.

Chesney-Lind, M., Shelden, R. G., & Joe, K. A. 1996, "Girls, delinquency, and gang membership." in C. R. Huff (ed), *Gangs in America*, 2nd edition, Sage Publications, Thousand Oaks, CA, pp. 185–204.

Daly, K. 1998, "From gender ratios to gendered lives, women and gender in crime and criminological theory," in M. Tonry (ed), *The handbook of crime and justice*, Oxford University Press, Oxford, pp. 85–108.

Daly, K. & Chesney-Lind, M. 1988, "Feminism and criminology," *Justice Quarterly*, vol. 5, pp. 497–538.

Decker, S. H. & Van Winkle, B. 1996, *Life in the gang*, Cambridge University Press, Cambridge.

Esbensen, F.-A. 2000, "The national evaluation of the gang resistance education and training (G.R.E.A.T.) program," in J. Miller, C. L. Maxson, & M. W. Klein (eds), *The modern gang reader*, 2nd Edition, Roxbury Publishing Company, Los Angeles.

Esbensen, F.-A. & L. T., Winfree, Jr. 1998, "Race and gender differences between gang and non-gang youths: results from a multi-site survey," *Justice Quarterly*, no. 15, pp. 505–26.

Fagan, J. 1990, "Social processes of delinquency and drug use among urban gangs," in C. R. Huff (ed), *Gangs in America*, Sage Publications, Newbury Park, pp.183–219.

Federal Bureau of Investigation 1996, *Crime in the United States, 1995*, U.S. Government Printing Office, Washington, D.C.

Glassner, B. & Loughlin, J. 1987, *Drugs in adolescent worlds: burnouts to straights*, St. Martin's Press, New York.

Jacobs, B. A. 1999, *Dealing crack: the social world of streetcorner selling*, Northeastern University Press, Boston.

Jacobs, B. A. & J., Miller, 1998, "Crack dealing, gender, and arrest avoidance," *Social Problems*, no. 45, pp. 550–69.

Joe, K. A. & Chesney-Lind, M. 1995, "'Just every mother's angel': an analysis of gender and ethnic variations in youth gang membership," *Gender & Society*, no. 9, pp. 408–30.

Joe-Laidler, K. A. & Hunt, G. 1997, "Violence and social organization in female gangs," *Social Justice*, no. 24, pp. 148–69.

Kandiyoti, D. 1988, "Bargaining with patriarchy," *Gender & Society*, no. 2, pp. 274–90.

Kanter, R. M. 1977, "Some effects of proportions on group life: skewed sex ratios and responses to token women," *American Journal of Sociology*, no. 82, pp. 965–90.

Katz, J. 1988, *Seductions of crime*, Basic Books, New York.

Klein, M. W. 1995, *The American street gang: its nature, prevalence and control*, Oxford University Press, New York.

Konrad, A. M., Winter, S. & Gutek, B. A. 1992, "Diversity in work group sex composition: implications for majority and minority members," *Research in the Sociology of Organizations*, no. 10, pp. 115–40.

Lauderback, D., Hansen, J., & Waldorf, D. 1992, "'Sisters are doin' it for themselves': a black female gang in San Francisco," *The Gang Journal*, no. 1, pp. 57–70.

Like, T. Z., Miller, J. & White, N. A. 2000, "Violence against urban African American girls," Annual Meeting of the American Society of Criminology, San Francisco, November.

Maher, L. 1997. *Sexed work: gender, race, and resistance in a Brooklyn drug market*, Clarendon Press, Oxford.

Messerschmidt, J. W. 1995, "From patriarchy to gender: feminist theory, criminology, and the challenge of diversity," in N. H. Rafter & F. Heidensohn (eds), *International feminist perspectives in criminology: engendering a discipline*, Open University Press, Philadelphia, pp. 167–88.

————. 2000, *Nine lives: adolescent masculinities, the body, and violence,* Westview Press, Boulder.

Miller, J. 1998, "Up it up: gender and the accomplishment of street robbery," *Criminology,* no. 36, pp. 37–66.

————. 2001, *One of the guys: girls, gangs, and gender,* Oxford University Press, New York.

Miller, J. & Brunson, R. K. 2000, "Gender dynamics in youth gangs: A comparison of male and female accounts," *Justice Quarterly,* vol. 17, no. 3, pp. 801–30.

Miller, J. & Decker, S. H. 2001, "Young women and gang violence: an examination of gender, street offending and violent victimization in gangs," *Justice Quarterly,* vol. 18, no. 1, pp. 115–40.

Miller, J. & Glassner, B. 1997, "The 'inside' and the 'outside': finding realities in interviews," in D. Silverman (ed), *Qualitative Research,* Sage Publications, London, pp. 99–112.

Peterson, D., Miller, J. & Esbensen, F.-A. 2001, "The impact of sex composition on gangs and gang member delinquency," *Criminology,* no. 39, pp. 411–39.

Rosenfeld, R., Bray, T., & Egley, A. 1999, "Facilitating violence: a comparison of gang-motivated, gang-affiliated, and non-gang youth homicides," *Journal of Quantitative Criminology,* no. 15, pp. 495–516.

Rusk, D. 1995, *Cities Without Suburbs,* 2nd Edition, Woodrow Wilson Center Press, Washington, D.C.

Simpson, S. & Elis, L. 1995, "Doing gender: sorting out the caste and crime conundrum," *Criminology,* no. 33, pp. 47–81.

Taylor, C. 1993, *Girls, gangs, women, and drugs,* Michigan State University Press, East Lansing.

Thornberry, T. P. 1997, "Membership in youth gangs and involvement in serious and violent offending," in R. Loeber & D. P. Farrington (eds), *Serious and violent juvenile offenders: risk factors and successful interventions,* Sage Publications, Thousand Oaks, Cal., pp 147–66.

Thorne, B. 1993, *Gender play: girls and boys in school,* Rutgers University Press, New Brunswick, N.J.

West, C. & Fenstermaker, S. 1995, "Doing difference," *Gender & Society,* no. 9, pp. 8–37.

West, C. & Zimmerman, D. H. 1987, "Doing gender," *Gender & Society,* no. 1, pp. 125–51.

Wright, R. T. & Decker, S. H. 1997, *Armed robbers in action: stickups and street culture,* Northeastern University Press, Boston.

Glossary of UK/ Australian terms by chapter

Chapter One

Canal: waterway

Estate: block of high rise flats (between twenty and thirty stories high) built after World War II to replace street housing; estates are social housing

Standing up: defending

Wheelie: wheeled rubbish bin

Chapter Two

Clip: slap

Dens: secret meeting places

Dustbins: garbage cans

Fall foul: invoke adverse attention

Fire poker: metal rod, used for reviving domestic fire

Footpath:	sidewalk
Hangers-on:	spectators
Larrikins:	working class youths who gathered in the streets to fight (1890's usage)
Ne'er-do-wells:	delinquents
Progging:	firewood
Push	a hooligan "gang" (1890s usage)
Scrap heap:	waste disposal site
Singlet:	vest
Skittles:	home-made game of bowling
Tea:	afternoon tea party
Whacks:	hits

Chapter Three

Ladette:	young woman characterized by enjoyment of activities typically considered to be male oriented, and by attitudes or behavior regarded as irresponsible or brash; (usually) one of a close-knit group
Lashing out:	assaulting

Chapter Five

Blue Peter:	very respectable children's TV program
Cardigan:	woollen jacket

Daftie:	a person who is unable to stick up for themselves and is viewed as "soft"
Dinna:	does not
Fenian:	Irish nationalist
Giving or getting a 'doing' or a 'battering':	physical assault
Grass:	inform (to the police)
Jakes, shams, and minks:	undesirable persons owing to their personal hygiene, state of their home or area of residence, etc.
'ken:	you know
Lassie:	a young woman or girl
Lezzie:	lesbian
Ned:	connotation of "ned" depends on social position; could be (1) a tough, streetwise person, adept at looking after self or, (2) a socially inferior person, inarticulate and inclined to resort to physical violence
Paki:	Pakistani
Pikeys and tinks:	gypsies or travelers
Quine:	young woman (north-east Scotland)
Rumbles:	play-fighting, usually involving groups of friends
Shat:	defecated
Slagging:	umbrella term covering a range of different types of verbal intimidation, including gossip, threats, ridicule, harassment

Stick up:	defend
Tart:	promiscuous woman
Wide-o:	untrustworthy person who requires watching

Chapter Seven

Borough:	local government
Estates:	blocks of high-rise flats (between twenty and thirty stories high) built after World War II to replace street housing; estates are social housing
Hallway:	interior entrance of house
Hump:	annoyed/ sulking
Landings:	outdoor passages connecting flats on each floor of the block to each other
Punter:	the purchaser of sex in exchange for money or moneysworth
Partner:	a regular lover, girlfriend or boyfriend
Stairways:	a stairwell running between the floors within each block of flats; although the floors of most blocks of flats are connected by lifts, all have stairways
Under wrap:	secret/ hidden

Contributors

CHRISTINE ALDER is a Principal Research Fellow in the Department of Criminology at The University of Melbourne (Australia). Her previous publications have been on topics including young women in juvenile justice, restorative justice and family group conferencing, policing young people, child homicide, and women human rights activists. Her community involvements include serving as a member of the Youth Parole Board of Victoria. She has also been a member of several government advisory committees regarding the development of youth policy and juvenile justice policy and practice. As a feminist, there has been an enduring concern with the interests of women, of all ages, across her publications, teaching, and community activities.

SIBYLLE ARTZ is Associate Professor in the School of Child and Youth Care at the University of Victoria. She has worked as a school-based Child and Youth Care Worker, as an outreach worker with delinquent and pre-delinquent street kids, as a special-care parent in group and foster homes, and as a contract Child and Youth Care Worker. Her research interests include the problems of practice in Child and Youth Care, the constructive use of emotion in everyday life, and family conflict and youth violence, with a specific focus on violence among adolescent females. She is the author of *Feeling as a Way of Knowing: A Practical Guide to Working with Emotional Experience* (Trifolium Books 1994) and *Sex, Power, and the Violent School Girl* (Trifolium Books and Teachers College Press 1998). In 1998, she was chosen as Academic of the Year by the Confederation of University Faculty Associations of British Columbia.

SHEILA BATACHARYA is a Ph.D. candidate at the Ontario Institute for Studies in Education, University of Toronto. She was born in Southern Ontario, Canada. As a community worker and educator, she has worked on issues pertaining to violence against women and youth, antiracism, anti-homophobia/heterosexism, and community economic development. Sheila is committed to promoting strategies for healing from violence and oppression which she is exploring as a yoga teacher and in her doctoral work on young women's experiences of trauma caused by violence.

MICHELE BURMAN is the Director of the Criminology Research Unit at the University of Glasgow. She has long-standing research interests in young women and criminal justice, and troubled and troublesome girls. Over the past fifteen years, she has conducted research in the areas of male violence against women, female offenders, the criminal justice response to rape and sexual assault, and, most recently, the role of violence in girls' everyday lives.

BARRY GODFREY is Lecturer in Criminology at Keele University. He has published on private policing in the nineteenth century and recently completed research on violence in England, Australia, and New Zealand, 1880–1920. His work now focuses on comparative cross-national perspectives on crime and policing in the nineteenth and twentieth centuries.

JODY MILLER is Associate Professor of Criminology and Criminal Justice at the University of Missouri-St. Louis. She specializes in feminist theory and qualitative research methods. Her research focuses on gender, crime, and victimization, particularly in the contexts of youth gangs, urban communities, and the commercial sex industry. She is the author of *One of the Guys: Girls, Gangs, and Gender* (Oxford University Press 2001) and has published numerous book chapters and articles in journals including *Criminology, Social Problems, Justice Quarterly, Journal of Research in Crime and Delinquency*, and *Journal of Contemporary Ethnography*.

JENNY J. PEARCE is Principal Lecturer in the School of Health and Social Sciences at Middlesex University (UK). She has also worked as a teacher and youth justice worker with young women. Drawing on her youth work practice, her teaching, research and publications focus on gender, community safety, and sexual exploitation. Her most recent research and teaching concentrates on preventative work with young women at risk of sexual exploitation and prostitution.

LAURIE SCHAFFNER is Assistant Professor in the Criminal Justice Department and Sociology Department at the University of Illinois at Chicago.

Dr. Schaffner is the author of *Teenage Runaways: Broken Hearts and Bad Attitudes* (Haworth Press 1999), as well as articles for *Crime and Delinquency, Adolescence, Social Justice, Hastings Womens Law Journal,* and *International Journal of Children's Rights.* Her work has earned awards from the American Sociology Association, the Society for Applied Anthropology, and the American Society of Criminology. She co-founded both the San Francisco For Girls Coalition (1996) and the Chicago Girls Coalition (2000) where community advocates, scholars, and young women come together to focus on the plight of girls in the juvenile legal system. Dr. Schaffner also served as a Juvenile Justice Commissioner for the State of California, City and County of San Francisco from 1998 to 2000.

NORMAN A. WHITE is Assistant Professor of Criminology and Criminal Justice at the University of Missouri-St. Louis. He specializes in developmental and life course explanations of delinquency, the causes and context of victimization, and race/ethnicity and crime. His current research includes a study of the social context of stranger homicide, and a study of social networks among violent offenders and the role of these networks in facilitating violence.

ANNE WORRALL is a Professor in Criminology at Keele University (UK), having previously been a probation officer and then a Lecturer in Social Work at Manchester University. She is also a Visiting Research Fellow at the Crime Research Centre, University of Western Australia where she teaches courses on women and crime. She has an extensive publications record, including *Gender, Crime, and Justice* (Open University Press 1987) co-edited with Pat Carlen, *Offending Women* (Routledge 1990), and *Punishment in the Community* (Addison-Wesley Longman 1997). She has also published a number of book chapters on the treatment of young women and girls by the criminal justice system. She is a member of the Parole Board of England and Wales.

Index